"ALL-AMERICAN MONSTER"

"ALL-AMERICAN MONSTER"

THE UNAUTHORIZED BIOGRAPHY OF
TIMOTHY McVEIGH

BRANDON M. STICKNEY

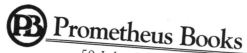

Prometheus Books

59 John Glenn Drive
Amherst, New York 14228-2197

...shed 1996 by Prometheus Books

Library of Congress Cataloging-in-Publication Data

Stickney, Brandon M.
      "All-American monster" : the unauthorized biography of Timothy
McVeigh / by Brandon M. Stickney.
          p.   cm.
      Includes bibliographical references and index.
        ISBN 1–57392–088–6 (cloth : alk. paper)
        1. McVeigh, Timothy. 2. Terrorists—United States—Biography.
    3. Oklahoma City Federal Building Bombing, Oklahoma City, Okla., 1995.
    I. Title.
    HV6432.S75   1996
    976.6'38—dc20   —dc 20
    [B]   96–20469
    [808'.06665]   CIP

Printed in the United States of America on acid-free paper

For Daniel V. Kane

Contents

I know my fate. One day my name will be associated with the memory of something tremendous—a crisis without equal on earth, the most profound collision of conscience, a decision that was conjured up against everything that had been believed, demanded, hallowed so far. I am no man, I am dynamite.

—Friedrich Nietzsche (1886)

Preface

The Lead Headline

The last person I expected to be calling me at four on a Friday afternoon was Dan Kane. He left the office by three every day after the circulation drivers had been on the road for at least three and a half hours. A stern leader, Kane had been my boss for five years at the *Union-Sun & Journal* in Lockport, New York. He was respected by many in the community for his pointed, often biting style. His leadership of the newsroom was difficult to work under at times, but any valuable learning experience will have its trying moments. Those who wanted to learn stayed on, while those who didn't found that Kane had little time for them.

"What are you doing now? You have some time, right?" Kane spoke with an uncommon urgency, and I tried to think of an answer, but nothing came to mind; I was still trying to awaken from an afternoon nap. "Nothing, I—"

It took a few seconds for me to tune in.

He continued, "Get out to Campbell Boulevard, 6289! Write it down—6289 Campbell. It's him! The guy they arrested in Oklahoma for the bombing is from Pendleton. Get an interview with the father. Get photos!"

He hung up and I turned on the television. All the stations were carrying the story: Timothy J. McVeigh of Pendleton, New York, a former soldier, was charged in connection with blowing up a federal building in Oklahoma City. And it all ran back through my mind—the faces, the shock, and the sadness that had been in the news since April 19, 1995, two days earlier.

The telephone rang again. "Why haven't you left your house yet?" Kane bellowed.

I met up with the newspaper's staff photographer, Dennis Stierer, and we rode together to the house in Pendleton. During the ten-minute ride I imagined myself, the local reporter, being able to get an exclusive interview with a family member or someone who had known this McVeigh character. Personally, I had never heard of the McVeighs before this day. I thought the name was pronounced "McVee," like Christine McVie from the band Fleetwood Mac. I figured we'd find this Tim person's broken father at the home. "How could my son have done this?" the elder McVeigh would ask as I feverishly wrote in my note pad. "Where, when did I go wrong?"

Dennis finally pulled his car up to a huge, bustling crowd of news reporters and local television personalities who were being held back by state police. FBI agents were inside the small, ranch-style home and nobody was talking to the press. I thought then that this was never going to be my story . . .

That night, city editor Kathleen Ganz and I found ourselves working late at the paper on our story assignments. I called Sheriff Tom Beilein at home and was told that the FBI had informed him about McVeigh and asked if any local arrest or crime records existed. Kathleen had interviewed neighbors of the McVeighs who said Tim had been an outgoing kid, full of promise, one who would do something someday—not the young man I had seen glaring on the television screen.

Preface

The following day, Saturday, was my day off from work and I slept in. It had been so difficult to fall asleep the night before, pondering the connection of my hometown to such a national tragedy. At 10:30 A.M., the telephone rang. It was Kane, who so rarely called me at home that I feared the worst. He had seen the Saturday edition that Ganz and I had worked on the night before. He also realized that this was the biggest story to hit the Lockport area in decades.

"I was once an enterprising reporter," he told me. "But I'm too old for that now. If I was a little younger, like you, I'd be trying to piece together this man McVeigh's life story. His biography."

I hadn't realized it until he called, but the horror story of the decade had just landed in my lap. I thanked Dan for the idea and began making calls. I grabbed the $2.58 remaining in the kitchen change dish and ran out to purchase copies of the *Buffalo News, Niagara Gazette,* and *Toronto Star.* I had to get started on a first chapter.

Most of what I began writing would never see the light of day. Drawn from the stories making headlines, some of the information was way off base. From conversations with two women outside the McVeigh home on Friday, I wrote that Tim McVeigh was known in school to hang out with a "less than reputable crowd." On Tuesday, April 25, 1995, I received a letter at the newspaper from Pam Widmer, who said that Tim had never hung out with a "less than reputable crowd." Rather, Tim associated with honor students and was a bright person with whom she enjoyed talking. I called Widmer immediately and told her of my plans for a book. She agreed to an on-tape interview. I soon learned that Justin Genter II, a computer specialist I knew, had also gone to school with McVeigh. My long road tracking Tim's life had begun. Kane's recommendation to write McVeigh's biography brought me to the word processor, but it was definitely Widmer's note that made me really want to dig deep. She proved how easily the mass media could misrepresent McVeigh. I strongly believed that it

uld take someone from Tim's hometown to tell his story accu-
ely. And this is what I stressed to those I sought to interview, as
ell as fellow reporters and literary agents who had taken an interest in my project. Could Tim write his own life story? Probably not, because it would be too full of political complaint and too
short on facts. Was another journalist already at work on such a biography? I rarely pray, but in this case I almost did, whenever anyone posed that question.

Being from McVeigh's hometown helped with many of the interviews. Some of the people who spoke with me, I already knew
from my previous work at the newspaper, covering city council
meetings and such. Some former classmates of McVeigh opened
their doors to me to speak on and off the record, as did McVeigh's
relatives. The unnamed source can be the reporter's best friend
and can make a story into a lead headline, instead of a small note
on the obituary page. Writer Bob Woodward proved that with his
now famous "Deep Throat" source. He still stands by his source
today. I refer to a speech he made a few years ago at the Governor's Mansion in Charleston, West Virginia. Sources are, Woodward told a gathering for the Arts and Letter Series, "often the best
way to understand and find out what's going on. I would rather
everyone speak on the record, but they don't." In the case of
McVeigh, for example, it took several sources just to piece together the eventual breakup of his parents.

I floated a small story in the *Union-Sun & Journal* in June,
based on my interviews with Genter and Widmer. I made note in
the piece that I was at work on McVeigh's biography, hoping that
this article would generate more contacts willing to do interviews.
The story couldn't have run at a better time. A day later, Richard
Burr, one of McVeigh's attorneys, visited the paper to tell me that
he had seen the story. He informed me that he was working with
lead attorney Stephen Jones. Burr asked if I could help him by
providing some of the information I had gathered. I told him my
goal, of writing a fair and accurate book, and asked him if I could

interview McVeigh. He left, saying he would get back to me. My request was never met, but I kept trying.

I also sought interviews with McVeigh's sister, Jennifer, and father, Bill. I wrote several letters to them, which went unanswered. But, when I visited their home in person, Jennifer and/or Bill would speak to me briefly on occasion. I visited other members of the McVeigh family and contacted members of the Hill family (Tim's mother's relatives). A few sat down with me and talked, once I swore never to reveal their names in print or in conversation. "I've received so many death threats," a female McVeigh family member told me. "If you write about me or quote me in the newspaper, I'll break your arm." She's a foot taller than me, so I honored her demands.

To my great surprise, Jennifer McVeigh agreed to an on-tape interview, in part, I suggest, because she believed that a published book by the ex-wife of Tim McVeigh's codefendant in the Oklahoma City bombing case, Terry Nichols, may have misrepresented Tim. Jennifer said she also thought that other types of media coverage were unfair.

Other than two letters to the *Union-Sun & Journal* from 1992, Timothy McVeigh had been silent. This made writing a book somewhat difficult early on because I needed to know more about how his mind worked. Finally, in early July 1995, McVeigh granted an interview to *Newsweek.* While short on quotes, the story helped me develop a timeline of events in his life. It also served to expose some of his feelings. I say "some" feelings because I don't believe he was entirely honest with the *Newsweek* interviewer, especially when it came to questions about his parents and his military service. My search for information was inspired by this report though, because I hoped I could do better.

I continued interviewing and researching, and a lot of late-night writing. I was aided when winter came and a reporter from a magazine known as *Media Bypass* called to ask me a few questions. McVeigh had granted an interview to Lawrence Myers, one of its reporters. The interview was to occur in December. McVeigh greatly respected military men, so it was not too surprising when he agreed to be interviewed by a former colonel from *Newsweek*. I had never served in the military, so my chances of being considered for an in-person interview were slim indeed. But Myers, who Tim took an interest in because of his early stories on McVeigh for *Media Bypass,* would come to my rescue. In preparation for his meeting with McVeigh, Myers had a great deal of information on Tim's later life, but he needed details from McVeigh's early years, Tim's childhood. My chapter four was written, so I offered Myers several questions based on my work, which McVeigh answered in the Oklahoma jail interview.

This biography really began to take shape in January of 1995 when Prometheus Books agreed to publish it, based on a detailed outline and one draft chapter. I took a month and a half leave from the newspaper in order to complete the first draft. I had gathered interviews and stories from family, friends, classmates, teachers, military buddies, political insiders, crime witnesses, and government employees. As the hundreds of stories weaved themselves together into a life, I found myself getting into McVeigh's mind, which allowed me to speculate on occasion. This well-informed speculation helped fill in the holes in Tim's life in portions of the text. What I found in my search and finally in the writing, was a seemingly ordinary boy, someone who could be found in almost any average neighborhood in America. His was not just a lack-of-self-worth-due-to-family-trauma story—the type of everyday tragedy that reportedly feeds the criminal element in our society. Timothy McVeigh's life is the tale of an all-American man desperately seeking a meaning to his existence and a direction to focus his considerable energies. Mickey McVeigh, Tim's mom, spoke an eerie truth when she said "he could be any of our children." Tim came from a small, upstate New York town, was trained to fight by the military, later came to believe that the government he served was corrupt, and allegedly blasted a hole in the heart of middle America.

The question posed to me was this: Was it McVeigh's nature that he could have been involved in such a bombing, or was he nurtured by those around him? I found both. As we'll see, he was a hard-working serviceman who seemed to enjoy military life. Yet he was encouraged to hate by the literature he read and by many of the people with whom he surrounded himself. McVeigh probably felt the road he was on was the correct one and may still feel that way today. But it takes an objective observer to see the difference. So, in this biography, I have tried to convey what it must have been like to be Timothy McVeigh, from his sometimes turbulent childhood to his frustrating and often paranoid adulthood. America has tried to understand McVeigh for many months, just as his classmates and fellow soldiers did during the years he shared a class or barracks with them. Television reporters have desperately tried to understand the young man charged with such a heinous crime. They have tried to make their viewers understand him. But it's impossible to understand McVeigh from one-hour television documentaries or a few minutes of reporting on the nightly news. Only in biographical form can we learn about the man and what influenced his life and actions.

The title of this book comes from a conversation I had with a couple who followed this case closely. It is also drawn from the September 3, 1995, issue of the *Sunday Times* of London. The magazine had a cover photo of McVeigh with the bold headline, "All-American Monster." The *Times* asked, "Did this small-town charmer blow a hole in the heart of a nation?" In the photo, Tim holds his long fingers to his boyish face as his deep blue eyes invite you in, to wonder.

Through long hours of research, conversation, and contemplation, I believe I have gained an understanding of McVeigh's inner forces. At times, I have stepped inside his soul, in a way, by detailing what his thoughts and words may have been at certain crucial times in his life. A few things McVeigh hoped to keep secret have been printed here. I believe the thoughts, words, and deeds presented in these pages are true and represent the best por-trait of McVeigh that could be revealed at this time, before the opening of the trial.

As in all such cases, the accused—McVeigh, Nichols, and Fortier—are innocent until proven guilty in a court of law.

I have tried to present a broad picture that affords the reader the opportunity to form his or her own opinion.

Brandon M. Stickney
Lockport, New York
May 25, 1996

Acknowledgments

At times, I had trouble believing that only my name was going to appear on the outside of this book. While I actually formed a life in words for Timothy McVeigh, many people went out of their way to assist me, from the beginning of this project on April 22, 1995, straight through to its completion. I will never be able to thank these people enough. Mentioning them here begins that process.

First, I'd like to mention my parents, Patrick and Michele Stickney, for their constant support, love, and encouragement. My wife, Jennifer Zimmerman, also fits this category for seeing this idea through the very worst of times and, of course, the best. If she had been the one to come up with the idea of writing this biography, this book would have been dedicated to her.

For the top-notch staff at Prometheus Books. Editor-in-chief Steven L. Mitchell, marketing director Jonathan Kurtz, and associate editor Mary A. Read truly cared about this book when it was still in the developing stages, and made telling this history worth the many hours of researching I undertook for months as a journalist.

19

Elizabeth Seib, my chief researcher and assistant, worked with me with undying devotion. Her care for the story and its completion came at many times before her day job as a bookkeeper in a law firm, her personal life, and her own writing career. Liz's assistance made deadlines come and go with ease.

My other researcher, Julianna Jacoby, was on call at all times and proved herself not only a good reporter who could string for *Time* or the *New York Times,* but also as someone who could realize such a project herself someday.

One of the ironies of this biography is that it took literary agent Jane Johnson of Michigan to sell the idea to a publisher here in western New York, where I have made my home for more than twenty years. Jane never became flustered when I flooded her with calls when I began writing this book. She also took the book on as a potential seller after a five-minute conversation with me. She is obviously someone who realizes the importance of a historical, current story when she sees it.

Martin Peterson of the computer-based Thunder Mountain Press of Montana was the first person to agree to publish this work. He realized that a print book deal was possible for McVeigh's biography and honorably turned the rights over at my request. Martin published my first book, *The Way the Gentlemen Ride,* on his computer bulletin board system, and made me believe in work that had previously received rejection from those too distant to even glance at page one.

Photographer Dennis Stierer has always believed in my projects and encouraged them to the point of giving up his professional time to assist, whenever asked.

My thanks to Lawrence Myers for being at the other end of the phone line to help sort the sordid facts.

A special thank you to the members of the McVeigh and Hill families who spoke on and off the record, and gave of themselves even though it hurt just to think of this subject.

Others who assisted and encouraged: Kim Alexis and her family, Lucy Arrigo, Margaret Arrigo, Mason Arrigo, Adrienne Atwood, Stephanie Bax, E.R. Baxter III, Beverly Beach, Cyd Bennett, Wendy Betts, Shirley and Larry Bossler, Lucille Britt and her family, Philip Burke, Christa Caldwell, Marcia Carlin at the *Skeptical Inquirer,* Stefano Castino, Brett and Carol Chamberlain, Brian Christy, Jude Cole, Michael Collette, Robert Creeley, Mike Cuzzacrea, Stephanie DeJoseph, Timothy Durfy, Ann English, Diana English, Rev. Rick English, Irving Feldman, Gary Fisketjon, Lisa Flagler, Kathy and Michael Geier, Tom Gewand, John Grimaldi, Steve Grimaldi, Brenda Giuliano, Geoffrey Giuliano, Jane Haenle, William Hannigan, Chris Harris, Christian and Sue Hayden, Monica and Larry Hayden, Sara Hayden, Jeanne Holman, Dr. Nasser Jafarian, Greg Johnson, Martha and Ron Kershaw, Geoff Koplas, Serge Kovaleski at the *Washington Post,* Alyce and Jacob LaPort, Brian Lasher, Bob Lehmann, Joan McDonough, Debbie and Gary McGranahan, David McIntyre, Charles McKelvy, Sherry and D.J. Mahar, Bob Marsh, Curt Maslowski, Steven Mayhew, George Maziarz, William Mazzo, Bill Miller, Stephanie Miller, Jamie Moses, Ben and Judith Moss, David Mullett, George Muscato, Kathleen Neville, Samuel Nixon III, Joyce Carol Oates, Michael David O'Hear, Fran and Maria Pahl, Timothy Pane, Brad Patenaude, Maria Patrick, Charles Rand Penney, Tuesday and Robert Poole, Gus Posey, Bill Prentice, Matthew P. Pynn, Caren Reese, Randy Reese, Robert Reese, Lester Robinson, Paul Robinson, Barb Root, Rosanna Sandell, John Sansone, Tom Scott, Serena Siegfried, Doug Stanky, Susan Stanley at the Canadian Broadcasting Corporation, Stan and Sally Stickney, Randall Tang, Bob Tetrault, Chris Thompson, Pete Townshend, Selena Truax, David Ulrich, Nicole S. Urdang, James Voelker, Judi and Jan Vullo, Brent Ward, David and Carol Zimmerman, and Todd Zimmerman.

Hundreds of others also assisted in making this project possible. Many others have requested anonymity.

Chapter 1

Amerika

Our sins are manufactured in heaven to create our own hell.
—Charles Bukowski*

April 18, 1975

He was one of the taller boys in class, seated in the second row, near the front of the room, because he liked to talk. Height was the only thing that made him stand out among the other children. Tim dressed casually, as did the others, and held his hand to his heart during the morning pledge.

". . . to the flag of the United States of America, and . . ."

Most eyes were on the stars and stripes in the corner, as the voices chanted in unison to the gentle rain outside the elementary

---

*Charles Bukowski, *Tales of Ordinary Madness* (City Lights Books, 1991).

school's windows. A few gazed up at the ceiling. Tim stared at the flag, feeling his heart beat under his right palm.

". . . to the republic for which it stands, one nation . . ."

He shifted his weight from left to right foot, as a boy notes how long he's been standing—in youth a second feels like a minute, and a minute an hour.

". . . under God, indivisible . . ."

And classrooms all across New York and its neighboring states held this individual ritual in honor of the founding fathers of freedom. A chant every morning at nine. This first lesson of America was led by the teachers, but taught to the children by their own repetition.

". . . with liberty and justice for all."

April 21, 1995

It was Friday afternoon and Niagara County Sheriff Tom Beilein was thinking about the weekend, ready to relax at home with his family. He was surprised when he picked up his office line and heard the monotone voice.

"Sheriff Beilein, it's special agent Joe Wolfinger."

The FBI's Buffalo chief. Beilein was taken aback. "Yes, Joe, what is it?"

"We're in town today. Can you run a local background check on Timothy James McVeigh, birthdate 4/23/68?"

The name was not familiar. Beilein said sure and wondered why. Wolfinger was grave.

"He's in custody in Oklahoma City. We think he's one of those responsible . . ."

Beilein knew the words that were coming next and faded from the conversation. Wolfinger's voice bled into the screams of the victims Beilein had heard on television; CNN's constant coverage of the bombing of the Alfred P. Murrah Federal Building. Beilein's heart sank. A hometowner was apparently mixed up in the deadliest terrorist attack in U.S. history.

Two days earlier, shortly before 9 A.M., a tall, lanky man with a brushcut, looking like a military soldier in plainclothes, lingered outside the federal building in Oklahoma City. The massive structure, which takes up a whole city block between Harvey and Robinson streets, was set up to be open to the public, like a shopping mall, not like a secret place that would house top government criminal investigation agencies like the Bureau of Alcohol, Tobacco, and Firearms and the Drug Enforcement Administration. The building was just coming to life with morning workers. The man outside fidgeted nervously, mumbling to himself, watching a yellow Ryder truck parked nearby. His heart pounding like a jackhammer, the man walked hurriedly from the federal building, heading toward a yellow 1977 Mercury parked outside the YMCA a block away. A partner of the man at the site, seen seconds earlier in the truck, seemed to disappear into thin air.

April 19, 1995, was just another day to most in the government building. But to the man who lingered outside and to thousands more across the country, this was a day of historic significance. Two years ago, eighty-one devotees of religious cult leader David Koresh died in a blazing inferno near Waco, Texas, which started after a raid by federal agents. Ten years ago today, a heavily armed Christian rightist camp dubbed the Covenant, Sword, and Arm of the Lord was raided by government agents because the Christian rightists had stockpiled weapons and poisonous gas, and had an association with another group, The Order, that had allegedly murdered a talk-show host because he was outspoken and Jewish. On this particular April 19, a white supremacist "hero" named Richard Snell was to be executed in an Arkansas prison for killing a black state trooper named Louis Bryant and a pawn shop owner named William Stumpp, who he mistakenly thought was Jewish. This was the date a radical group calling itself the Montana Militia had proclaimed "National Militia Day"; and April

19, 1972, was the bogus birthdate listed on the driver's license
Timothy McVeigh carried as he sped away from the Alfred P.
Murrah Federal Building in an old Mercury. It was also the anniversary of the battles of Concord and Lexington, where the first
shots of the American Revolution were fired in 1775.

The time of day, shortly after 9 A.M., was also important. It
was to be the time when a fictional group of select Americans
angry about gun control and race relations would bomb an FBI
building in Washington, D.C. This story was the creation of former American Nazi party official William Pierce, a former physics
professor and author of *The Turner Diaries,* one of McVeigh's favorite books. Tim glanced into the rearview to catch the gray-
white structure for memory's sake and remembered a quote used
by true believers of "freedom"—that sometimes the innocent have
to die to further the cause of liberty. Pierce's hero character Earl
Turner said, "Most of the victims of our bomb are only pawns. But
there is no way we can destroy the system without hurting many
thousands of innocent people." Tim McVeigh grinned. About two
miles from the Murrah building Tim pulled the car to the side of
the road. On this clear day he could see the tip of the building from
the outer edge of the city. Tim decided he would watch.

In the Murrah building at 9:02, when most workers were having their first cup of coffee or settling in, a deafening boom
blocked their ears and made everything around them disintegrate.
As the sound of falling rubble dissipated, it was replaced by
screams and sirens. Those horrific shrills and whines would last
for hours as reason gave way to chaos and pure animal instinct
took over. Charles Watts, an attorney who was in a nearby building, told *Media Bypass* magazine that he felt two explosions,
which would have been the initial blast immediately followed by
a strong shock wave.

It was like two distinct happenings. We thought the [bankruptcy
court] building we were in was the one being bombed, as I

guess most people in downtown Oklahoma City did. The alarms immediately went off in the building. Never have I ever experienced anything like this. This was a huge, huge explosion.[1]

Other than Watts, a Vietnam vet, very few knew what had happened. In the federal building, they woke remembering they had been at work and wondered how they'd arrived, covered with blood and dirt, in hell.

The shock waves from the powerful blast had caused the building's cement floors to fly upward and then hurl down as the walls tore away from their supports. Hot gas that had formed in the blast moved at more than seven thousand miles per hour, pushing everything forward and then pulling it back out.

Calls flooded emergency lines. Who could have realized that the city of Oklahoma and its life would be changed forever? It was as if Judgment Day had come for the Earth's sinners. The anger of three men, yet to be known, had struck the office building with all the force of an apocalypse, and its remnants—a towering cloud of black smoke—rose like a victory flag of evil over the city. *Oklahoma Rescue* author Jon Hansen, one of the city's assistant fire chiefs, described the scene:

> To the east, the sky was full of dust and dense black smoke. You couldn't see anything through it—that's how thick it was. It darkened the streets, covering at least a square block. . . . We scrambled to our vehicles and headed east down Fifth Street.[2]

In that split second of the blast, about 160 adults and children were killed instantly. Some were blown to pieces like the walls of the building itself, while others were burned beyond recognition. Still others lay trapped inside the rubble, waiting to die. At least five hundred people were injured in the area around the blast site and in nearby buildings. Glass rained through the city at that moment like a hailstorm, slashing everything in its path. The death toll would finally reach 169, as bodies were discovered and several of the severely injured died in hospitals. Assistant Fire Chief Hansen said:

> I was stunned to see the chaos in front of me. Smoke was pouring out from behind the Water Resources Building two blocks ahead at Fifth and Harvey. My first thought was that a plane had crashed. It never occurred to me that anyone would intentionally set out to cause this kind of destruction.[3]

Charles Watts made his way to a smashed window of the bankruptcy court building and he could see the Murrah Federal Building in the hazy distance. Watts recalled to *Media Bypass*:

> The front of it had all been blown off, but you could see daylight coming from the windows in the back. The thing that I guess is still the most sobering of anything was that there was nobody moving. There was no movement at all inside the building. We all knew at that moment there had been massive, massive . . . loss of life.[4]

Four blocks of the city felt the initial blast, and its effect was noted many miles away. A driver for United Parcel Service, parked ten minutes outside of the city, saw the windows of his truck fly out and shatter before his eyes, from the sheer force of the blast. A worker who had been gazing out his office window one block away from the federal building saw a veil of white dancing at the Murrah's rear as millions of sheets of typing paper fluttered down like confetti at a parade. Soon, media helicopters would be overhead, showing the world of CNN watchers this breaking story of confusion and mass murder. The world of network nightly news would see the screaming, bloody faces and wonder why.

No one in the rest of the world had ever really heard of Alfred P. Murrah, until the tragedy. He was chief justice of the Tenth U.S.

Circuit Court of Appeals in Denver from 1940 to 1970. The native Oklahoman had died twenty years before this nightmare day. Murrah himself would have nothing to do with the bombing, except that the building named for him contained a target for terrorists that was missed in the end, but their deluded political point was still made.

Assistant Fire Chief Hansen said he found that the source of the black cloud overhead was a parking lot of burning cars. He breathed in the dust hanging in the air and saw the streets littered with bricks and debris. "The coating of broken glass made the entire scene glitter in the bright morning sun," he said. "Dazed people wandered the streets . . . people were running—some for help while others were running to help. Paper rained from the sky."[5]

Rescuers descended on the injured and sought out those still trapped in the gaping hole that was the federal building, while police and investigators tried to sort out the details by interviewing witnesses and scouring the remains for clues. The building had been intentionally bombed. That didn't take too long to figure out. The questions were who and why?

An almost immediate search was begun to locate two John Doe suspects, who had been seen by witnesses minutes before the blast. Federal agents were looking for two white males in their twenties. Witnesses tied the two men to a Ryder rental truck that had been outside the building that morning, and to a car that sped away from the site shortly before the enormous explosion. According to FBI Agent Weldon Kennedy, the two were believed to have rented the truck that carried the bomb. On April 20, two sketches of the suspects were released to the media and police agencies nationwide.

The terrorists responsible for the bombing were seemingly successful, striking the United States at its weakest, a wide-open federal building, easily accessible to an armed attack; they killed children housed in the building's day-care center and crippled important government offices inside. More people would have been killed if there had been a building across Fifth Street from the Murrah rather than a parking lot. Seven other buildings were severely damaged: those housing the *Journal Record* newspaper, the Water Resources Board, the Athenian restaurant, the YMCA, the offices of Southwestern Bell, the Post Office, and the Regency Tower Hotel. Two Water Department employees and a receptionist at the Athenian perished in the blast. Though much of the Murrah building was left standing, its basic structure was destroyed, like the lives of thousands that would be affected by the incident, looming aftershocks of an earthquake. Assistant Fire Chief Hansen reports in his book *Oklahoma Rescue*:

> It was instantly clear to all of us that we were in the middle of a major incident. For a moment I just stood there, stunned by what I was seeing. The entire front of this huge building was gone. My mind raced ahead, wondering about the fate of the hundreds of people inside. I knew we had what we refer to in our business as a "mass casualty incident." As I made my way to the front of the federal building, which faces north, I saw toys lying among the debris in the street. And it hit me. There was a day-care center inside. My heart sank. Then I turned to survey the entire scene. To the north, I saw the *Journal Record* building. The roof on one side of the building was gone. I looked toward the YMCA across the street and saw tremendous damage there. I remembered the Y had a day-care center, too. I could see kids already being brought out. Some were cut and bleeding, in pretty bad shape . . . throughout the two-block area, there were dozens of people injured, adults and children. Some were walking on their own and others were being carried. Along with the toys . . . furniture and other materials had blown out of the Murrah . . . there were cars that looked as if somebody had picked them up, crumpled them, and thrown them back down onto the pavement. . . . The entire block looked like something out of war-torn Bosnia. . . . We were tortured by the victims we could see trapped in the debris.[6]

Oklahoma Police Officer Brad Lovelace made it into the Murrah building and began carrying the wounded to safety. He recalled to the *Sunday Times* of London that he will never forget the children who survived.

> I came to a room that terrified me. It was badly damaged, but I could tell that 15 minutes earlier it had been a functioning day-care center. I saw three little girls aged between four and six. They were in shock. I picked up the two smallest girls and told the eldest that I would be right back to get her. Tears welled up in her eyes. I got down on my knees and said, "I'll be back." She nodded. I carried the two smaller girls out to the medical center. When I returned, the older girl was still there. When she saw me, she said nothing, but put her arms out toward me.[7]

The nine-story Murrah building had housed America's Kids Day-Care Center, the Social Security Administration, a credit union, the Highway Administration, the Agriculture Department, Housing and Urban Development, the Secret Service, the Drug Enforcement Administration (DEA), Marine Corps. recruiters, U.S. Customs, a general accounting office, *and* the bombers' alleged bull's-eye—the Bureau of Alcohol, Tobacco, and Firearms (BATF). It had also once housed Federal Bureau of Investigation officials. But the main target, according to close observers of the Oklahoma bombing probe, was Robert Ricks, the lead spokesman for the BATF at the Waco, Texas, confrontation with David Koresh and the Branch Davidians. Ricks, who was not in the building at the time of the blast, is currently director of the Oklahoma Transportation Department. Of course, the bombers' plan encompassed far more than just killing one man. It was a show of force by a small group with ideas more chilling than the act of terrorism itself.

Timothy McVeigh was by now many miles outside the city. He had spots on his eyes from the bright orange flash of the explosion he witnessed. McVeigh still tingled from the way the blast had made his bones shake, an experience he'd had before, but not with such strength. To him, it was the strength of justice, for all things that were right. McVeigh was traveling at his normal 75 miles an hour, with the radio mumbling something along the AM dial.

McVeigh was armed with a loaded pistol and the recollection of a quote from the philosopher John Stuart Mill about war being "ugly" but necessary when men's rights are in jeopardy. In McVeigh's mind, war against the federal government had been declared and the first act of the underground carried out. His destination now was a Kansas dump site where he could ditch the car and then head to his own tiny camp near a military base, where someone who looked like him, a soldier, could blend in with the town crowd. But how would the government and the people know it was he who struck back? What could he do to be known for this patriotic act? To him there would be more attacks. This was just the first. McVeigh apparently did not know that the vehicle he piloted had no license plate and that this would be his final trip up Interstate 35.

Investigators and firefighters soon revealed to reporters, who had arrived about as fast as the rescuers, that the explosive had been made of fuel and combustible fertilizer packed into the rented Ryder truck. One of the truck's axles bearing a traceable serial number had also been found. Oklahoma Governor Frank Keating pointed out the twisted axle to some television reporters and cameramen during a walk two blocks from the crime scene. A report said he had apparently come across the truck part by accident and made an offhand comment about how the entire area was to be searched for clues. But this bone of evidence, this metal hunk of death machine, once tested and traced by the FBI, would eventually lead to three men being charged for various crimes associated with the bombing.

According to specialists, the making of such a powerful bomb required no great knowledge. In fact, a child could set one off if trained properly. Instructions on explosives are available at libraries, in magazines and newsletters, and on various computer networks. Bombings not unlike the one in Oklahoma City have been detailed and romanticized in such books and movies as the right-wing tome *The Turner Diaries,* about a people's revolution, and *Blown Away,* a Tommy Lee Jones film about an insane bomber.

Favored by terrorists, car and truck bombs are quite effective in striking at an enemy or achieving revenge. Large quantities of explosives can be transported right to the doorstep of the desired target. When a car bomb is used on a building like the Murrah, the first wave of the explosion shatters windows and rips vertical supports away from the foundation as it creates an upward wave of motion. A shock wave penetrates to the interior, pressuring floor slabs, causing them to fall. The shock then creates pressure on the roof and sides of the building. A vacuum is created, causing a wind that can carry debris great distances. The explosion also forms a crater in the ground, creating an earthquake-like atmosphere, shaking the entire site. Charles Watts told *Media Bypass*:

> There were a lot of people who were injured and terribly upset, and people who were looking on in horror. Lots of people were making the comment, "What can we do? I wish there was something we could do." And that terrible sinking feeling of helplessness.[8]

A task force of more than 350 federal agents, many of whom had friends and co-workers in the Murrah building, was sent to the site for the probe. What the agents found reminded some of previous vehicle bombings in far-off Argentina, Lebanon, and other countries. Major media agencies drew comparisons to the attack on the American embassy in Beirut more than a decade earlier. Shortly after the explosion, agents were watching a videotape recording of the scene captured by an automated bank teller camera across the street. The Ryder truck could be seen on the tape. By tracing vehicle serial numbers from the located axle, investigators journeyed to a Junction City, Kansas, body shop and rental firm to which the truck had been assigned.

As the rescue work continued, President Clinton promised the nation that those responsible would be apprehended and justice would be swift. He met with a group of children to reassure them and all Americans. Bombings were common in the Middle East and in countries like England and Ireland where the natives have grown angry with the government over decades. But this, like the World Trade Center, seemed to be part of the beginning of something new for America, the first chapter in a modern history book of civic horror. The Twin Towers bombing in New York City, just a couple of years before, had Middle Eastern connections. Was this to be a regular occurrence in America? Were all of our major cities targets? These were questions to be answered right away by the U.S. leaders before mass hysteria spread among the people. Clinton tried to stay in control. He told the nation in a radio address from the Oval Office, with twenty children present, that parents should talk with their youngsters about the Oklahoma disaster. Not knowing whether another bomber was waiting in the wings to strike another building in some other city, Clinton pleaded:

> Tell them that they are safe, that their own school or day-care center is a safe place and that it has been checked and that you know it's safe . . . when we catch the people who did [the bombing in Oklahoma], we will make sure that they can never hurt another child again, ever. And most important of all, [during] the next several days go out of your way to tell your children how much you love them. Tell them how much you care about them. Be extra sensitive to whether they need a hug or just to be held. This is a frightening time. If your children are watching news about the bombing, watch it with them. If they have questions, first listen carefully to what they're asking and then answer the questions honestly and forthrightly. Then reassure them.[9]

In the days that followed, rescue efforts at the bomb site slowed as resources and energies dwindled. Oklahoma Fire Chief Gary Marrs held press conferences to release information and to answer the many questions his city and America had. There were some questions he couldn't answer, but he knew his teams, and the thousands of people called in and those who volunteered, were doing everything they could, even risking their own lives in the shaky structure that was left behind by the bomb. Marrs said late in the search that there was little hope for those at the bottom of the rubble. The Murrah Federal Building had become a tomb and the stench of death flooded the city. And yet Oklahoma City and the nation could gain solace in the fact that while many were badly injured, *three-quarters* of those who were in the Murrah building survived. They stood as living bodies of evidence, victims waiting to face their attackers. According to Assistant Fire Chief Hansen,

> Most of the surviving workers and visitors on the lower floors had made their way out on their own. Others had been assisted by rescue workers or those who were not too badly injured themselves. From the street, everyone could see the frightened individuals who had approached the ragged edge of what was left of the front of the building.[10]

About 515 people worked in the Oklahoma City federal building. The list of casualties, published a few days later in the *Daily Oklahoman,* read like the Vietnam Memorial Wall in Washington. They were all innocent people, brought together by a tragedy still too awesome to believe. They never met their killers, but the rest of angry America would, just a couple days after Black Wednesday.

The yellow Mercury sped out of Oklahoma toward Kansas where anonymity waited like that girl from Lockport, who'd always said no when he asked her out. The Earth had shaken just forty minutes ago. The war had begun. Sgt. McVeigh gave the old engine a little more gas as he headed toward a town near Fort Riley, where he could disappear for a while. It was 10:19 A.M. when he heard the siren and glanced in the rearview. It was a black and white Oklahoma Highway Patrol car coming up behind. Another speeding ticket, Tim thought. He'd probably never pay this one. Why bother? Terry would think it was funny that he had been stopped on the way back.

Trooper Charles Hanger followed the Mercury Marquis to the side of the road. When he wanted to run the license he couldn't. The four-door car had no tag, but it had pulled over right away. Tim McVeigh had no idea that he was being stopped for both speeding and no license plate, so he figured he'd get the speeding ticket and be on his way. There was no reason to pull out his gun at this point.

Chapter 2

The Gambler

Looking back now across fifteen years, I could see with great clarity the fear I had lived in, which must mean that in the interval I had succeeded in a very important undertaking: I must have made my escape from it.

—John Knowles*

The known history of the McVeigh family begins an ocean away in nineteenth-century Ireland. Hugh McVeigh, Timothy's great-great-great-grandfather married a pretty, red-haired girl named Doris O'Shea. Hugh and Doris had a son, Edward, in 1840 who while growing up would help with the farm in his early years, before marrying and coming to the United States. Not knowing how to write his name, Edward signed early documents with an "X." By mistake, U.S. immigration officials pronounced his name "McVay," instead of the traditional Irish and English "McVee." As it is told, the incorrect "McVay" was so often used that the name stuck over the years.

---

*John Knowles, *A Separate Peace* (Bantam Books, 1966).

Edward was a man of solid build, a real trailblazer. He and his wife, Margaret, settled in the town of Lockport in western New York, about thirty miles from the well-known Niagara Falls. Edward came to America looking for work. His poor neighborhood in Ireland offered little in the way of a future, and to many his age, the land across the ocean was a call to promise. Edward found land plentiful and cheap, and there was a demand for what he could do best, farm. The two made their home in a quaint wooden cabin on the Erie Canal side of Murphy Road. While he worked many hours during the day, and enjoyed a bit of liquor with the canal boat workers, McVeigh always found time for his wife and the duties of the cabin. Local vendors always had plenty of food and goods for sale and you didn't have to travel far for supplies as the canal port atmosphere offered items from all over the state, passing on boats to shops and stores.

Edward and Maggie had a daughter, Alice, and soon after, a son, Hugh H., named after Edward's father. News came by letter a few years later from Ireland that the elder Hugh was ill. No one was sure what was wrong with him, but he suffered from a shaking. He finally died after a long period of suffering. Edward and Maggie were sad because they could not leave America to visit the others back home. This made the bond among the small clan of Lockport McVeighs stronger, a bond that would last for many years.

Young Hugh H. McVeigh and his sister were nurtured and supported by their parents. As an adult, Hugh carried on the strength by purchasing his own property on Bear Ridge Road, outside Lockport, and invited his parents to join him on the land. His father, Edward, could not part with the cabin he loved so dearly, but wished to honor his son's offer. Edward, Hugh, and some local friends banded together and moved the home onto the new property.

After his wife's death, Edward moved to Buffalo, thirty miles to the south, where his daughter, now Alice [McVeigh] Smith, lived. Edward died in 1926 of complications from arteriosclerosis.

Around 1910, Hugh married Wilhemina Wortbroker, a well-to-do native of the Lockport area. Their marriage was the talk of the town because of Hugh's ancestry and Minnie's social status, not to mention her charming good looks. They had two sons, Edward W. McVeigh, and Hugh, Jr., as well as three daughters, Marion, Helen, and Dorothea. The five children attended local schools during the mornings and then helped their father with work on his land. The elder Hugh became well known in Lockport and the nearby town of Pendleton for his ownership of hundreds of acres of land, which he used for farming. He was invited by some locals to run for government office, but he declined the offer because of his already heavy work load. He is remembered as a confident man and hard worker, proud among the early pioneers.

One son, Edward W. McVeigh, Timothy McVeigh's grandfather, was born December 31, 1912. He was different from his male bloodline and sought true adventure. Ed was taught the importance of a gun as a boy. His father and friends took him along when they went shooting, and Ed accompanied his elders on many hunting trips into the deep woods of western New York. Every fall, the cracks and pops of shotguns could be heard throughout Niagara County. Deer hunting contests were popular, and bringing in a ten-point buck was the mark of a hero, especially for a young teen. Shotguns in hand, and a bit of whiskey for the cold spells, the hunters gathered at the edge of the Bear Ridge woods and headed out for the day. Ed was in his glory as he received all the attention while the lessons of men were taught.

In his teens, Edward McVeigh proved himself to be a real cowboy, gaining quite a reputation for breaking wild horses in Lockport. The horses, which breathed steam like fire, were taken into Lockport by railcar to the Henry McAfee Ranch, and were trained by McVeigh and other hands to plow fields.

Miron Wasik, now seventy-six years old, mused with the *Buffalo News* about his early years in the field with "Eddie" McVeigh. Wasik said he could still recall the times that he and Ed went into the corral and climbed onto the wild horses—towering monsters, with veins like power cables popping out of their necks. Glaring with their angry baseball-size eyes, the horses thought better than to be climbed on, much less ridden: "Eddie and I got kicked and thrown off more than once and some of the horses bit. Eddie was afraid of no horse and there wasn't (one) he couldn't ride."[1]

Edward took a shine to a girl named Angela Litz. After a courtship, they were eventually married and had two boys, William and James. To support the family, Edward took one of the better-paying jobs in the area, that of ice cutter. He broke down large ice blocks from a frozen pond, and helped move the ice to the railroad. The ice was used for railroad storage cars that were "refrigerated." A few years later, Ed was hired at Harrison Radiator, an automobile radiator manufacturer and a growing company in the city of Lockport. The company became the backbone of the area as the demand for its products and services grew. Ed would stay at Harrison for thirty years, paying for his children's education and plenty of frills as a millwright when times were good.

In a land famous for its bowlers and other sporting competitions, McVeigh joined a league and was the second local McVeigh to make a regional name for himself, his land-rich father being the first. He began bowling in the 1950s and soon his high-scoring games made news in the local paper, the *Union-Sun & Journal* of Lockport. There was talk of him one day joining the National Bowling Hall of Fame.

Ed McVeigh's other interests included the ritualistic group Knights of Columbus, local #319. He had also belonged to the South Lockport Volunteer Fire Company, which protects a residential area south of the small city, and north of Pendleton.

Edward's wife died young in 1972. His living relatives told the *Buffalo News* that Edward spent years taking care of Angela, prior to her death after suffering from multiple sclerosis. He worked to care for her and other needy people, as a van driver for the American Red Cross. In 1973, Edward McVeigh retired from Harrison Radiator, concentrating on his devoted family and the bowling game he'd come to enjoy so much.

McVeigh passed that love of bowling on to his sons, Bill and James, but especially Bill, who, in his adult years, would also make headlines in the local newspaper for sporting achievement. As a boy, Bill learned to appreciate horticulture. He and friend Wilma Donohue enjoyed getting together on June mornings to pick cherries in the orchard across from the Donohue home on Main Road.

Bill and James McVeigh attended St. Patrick's Roman Catholic Elementary School at 76 Church Street in the city of Lockport and then DeSales Catholic High School on Chestnut Ridge Road in town. Those school days were quite strict. The boys and girls were ruled with an iron hand and were not allowed to mingle. DeSales in the late 1950s and 1960s was like any other Catholic school in the nation, attempting to rule with the fear of God during a time when the new generation was turning away from the church and seeking the freedom of experimentation. Priests and nuns at the schools had the right to brutally discipline students with corporal punishment for their daily sins. A DeSales student, Mildred Hill, would one day be Bill McVeigh's wife and Timothy McVeigh's mother. A classmate of Hill's, Edward Tracy, offered this recollection:

> There were about 125 students in my high school class. The boys were taught by priests and the girls were taught by nuns. Girls and boys were not allowed to cross over [to each other's buildings]. There was no contact allowed. When Mildred was a student, she was required to wear an extremely ugly blue uniform and blouse. There was a great deal of supervision at the time. We had dances every Friday that cost a quarter. The girls were neatly dressed and rigidly supervised.[2]

Bill McVeigh met Mildred "Mickey" Hill in school, but they did not have an immediate relationship. Bill graduated in 1957 from DeSales, living through the stern discipline on the boys' side where you weren't "even allowed to loosen your tie on a hot day," according to Tracy.

Mildred M. Hill was born in 1945, the daughter of Dorothy and William Hill of Ransomville, a town near Pendleton. Mickey was a pretty girl who grew up among the cornfields of her hometown and took the bus to Sanborn Elementary School on Route 31. Her teacher was Mrs. Fanny Daley, a well-liked educator who was a stickler for spelling and math. Mickey was outgoing and gregarious, coming from a family of fun lovers. Classmate and childhood friend Jerry F. Boone wrote about young Mickey's high school years in his column in the *Oregonian,* a Portland-based newspaper:

> Bus eighteen was how we got to school in those days. Mickey and I were country kids and shared the forty-five-minute ride [to DeSales]. The bus began its run in the village of Wilson along the south shore of Lake Ontario. It meandered via rural gravel and paved roads through towns with names such as Ransomville, North Ridge, Pekin, Cambria Center, and Pendleton. This was farming country. Apples for sauce. Pears for the cannery. Grapes that went to Welch's juice. Land that wasn't orchard or vineyard was pasture for dairy cattle or hay for winter feeding. Mickey and I lived less than two miles apart on Lower Mountain Road. My family's farm was across from the town's commercial center—a gas station and a tavern just down the road a piece from the community church, the two-truck fire department, the town hall, and the highway department. On summer days, Mickey and her sister [Jean] would ride their horses down the edge of the highway and tie them up at the end of our driveway while they went into the Hillside Tavern for a Coke. I was jealous then. I wanted a horse. I probably also wanted Mickey.[3]

Mickey Hill helped manage the girls' basketball team in high school, worked as a part-time librarian, and was a member of the French Club. She graduated from DeSales Catholic High School in 1963. While Bill McVeigh served two years as a draft recruit in the army as a truck driver at Fort Campbell, supporting the 101st Air Division, Mickey attended Hartford Airline Personnel School, gaining the knowledge she'd need for future travel agency jobs.

Bill came home from the army with his twenty-something body in great shape, just as in his football years at DeSales. Mickey was attracted to him at an alumni party for DeSales graduates. They had a couple drinks together and remembered those silly days at school when every move they made was watched by the teachers. Mickey's older sister, Jean, went to Morrisville College and earned a nursing degree. She married Louis Zanghi and settled in Rochester. In conversation with Julianna Jacoby, a member of my research staff, Jean said Mickey brought Bill to Rochester to meet them. "We both immediately liked Bill," Jean said. He was in the service at the time. She remembered him as reserved. Jean told Bill then, "You may come in quiet but you're not that way for long, if you want to get a word in."[4]

Mickey seemed to appreciate Bill's nature as the strong, silent type, and Bill was fond of Mickey's chatty, "let's have fun" attitude. Bill completed his two years of required military service and not long thereafter his father was able to secure a job for him at Harrison Radiator. Mickey wanted to work, too, so she took a position at Argy Travel Service Company in Niagara Falls.

Bill and Mickey were wed on August 28, 1965, in a traditional ceremony at Immaculate Conception Church at North Ridge in Cambria, a town between the two lovers' birthplaces. Mickey's parents and members of the McVeigh family were in attendance. Mickey was given in marriage by her father, William, and Jean (Hill) Zanghi's daughter, Theresa, was the flower girl. James McVeigh, Bill's brother, was the best man. The Rev. Francis Cronin, a native of Niagara Falls, celebrated mass at the double-ring ceremony.

The families celebrated with dinner and a champagne reception at the Cambria Community Center, where the music and good times flowed until well after midnight. Bill and Mickey then left for a honeymoon trip to the Adirondack Mountains in upper New York State.

Bill and Mickey settled into a tiny apartment above a garage at 8 Pound Street in the city of Lockport. In late 1965 they had their first child, a girl, and named her Patricia. As the first child grew out of baby blankets and stroller, the McVeigh apartment in Lockport shrank rapidly. Bill learned of a house for sale in the town of Lockport. A bowling buddy, Leo LaPort, Sr., was offering a green home at 5063 Lockport-Junction, which was next to his own house. The ranch-style structure had two bedrooms and would be perfect for the McVeighs because Mickey was now expecting her second child. Leo LaPort, Jr., also a bowling friend of Bill's, recalled that time fondly: "[Bill] was working at Harrison. He bought the house off Dad. It's still there, as a matter of fact. They lived there for a couple years. I remember Mickey being pregnant with the baby [Timothy McVeigh]."[5]

Timothy James McVeigh was born at 8:30 A.M. on April 23, 1968, at Lockport Memorial Hospital. Tim had his dad's deep blue eyes as well as his pronounced nose and chin. His scattered hair was as white as a ghost. He didn't seem to cry often, and Patty, who was now three, would stare at him lying in the crib.

Timothy's father was involved in a big softball rivalry at the time—sandlot games organized through local taverns and restaurants. He worked hard at the game. Leo LaPort, Jr., said Bill was known for his strong arm out on the field, and the newspaper, Leo notes, even wrote a feature article about Bill McVeigh's game.

The family soon outgrew the Junction Road house and Bill built a slightly larger home at 5321 Hinman Road in the town of Lockport, three miles from Junction Road. They lived there for several years while Bill McVeigh used the money he was earning to construct a two-story wood "dream" home with brick fireplace at 4675 Meyer Road. During their time on Hinman, Mickey had her third child. Jennifer Lynn McVeigh was born on March 5, 1974, at Lockport Memorial Hospital. In 1977, the McVeighs' dream home on Meyer Road was completed and they moved in. Its four bedrooms, two and a half bathrooms, and two-car garage, all situated on more than an acre of land in a country neighborhood, were perfect for raising children.

Tim's adventurous childhood years were spent there, on a street with a home about every forty feet, but with acres of vacant land behind each one. His father, Bill, and grandfather Edward kept Tim busy with fishing, plenty of catch games, and trips to the bowling alley.

Tim's older sister, Patty, had the most guarded childhood of the three. Because she was the firstborn, the devoutly Catholic McVeighs watched her closely and she accompanied them every Sunday to Good Shepherd Church in Pendleton. Patty attended Starpoint schools on Mapleton Road. The school complex comprises several different buildings all connected by long hallways. Starpoint has kindergarten through twelfth grade classes with many noteworthy teachers and spirited athletic teams. The school district itself ranks among the top ten in western New York, according to local polls. Despite the warm, inviting environment of the school, there seemed to be no "community" feeling with a student body dispersed over the five towns of Pendleton, Lockport, Cambria, Wheatfield, and Royalton. It had a scattered, random population, housed in an educational complex positioned amid the cornfields surrounding the town of Pendleton. A longtime teacher at Starpoint, who agreed to be interviewed but requested anonymity, stressed that the girl he knew as "Trisha" McVeigh was a top student, who excelled in all areas: "She was a fine athlete, too. She was the real athlete in the family, real solid. I was coaching at the time, and she was a finalist for the title 'Girls' Athlete of the Year.' She was bubbly, outward."[6]

Tim developed into a boy-about-the-neighborhood when he lived on Meyer Road. He made a lot of friends quickly in the summer because the McVeighs were one of the few families in the area to have a pool. Tim was also looking for attention, according to neighbors and school friends. In appearance, Tim was a carbon copy of his dad, as Bill was of Edward. But his social skills were far more developed, like his mother, Mickey, who was very at ease with people and who would greet the neighbors and discuss the news of the day. Tim's social life developed in much the same way: as Mickey was a magnet for men, Tim was a magnet to the other children. Tim McVeigh hung around Brad Waugh on Meyer Road, and at times, Brad's brother, Jonathan, and sister, Trisha, could tag along. It was on Meyer Road that Tim first met Vicki Lyn Hodge and her brother, Steven. The Hodges lived across the street, and Tim enjoyed Vicki's company. It is believed that she was his first childhood crush.

Unlike his father and his older sister, Tim lacked athletic co-ordination. Family friend Leo LaPort, Jr., said Tim inherited his mother's love for life, but not the McVeigh thirst for sport.[7] The Waugh children's father, Jim, told the *Union-Sun & Journal*:

> [Tim] was not very athletic, kind of a lanky kid. But he was a hustler. The kids in the neighborhood were always asking for money because they wanted to go to Tim's house. . . . He always had something big going.[8]

Tim, who has also been described as "theatrical" by one neighbor, constructed a roulette wheel in his front yard, much like one he saw at a church picnic. Bill McVeigh would sometimes assist with bingo and other activities at Good Shepherd Church, occasionally bringing the family along. Tim loved the weekend festivities in the churchyard, where the Pendleton community joined in wholesome entertainment. So, he set up his own wheel at home, figuring he could get everyone to come to his house and leave some cash behind. "I'd front the money and the kids would go over there and lose it all," says Jim Waugh. At Halloween one year, Tim set up his own haunted house in a side yard and charged each kid one dollar to tour it. Mrs. Waugh saw that Tim had a future in something big, but she wasn't sure what.

> He was just different . . . just entertaining. I used to laugh to myself and say, "My God, this guy is going to do something one day." He was always thinking of ways to raise money for himself.[9]

Tim attended Starpoint's Fricano Elementary School on Mapleton Road. He was bright in the early years, like his sister Patty, and sought attention there, too. Tim was the talk of the third grade class when he learned *gay* wasn't just a reference of humor among children but a term used to describe people who were homosexual. The dictionary listed *gay* as meaning merry and cheerful. Classmate Justin Genter II remembers:

> He used to sit at the lunch table next to us. The big thing then was he told someone he was gay. And everybody would ask him, "You're gay?!" And he'd say, "Yeah, I'm gay—I'm happy, yeah." He'd try to make a joke to get attention. He did definitely stand out, trying to be funny. But I'm not sure what he had in mind with that.[10]

In 1977 when Tim was nine years old, an act of nature would affect him enough to formulate his idea of readiness and have an impact on the rest of his life. It was winter and a storm headed toward Niagara County. In an area accustomed to its share of snow, the locals thought they were ready for another of winter's harsh realities. But the storm turned into a blizzard by late afternoon on Friday, January 28, and by nightfall, thousands of people were stranded at work, at friends' houses, and in their own homes. Tim McVeigh was at home with his dad and sisters, Patty, eleven, and Jennifer, three. The winds raced at seventy miles an hour as the storm raged outside. The telephone rang. It was Mickey. She was stuck with friends at the Sheraton Hotel in Lockport. They had gone for drinks, she said, and she could not leave, even though she was only about three miles from home. Bill called his work and said he couldn't go in because he had to take care of the kids. As Tim lay in his bed that evening, listening to the winds howl through the trees and the hum of sheriff's department snowmobiles pass on the road, for the first time he felt deserted by his mother. This was a time of emergency and Mom couldn't come home. He hoped she would be okay and wondered why, in such a storm, she had gone out in the first place. Tim heard his dad talk-ing to someone again on the telephone in the kitchen. He pulled the covers up to his face and wished the downstairs door would open, and his mother's voice would echo in.

There was no school for two and a half weeks and many busi-nesses were closed for the next three days. Fifteen feet of snow had fallen. The newspapers and television stations were pro-claiming the Blizzard of '77 the worst in twenty years. Pendleton was hit the hardest in Niagara County, where roads became thirty-foot snow drifts, and the power to many homes was cut off. After the second day, Tim's house lost telephone service, along with many others on Meyer Road. Mickey McVeigh didn't come home for about two days. But Bill recalls his son enjoying most of the blizzard experience. He said Tim and his friends took their sleds and climbed the high drifts to a lower roof of the McVeigh home, where they slid down to the deep snow below. This play went on each morning after breakfast.

Dan Kane, managing editor of the *Union-Sun & Journal* in Lockport, recalls the blizzard:

> The Blizzard of '77 was a very severe storm. It was the most se-vere storm I've ever been in and I come from the South—Day-tona Beach, Florida—where storms and hurricanes and torna-does are commonplace. The community that was probably the hardest hit in western New York was the town of Pendleton. I remember weeks later, going to Pendleton, to Five Corners, and having to walk through a tunnel of snow and drifts to get to the grocery store, and this was two weeks after the blizzard sub-sided. But those tunnels still remained. The place was almost in-undated with snow. So if that left an impression on me as an adult, you can imagine what it would have done to a ten-year-old kid who liked nature and liked to be out in the elements. So I can understand if it had a lasting impression on Tim.[11]

New York Governor Hugh Carey asked President Jimmy Carter to declare Niagara County a disaster area, and the request was granted. The Blizzard of 1977 is still remembered as the worst in western New York history. Three people died in Lockport: two in a house fire that could not be reached by firemen in the storm, and one of a heart attack in his car. Eight people died in Buffalo, most from freezing to death in their stranded cars.

After the snow subsided and the main roads were finally cleared, the county struggled to get back to normal. To be prepared if more snow hit, the McVeigh family began storing food, water, and supplies in the basement. Tim asked his dad if they could also keep a generator down there, in case they ever lost power again. Bill thought that was going too far and said no. When Mickey returned, she had a few stories to tell about her stay at the hotel.

Tim McVeigh carried with him the fear of being unprepared and alone. Its effect on his life would surface later as an emphasis on survivalism. Young Tim also realized that Mom may not always be there for him in a time of fear. These were two powerful lessons to learn for a fun-loving nine-year-old boy with the world at his feet.

The McVeighs seemed the average American, small-town family: a home, three kids, and a General Motors car. But something was missing for Mickey. Bill McVeigh worked often and Mickey traveled a lot as a travel agent, dividing her time among Patty, Tim, Jennifer, and her social life. There was always plenty of beer and good times at the local bowling alleys. Bill would stop in before the night shift at Harrison and bowl a frame. He should have kept in mind his high school lesson on Alfred Lord Tennyson, who said, "worse than being fooled of others, is to fool one's self." It wasn't until Bill McVeigh left the Alley Brandt's building that the good times began, as Mickey's pretty eyes began to wander.

Trooper Hanger stepped up to the car and looked inside. The lean man in the front seat gazed up at him with a smile, as the trooper told the driver why he'd been stopped, and asked for identification. Just past the trooper and Tim's cars, a brown pickup truck pulled to the side of the road. Whoever was driving the truck seemed to be interested in the scene, maybe a friend of McVeigh's. Stopping for just a few seconds, the mysterious truck pulled back out onto the highway and continued on. As Tim reached into his right rear pocket for his wallet, Trooper Hanger saw the silhouette of a pistol under the left side of McVeigh's new jacket. Hanger's mind shifted immediately to what he had learned years ago in training—take charge of the situation and get the person out of the car! The trooper told the driver to pull his jacket back, unsnapped his own gun, and calmly asked Tim if he had a weapon. When Tim responded yes, Trooper Hanger grabbed hold of the left side of McVeigh's jacket and placed his police-issued weapon to the back of Tim's head. McVeigh had no chance to do anything, even if he'd wanted to. At gunpoint Tim was ordered to get out of the car and place his hands on the trunk.

Chapter 3

Our Town

There was the truth of virginity and the truth of passion, the truth of wealth and of poverty, of thrift and of profligacy, of carelessness and abandon. . . . And then the people came along. Each . . . snatched up one of the truths and some who were quite strong snatched up a dozen of them. It was the truths that made the people grotesque.

—Sherwood Anderson*

In Pendleton, New York, as in many American small towns, traditional ways of life become embedded in the community: for example, the daily routine of a wife maintaining a clean, comfortable house for her husband and children, the mother being home when the kids return from school, dad hard at work, dinner on the table every evening, and a front yard kept immaculate by the work of dad and the children on weekends. While much of this changed in the early 1970s with women's liberation and the romantic notion

---

*Sherwood Anderson, *Winesburg, Ohio* (Penguin Books, 1976).

51

of the singles lifestyle, there are still many townspeople today who are ruled by religious faith and a commitment to tradition. The stresses and strains of this volatile decade formed three factions in the community of Pendleton: those who led quiet lives and attended Sunday mass, those who abandoned all tradition and looked with scorn on the old ways, and those who fell in-between. The in-betweens gave the impression that they lived by the old ways and even fooled themselves from time to time, but when no one important was looking they would sneak out to live the wild life. The members of the McVeigh family represented all three of these groups as the 1980s grew closer. It was only a matter of years before the clan would feel the separation of its opposing forces.

Today, Pendleton is populated by many hardworking families. It's a friendly community—one of the smallest in western New York—where a stranger is always made to feel at home. In the summer, the athletic field near the town hall is full of young people playing baseball and tennis. Picnics and yard sales dot the highways. On Monday nights some locals and retired citizens gather for a drink at Brauer's Tavern, or for chicken and biscuits and a game or two of cards. Bingo is held each week at the church recreation hall.

The name Pendleton comes from a renegade, the town's founder, Sylvester Pendleton Clark. This rowdy gent with heart-shaped face and deep-set eyes was a member of an antigovernment group that refused to pay taxes in 1817. Clark's dispute with the American government led him and his friends to settle on Grand Island, a large spot of former Indian land connected to Buffalo today by a bridge across the Niagara River. Grand Island isn't far from Niagara Falls, and is about a thirty-minute drive from what we now know as Pendleton. Historian and author Christopher J. Carlin wrote of those days:

> The people who settled [in Grand Island] were considered outlaws. This population organized a small, independent govern-

ment of its own. The head of the government, Clark, had assumed the title of governor.[1]

Paradise was eventually lost and the group was kicked off the island in 1819 by a state militia that burned the settlers' homes to the ground. Many went north to live in Canada, but Clark, a natural-born American, traveled east and used much of the money he'd gained in Grand Island to purchase land in Niagara County. He named his land purchase Pendleton, after his mother's maiden name. The town itself was established on April 16, 1827, and was home to the Three Willows Site, where Seneca boats stopped to load and unload supplies. Revolutionary War heroes John Van Slyke and Noah Strickland made the town their home. The digging of the Erie Canal inspired people, including Irish immigrants, to stay in Pendleton and raise their families.

Niagara County is named for the falls, and borders a long stretch of Lake Ontario. A long, warm spring climate has made it the ideal place for farming vegetables and fruit. Homes that were not built of wood were constructed from stones found in creeks and in the lake. Lake ports were established in the Niagara towns of Olcott, Wilson, Lewiston, and Youngstown.

The digging of the canal, which began in 1821 in Niagara, opened more area for settling during the four-year period of its completion. In addition to Pendleton, the towns of Lockport, Royalton, Hartland, Somerset, Newfane, Porter, and Wheatfield were all eventually established.

Despite the large settlements that made cities out of Lockport, Niagara Falls, and North Tonawanda, Pendleton has remained much as its founder left it, surrounded by deep woods and fields. Pendleton has a few government offices, two bars, a pizzeria, a gas station, and the Starpoint school system named for the five towns it represents, as many kids are bused to the school from the surrounding area.

Pendleton's population of five thousand also remains as it was decades ago. Most are white Catholics and Protestants who live their entire lives in the town, or leave for some schooling and then return. The eastern part of Niagara County is well known for having residents who never leave. The reasons for this inertia are generally the same: a desire to remain with family, an economic inability to leave, and fear of the outside world. Other than history classes, the children learn about the rest of the world through television. It's a common belief that outside eastern Niagara, the crime rate is higher and the weather inclement. "At least we don't have tornadoes or earthquakes," is a common refrain among locals.

Because of the geographic separation, racial prejudice born from ignorance has been passed on for generations, from early immigration to today. The predominantly white Niagara County had an initial settling of black Americans around 1850 when a law was passed that fugitive slaves found in free states had to be returned to their "masters." The Underground Railroad had stops in and around Lockport, New York, as slaves passed secretly through the area while seeking freedom in nearby Canada. Frederick Douglass worked with the "railroad" from his home base in Rochester, where he ran his newspaper *The North Star,* named after the celestial light that guided the railroad's "conductors" like Harriet Tubman and other fugitives along the winding trails at night. Some African Americans settled in budding Lockport and found jobs on farms and in factories. Their children, for many years, were not allowed to attend schools with white children in Lockport, and it took black rights leader Aaron Mossell most of his adult life to convince the Board of Education that all students should learn together. Mossell planted the seed in the community that a "public school system" would be better than the "private" system for whites only. Integration in Lockport schools did eventually take place in 1876.

These efforts on behalf of blacks in the area were not without cost. Racism festered. Local records from the Niagara County historian's office detail the birth of a new political party that not only gave the Republicans competition in annual elections, but also scared the local police and residents on several occasions. That party was the Ku Klux Klan. It rose to power when the fight for jobs in western New York became a racial issue, and scapegoats were sought for some economic problems the region was experiencing. The Klan's influence soon ran from little Olcott near Lake Ontario, through Pendleton, and all the way to the city of Niagara Falls. Membership, of course, was nationwide for the group born in the South years after the Civil War. The group's influence took several years to reach the North. Scary headlines in the Lockport and Niagara Falls newspapers during the 1920s read "Fiery Cross Burns in Town of Hartland," "Niagara KKK Plans Demonstration," "Former Deputy Arrested in KKK Probe," "Klansmen's Olcott Outing Was Gala Occasion," and "Capacity Audience at Klan Meet."

According to historian Chris Carlin, one of the first major events involving the KKK in Niagara County was a massive parade on July 4, 1923. Close to ten thousand Klansmen and their families walked through the streets of Niagara Falls, and burned a number of crosses near Gill Creek. In a ceremony there, more than five hundred new members were initiated into the "Invisible Empire." A group opposed to the KKK arrived at the site but were ushered out by Klan members who stood shoulder to shoulder and walked the field, herding the unwanted people away.

Another newsworthy event occurred on October 18, 1923, when sheriff's deputies James Deasy and Bernard Murphy investigated a KKK gathering five miles east of Lockport, in Sanborn. KKK members, armed with shotguns, stood outside the gathering by the road, preventing anyone from entering, unless they intended to join the Klan. The deputies left, but later returned with police reinforcements only to find themselves vastly outnumbered. During a chase, the KKK fired at the fleeing deputies but no one was hurt. Two Klansmen from the Falls were arrested and jailed in Lockport. One day later, during an investigation by the police, KKK member and former deputy Roy Cramer of Pendleton was charged with threatening people outside the gathering but the charge was dismissed by County Justice Budde. A grand jury later indicted Cramer and the two Falls men on related charges.

In 1925, Customs Agent Orville Preuster, brother of a former KKK leader, was killed by a bomb blast outside his Falls home. The incident set off a number of demonstrations by the KKK, who, along with the police, conducted their own investigation. The murderer or murderers were never caught.

Another Klan gathering of ten thousand or more was held in 1925 at the Niagara County Fairgrounds in Lockport. The carnival-like atmosphere was topped off by an early-evening address by national Klan speaker Dr. G. A. Brown, who criticized Jews, blacks, and anyone he considered "foreign born." He also reaffirmed the Klan's commitment to "white supremacy." Shortly before 1930, the Klan lost much of its influence when Lockport lawyer Merton Doty used a run for office as a way to expose the group's hatred to the masses in Niagara. Though Doty lost the county surrogate judge race, his campaign caused the KKK to slowly lose its hold in the local municipalities. The articles on file in the Niagara historian's office do not detail the Klan's demise, and it is unknown when the official KKK meetings finally stopped. The office does have a list of Klansmen, and the document contains the names of the grandfathers of many prominent women and men in leadership positions in Niagara County today. The name McVeigh does not appear there, but the name Hill does. My research has failed to match the Hill in the KKK list to the family historically united with the McVeighs.

Animosity and ignorance toward "non-whites" still exists in western New York and it struck hard when the national economy spiraled downward in the late 1970s and again in the 1980s. Henry L. Taylor, Jr., director for urban studies at the University of Buffalo, said problems of race in and around Buffalo still center on economic issues. Professor Taylor wrote in the February 25, 1996, issue of *Buffalo Magazine* that despite the increase in the African-American population:

> Race and class divisions are still strong here. . . . Race plays a big role in deciding who works and who remains jobless. On the Niagara Frontier, the race problem is really a problem about jobs and who gains access to them. In 1992, the *Buffalo News* conducted a poll on racial attitudes in Erie County. It found whites viewed blacks as less intelligent, less hardworking, and less trustworthy than whites. Similar results were found in a poll conducted by WKBW-TV [in Buffalo]. . . . Whites—to separate themselves from blacks—practice economic segregation, oppose mass transit to suburbia, [and] fight against programs designed to help blacks out of dire straits. . . . In the quietness of their suburban homes, they fan the flames of economic and social crisis.[2]

Prejudice is very prominent in the hometown areas of the McVeighs. One would have to be deaf not to take in at least two or three racist remarks at a social gathering or public place. Whether it be the man on the street or a local politico, prejudicial sentiments are passed on in conversation as if the year is 1900, not 1996. Letters to the editor of the *Union-Sun & Journal* talk of restricting immigration and stopping imports to "save" the economy of America. Buffalo-based editor Barbara Banks reflected, "A large part of the problem is that nobody wants to admit racism is a problem. We all have stories to tell. For most of us, being black in Buffalo, like being black in America, is an ongoing, sometimes frustrating, struggle."[3] Clifton Gibson, president of Discipleship Organization for Minority Order in Resources and Education in Lockport, says prejudice spreads in rural communities like Pendleton because of the absence of diverse culture. During an interview for this book, Gibson stressed:

> Pendleton is even more rural than Lockport. Still, today, there is racial tension. When you don't understand something, you fear it.

We are now starting programs in the middle schools to promote
understanding and deal with problems that have developed.[4]

Hate, dislike, and discomfort with people of color or of Eastern
descent is common, but subtle.

In the 1850s, the railroad through Lockport and an increase in
commerce helped establish the area as an industrial and manufacturing area, not to mention the tourism value of Niagara Falls.
Harrison Division of General Motors was established in Lockport
and attracted many teens who had just completed high school and
were seeking its high-paying assembly jobs. All the area towns
had youth to send to Harrison, and during the war, the women
stepped into those jobs to continue production.

Pendleton produced Gertrude Warren, the founder of the international 4-H clubs, which were based on farming and teaching
children this work for the preservation of the lifestyle back home.
Another well-known figure, author Joyce Carol Oates, was raised
in Lockport and Pendleton. She attended Good Shepherd Church
with her parents, and had junior high classes at North Park School
in Lockport. Oates, now a Princeton University professor, recalled her difficult hometown days to Marian Christy of the
Boston Sunday Globe:

> Growing up on a farm, you learn about life as a ceaseless strug-
> gle. Farmers are beleaguered. They think of nature as an on-
> slaught. Torrential rains that beat down the wheat. The lack of
> rain dries the corn. Those tomato worms. Those slugs. As a
> child, I fed the chickens, worked in the strawberry patch, and
> tended the vegetable garden. But it was also a life that brought
> me a sense of solitude. I wandered a lot near the creek. I learned
> to be alone with my thoughts.[5]

Oates talks of her father's struggles also, and how her parents
were "cheated out of the opportunity to develop their talents." Es-

tablished as a working-class society, the county has offered little over the years in the way of culture, or exposure to the outside world. It is a vacuum where many seem happy but hide their true selves, like the characters in *Winesburg, Ohio.* Some are like the twisted apples left behind by pickers, which Sherwood Anderson describes in his book about small-town America.

> On the trees are only a few gnarled apples that the pickers have rejected. One nibbles at them and they are delicious. Into a little round place at the side of the apple has been gathered all of its sweetness. Only a few know the sweetness of the twisted apples.[6]

In addition to Oates, many top talents and achievers left Niagara to become recognized nationally in their fields. Lockport natives include volleyball inventor William Morgan, vice presidential candidate and congressman William Miller, Space Shuttle pilot Bill Gregory, and supermodel Kim Alexis. Also, Rep. Miller's daughter, Stephanie Miller, had her own syndicated late-night talk show on national television. On a smaller scale, there's Brock Yates, a recognized automobile authority and founder of the Cannonball Run, a car race across America that inspired the movie of the same name, starring Burt Reynolds and a huge cast of other well-known Hollywood celebrities.

In the late 1970s, the national economy took a turn for the worse. Its effect was felt soon after in Niagara County when Harrison Radiator began laying off workers and stopped accepting new applications. Employees from GM's Detroit office were called in. High school graduates, who had planned on a Harrison career like their fathers, had nowhere to turn in the decade that followed. Their options were limited: find a low-paying job at home; get a college education and leave; or enter military service. Timothy James McVeigh, not quite ten years of age when this dramatic change hit his hometown area, could look up to a father who represented a dying breed—those who had a high-paying career at the local factory locked up after school or the service. Tim would represent the current generation, a group with few choices, making its mark on history with an "X." The local Niagara economy spiraled down as more factories and stores closed, until it stopped at a dormant state, from which it is only now emerging. Tim's generation was left behind by Anderson's fictional apple pickers.

As jobs disappeared and "for sale" signs littered the neighborhoods, property taxes increased. The town voice, in addition to rumors about who was in bed with whom, now had a distinct grumbling sound. Why were taxes going up when salaries weren't? Why were public employees getting raises when private firms were laying off? An anger grew and it was directed at the local government. Interest at meetings of government bodies shifted from budding politicians to disgruntled taxpayers. Then there was welfare, a government program that many felt paid people to stay home and drink beer. Those who were perceived as choosing not to work attracted and aggravated the anger of Niagara County residents. Hardworking people like Bill McVeigh would have discussed these disappointments with friends and relatives, the way people discuss the weather. It became a popular topic.

In the summer of 1985 reality came knocking by way of a call from an unidentified source to a newspaper. The *Union-Sun & Journal* reported the next day that pounds of surplus government cheese and other food earmarked for distribution to the poor had been left to spoil in a Niagara County building. High-ranking county officials scrambled to offer an explanation for the "cheese fiasco." Weeks earlier officials ran out of food during a distribution day for Niagara Falls residents. Rumor had it that the cheese had been set aside for use by a North Tonawanda pizza-maker who had connections to the county and that a few other county employees were taking the food to their homes. Daniel Penale, a Work Experience Program director, was blamed and suspended. But he would be back later, stressing that he was made the "fall guy" by two county legislators and a Social Services commissioner.

Still, to the town voice, there was a lot more going on behind "Cheesegate" than was being told. The *Union-Sun & Journal* story, which made national headlines when picked up by the Associated Press, hinted at full-blown corruption among politicians in Niagara County. The rumor mill was now going full speed in the towns. Since 1972's Watergate, all the remaining trust that many Niagara residents had in any of their political leaders was completely lost. Taxes increased again the following year as pay hikes were handed out to the county employees who, many believed, couldn't keep a simple food program from going bad. Bill McVeigh, like every other taxpayer, would have complained bitterly to his family and friends about the government, which obviously had major problems nationally, and now in his town.

Cheesegate was never forgotten, but it was replaced in the public mind a few years later by a drunken trip to Florida that some politicians took and was later found to be paid for with tax money. Finally, the federal government became interested in the shady deals that were going on in Niagara County.

In the summer of 1991, state and private audits revealed inflated county costs of $1.5 million. To residents, $1.5 million was a lottery winning or an inheritance. To Niagara County politicians—those who hoped the figure would hide itself—it was a drop in the bucket of their multimillion-dollar annual budget. But to the federal investigators, $1.5 million in bogus costs was the stuff that makes for a good probe. So while the feds requested ten years' worth of county records and paid visits to the homes of some scared government workers and representatives, taxpayers planned peaceful protests. At county budget meetings as well as those of the city and schools, property owners asked more questions than ever before. In the tradition of Pendleton Clark, some residents threatened to stop paying taxes because of the money's obvious misuse by the local government.

The situation worsened in the fall of 1991 when *Niagara Gazette* reporter Karen Eckhardt broke a story about the county parks department renting four county government-owned homes to friends and relatives of county officials. The "rents" were about $150 a month for top-of-the-line houses in scenic lakeside or park areas, which could easily have brought in rents of $500 to $600 a month. In the months that followed, public discontent and the FBI's investigation grew better than the corn. One FBI agent called Niagara the "most corrupt" county he ever saw.

County officials began falling like dominoes in the next two years. Niagara Sheriff Francis Giles, Undersheriff Donald Plant, Social Services Commissioner Louis Scozzafava, Parks Commissioner Ronald Shiesley, Niagara Falls businessman John Gross, Legislator Mark Scott, North Tonawanda Councilman Mark Narowski, Falls Building Inspector Robert DiCamillo, Jail cook Clyde Rankie, and Lewiston landfill owner Steve Washuta—people with high-paying government or private jobs—all were charged or pled guilty to crimes ranging from bribery to theft of food. The reports of pleas and charges seemed never to end from 1991 to 1994, and several people, including Sheriff Giles, served jail terms. U.S. Attorney Dennis Vacco reflected on the federal probe of Niagara County in a *Gazette* report:

> The corruption was indeed at multiple levels in Niagara County. Even after the probe was disclosed, there was an attitude of business as usual in Niagara County, which allowed [an informant] to continue to accumulate valuable information. . . . Despite all the public attention given to the investigation, several people continued to engage in unlawful conduct.[7]

Oddly, Vacco commented that the 1986 bombings of several Niagara Falls tourist booths were in part responsible for sparking the investigation. Apparently, more people than just taxpayers were angry with the government over the corruption. Vacco did not elaborate on the bombings. One man who cooperated with the probe claimed he was an alleged target of the bombers, who were apparently his former employees and upset over salary differences.

It will be many years before the people of Niagara County allow the crimes of their leaders to fade into history. Many still grumble today about the dirty deeds that brought down a whole local government, and cost thousands more in taxes for the prosecution. In Niagara, every taxpayer had something to be angry about. Every time a government bill appeared in the mail, no one was quite sure where the tax money would go in the end.

And the distrust in government on the local level translated to the national level over the loss of President Kennedy, who once visited and was supported in Lockport; the Watergate scandal; the National Free Trade Agreement, strongly opposed by the Harrison unions; the tragedies at Ruby Ridge, Idaho, and Waco, Texas, that found citizens strongly suspecting that their government overstepped its legal bounds.

The peaceful morning traffic continued to cascade by them on the highway. Trooper Hanger took the loaded gun from under Tim's coat and confiscated a five-inch knife he found tucked into Tim's belt. Even though Tim had a New York State permit to carry a gun, and informed the trooper of his right as a citizen, possessing a loaded weapon while traveling was illegal in Oklahoma. Tim was handcuffed and placed in the back of the trooper's car, and would be brought in on five charges: speeding, driving a vehicle without a license plate, operating a vehicle without insurance, unlawfully carrying a weapon, and unlawfully carrying a loaded weapon in a motor vehicle. Sometime during the ride to jail, McVeigh slipped a business card he'd had into the seat of the patrol car. He might have thought the card, for Paulsen's Military Supply of Antigo, Wisconsin, would get him into trouble, since a note on the back read that "more TNT" was needed in May. While the cruiser continued its trip, McVeigh could feel that the Kansas border was farther away than it had ever been.

Chapter 4

Changes

For sweetest things turn sourest by their deeds
Lilies that fester smell far worse than weeds.
—William Shakespeare*

A .22 caliber. Grandpa McVeigh thought it would be the perfect gift for the thirteen-year-old boy, and little Tim was delighted. For many years Edward McVeigh had told Tim of the days when Niagara was still untamed, of the wild horses he broke when he was just a boy, and of the hunting days. The rifle felt heavy, not from weight but from the responsibility it carried. Ed stressed to Tim that this was a big step and he always had to be careful when cleaning and loading the gun. Tim McVeigh couldn't wait to get out into the yard and try it out. Under Edward's watchful eye, Tim seemed to bloom with the gun, an excitement unmatched in other activities he attempted. Grandpa was overjoyed because soon Tim

---

*William Shakespeare, *The Sonnets* (St. Martin's Press, 1980), no. 94.

would learn the value of collecting beautiful, well-crafted firearms. His son, Bill, had not taken a real interest in guns, other than owning the traditional shotgun to protect the home. Ed was a real gun collector, and even stopped at the occasional gun show in town to meet with dealers and others who shared his interest. Ed thought that soon Tim would develop the same liking for guns, know their value, and Ed would have a lifelong gun buddy.

Their relationship also benefited. Tim was becoming a man. Only a man could handle the difficult road ahead Edward saw for Tim's parents. There was a thorn pressing at the side of that marriage. Only a fool could be blind to it. Edward felt sorry for Tim, and for the girls. In the old days, a couple worked through their problems, fought it out, and a man was damned if he let his wife, the mother of his children, stray from sight. A man was damned! But Ed knew his son's ways. He had raised a forgiving gentleman, who kept his emotions inside and was the first to turn from a fight. Maybe that had been a mistake. Bill had the soul of a soldier, but the heart of a priest. Edward knew his son was not prepared for everything Mickey seemed ready to dish out.

"That's it, Tim. Eyes forward." Edward watched the boy aim the gun out at the pop can target, and braced for the first shot.

Sometime after 1976, while the McVeighs were at the Meyer Road home, Mickey began spending more time with girlfriends, namely Louise Braunscheidel. The two were inseparable during those years. Disco music was hot and "nightlife" was the scene in Lockport. Women wore tight pants and shirts that flared at the sleeves and inseams. The men wore their shirts open to display gold necklaces and chains. The Bee Gees kept saying on the radio, "You should be dancin'!" and the crowds responded in their platform shoes, polyester jackets, and Elton John glasses. The Lockport area had a few bars that were hopping, like Briandi's, Old City Hall, and the Sheridan Hotel lounge that had red kissing booths and live bands. The hotel bar was so packed with swingers, many had to wait outside for their chance to get in. Country girls like Mickey McVeigh would stop in the city from time to time for their moment under the disco lights, and sometimes they'd stop at Pendleton's After Dark club for a nightcap. Bill McVeigh missed much of the nightlife because he either had to work, or just disliked that type of adult play. Bill's bowling and church friend Richard Pierce, a Meyer Road neighbor, recalled Mickey's attraction: "She was going out with her girlfriends—shop till you drop types. She was not home that much. That was a problem."[1]

To a man, meeting Mickey McVeigh was a treat. She went from having that Jacqueline Kennedy 1960s look to the liberated bombshell with a million-dollar smile. Mickey was always charming, but after becoming a mother, she seemed to turn into a man magnet. All those who spoke of her during interviews recalled a friendly, open woman who could turn heads everywhere. She invited you in, and if you wanted to stay to see what would happen, that was okay, too. A family acquaintance, Dan Kane, remembered meeting Mickey years after her divorce from Bill:

> Mickey was a very, very attractive lady. Tall, thin, great legs. As I remember, she used to be partial to shorts and little halter tops . . . slender, more than average height . . . and well endowed. She had lighter hair, brown eyes, I think, and was friendly. She liked to go out and dance, liked to be seen. To be looked at and to look. I remember being attracted to her myself and thinking, "God, if I wasn't taken already, here's a woman who looks like she'd be fun to go out with." That was her reputation—going out and having a good time.[2]

Bill's friend Leo LaPort, Jr., offered another look at Mickey, saying she "was taller than normal, pushing five feet, ten inches, and had nice facial features. She was a good-looking girl."

Tim and Jennifer were often babysat by their older sister, Patricia, while Dad was at work and Mom was out. Tim began to realize something was wrong. Bill knew, but what was he to do? They talked and Mickey would say she was just out seeing some friends and happened to be out late. Nothing to worry about. A friend of Edward McVeigh's, who spoke to me in confidence and off the record, noted that Grandpa McVeigh also knew what was happening.

> He said Mickey was her own woman and no matter what Bill said, she was going to do what she wanted. She was one of strong will. Eddie was worried about his son and the children. He thought this was the first time that this happened on his side [of the McVeigh family].[3]

Mickey McVeigh continued to play at the Allie Brandt bowling alley, where the after hours lifestyle was more attractive than home life. Ralph Conne (not his real name) worked at the counter, where he would dispense bowling shoes, tally the games played, and accept money from patrons. Allie Brandt Lanes, in those days a thriving complex in Lockport on Lincoln Avenue, had a sparsely decorated bar and a separate lunch counter that served mainly hamburgers and fries. The well-lit bar was populated by men who were between games or frames. League play is still more popular than individual games, and most who bowl there have known each other for years. There is also a game room with pinball and video games for the children. The whole scene is something out of the television situation comedy "Roseanne," where friends meet and word of mouth spreads quickly. Mickey was allegedly fond of sneaking out on Bill with one of his "friends" or another man she had met. Ralph Conne spoke intimately about Mickey's trysts, which he witnessed as an employee of the bowling alley. Conne said Mickey made her unfaithfulness obvious:

> I know for a fact that she was cheating. You could tell what was going on. It was the type of thing where the guy would finish his drink and leave. Five minutes later, she would finish her drink and go out there. That was the way it happened. It was obvious.[4]

Their differences—Mickey's thirst for good times, and Bill's homebody nature—drove them apart. Bill's friend Leo LaPort, Jr., said, "Mickey would just want to stay out all night. She could make conversation with anybody." The town voice learned of the infidelity and rumors flew. Many people, especially those close to Bill McVeigh, felt sorry for the cuckolded husband, and were disappointed in Mickey. But the cheating didn't end. It got worse, with Mickey actually "flaunting" herself in front of Bill to show her unhappiness in their marriage. Richard Pierce philosophized: "She lost interest in being a housewife. He [Bill] was a good father and a family man. He wasn't the one causing the problem. [She] just wanted to get away from the house, I guess."[5]

She seemed to like the bowling/night life so well that she later obtained a job at South Transit Lanes, also in Lockport. In a May 7, 1996, letter to the *Fort Pierce Tribune* (a newspaper in the Florida town where she resides), Mickey tried to explain her absences from the family in those difficult days. Mickey also seemed to try to place some blame on Bill.

> I had a day job with a travel agency and my husband worked swing shift at a local GM factory. He worked six days a week, fifty-two weeks a year with no vacation time. I traveled for my job about every four to six weeks. They were one- or two-day trips. When Tim was eleven, I did leave for six weeks.[6]

Meanwhile, Tim's interest in weapons was encouraged by his father. Bill bought Tim his first shotgun when he was fifteen years old. Unlike his peers from school, Tim was not fond of hunting. Instead, he liked target practice and the study of guns. When he could, he read *Guns & Ammo* magazine to learn more about collecting and gun hobbies. In his later teens, Tim attended a local gun show and met others who shared his interests. He respected hunters, but didn't have the interest in joining them. It just wasn't necessary, and didn't carry the excitement factor that the practice with clay targets or shooting into the sky did. After being shot, an animal, like a rabbit, usually just fell and that was it. More and more targets could be shot into the sky, and one could shoot all day, without getting into the disgusting mess of dragging home and gutting an animal after killing it. Sometimes, Tim would bring one of his guns to Starpoint to show the others. He found that a gun really got the attention of the other kids, attention he was not getting at home from his absentee parents. Sure, he attended a Buffalo Bills game with his dad now and then, but Bill was usually at work. And who knew where Mom was.

A Starpoint classmate of Tim's, Justin Genter, pondered the early love of guns that Tim was known for. He said Tim didn't hang around the hunters, or even the kids who wore camouflage to school. Genter said Tim was the subject of some good-natured kidding in the hall because he was "kind of a dork" but he wasn't involved in fistfights. Tim's interest in weapons was stronger than most others, though.

> He told people about his BB pistol, a CO_2 one. I remember him demonstrating holding it out in police fashion, demonstrating how fast he could shoot fifteen rounds, as fast as he could pull the trigger.[7]

Timothy's other passion in youth was collecting comic books. Meyer Road neighbor Jack McDermott, a few years Bill McVeigh's senior, recalled spending time with Tim and encouraging his love for collecting and reading. The neighbor would take Tim to the House of Fantasy comic store in Niagara Falls. McDermott told Peter Jennings in an April 11 ABC News special report:

> Tim would buy every week four or five different editions that he felt he was going to read, to begin with, but he was also going to be able to save them and they would accumulate value over a period of time. . . . I said, "Well, what are you going to do with these things?" He said, "This is going to be my college fund."[8]

The situation at home eventually proved unbearable for the McVeigh parents. There were some short periods of separation, apparently caused by Mickey's devotion to her travel job, and then longer ones. Bill McVeigh confided in his pastor, Father Paul Belzer of the Good Shepherd Church. Father Belzer told CNN, "Tim was in about eighth grade when his mother decided things weren't going well. She took the two daughters and moved to Florida."[9] Members of Mickey's family, the Hills, lived in Florida and that proved to be a place where Mickey could attempt to get her life together. Bill stayed with Tim at the Meyer Road home, and Mickey finally came back. Friends say Bill and Mickey tried to work their differences out because they knew she had a great responsibility with the children. Bill would still take Mickey back anytime; his love was undying. Mickey apparently didn't feel the same. Mickey said in her 1996 letter to the *Fort Pierce Tribune* that: "My children had a choice on whether to stay with their father or go with me. Tim chose to stay with his dad."[10] Tim, who apparently suffered the separations and parental problems from the time he was about ten until his late teen years, rarely talked about his home life, choosing instead to keep that frustration and anger inside, much like his father. Richard Pierce remembers the initial difficulties for Tim and his family:

> Tim was like any other teen. He was hurting and confused, thinking, "Was it something I did?" [To Bill] it was devastating. He handled it well though. You knew he was hurting [but] he never complained. It might have been embarrassing. Embarrassing for him with his relations in the church. We were the ones who were most aware of it and the ones who really cared. Someone at Harrison wouldn't really care about that. Bill was kind of a victim in a way, of a woman who wanted to go out and really do her own thing.[11]

There were many tears, but they never washed away the empty feelings inside. Meyer Road neighbor Pat Waugh told the *Union-Sun & Journal* that after the separation, the happy-go-lucky kid they knew as Tim became different, not as open. She commented:

> Tim changed and his sister Patty became very angry. As [my] kids became teenagers, I did not want them to go over to [Tim's] house because there was no mother there, and with their father at work, they were unsupervised.[12]

Tim McVeigh soldiered the problems by developing his interest in weaponry. He, friend Dave Darlak, and some others allegedly formed a survivalist group in their teens to be prepared in the event that World War III broke out, a notion of nuclear holocaust imbedded in their heads by the 1980s film *The Last Day.* While other folks were able to handle the film at face level, it frightened the children and young adults who were allowed to stay up late enough to watch. *The Last Day* chronicles World War III's effect on a small town, and how a group of people are able to survive using special tactics. Tim would have seen the movie with just about every other youth in America. In his family's disintegrating state, the impact on Tim would have been strong—his world was facing real and fictional extinction.

"Chicken McVeigh," as Tim was called by some classmates, became more social at school. Though careful not to discuss his family or the problems at home, he was more outgoing. Tim was encouraged by his sister Patty's success in sports at Starpoint. Patty was known as a "jock" who hung around the crowd of girls who wore no makeup to school and rarely dressed up to impress the boys. She generally wore her hair long and "feathered" back as was the style in the early 1980s. She liked the band .38 Special, and even quoted one of its songs as the quote to remember her by in the 1984 yearbook. Patty excelled in varsity softball, basketball, and volleyball, playing on these teams from ninth grade to twelfth. Eager to fit in, Tim tried out for football in his freshman year. He was one of the taller boys in his class and that helped during tryouts with the Spartans, according to classmate Keith Maurer, who spoke to *Media Bypass*: "He wasn't the best athlete in the bunch . . . but he always played hard. When we tried out for freshman football he was pretty big for his age and he made the team."[13]

Tim also made the track team with his friend Doug Gorman. The team only won one match, against Akron, 77 to 64. It lost the other six matches against teams from outlying towns that season.

Patty McVeigh said goodbye to Starpoint in 1984. Among many friends in her brief yearbook biography, she listed, "Mom, Dad, Tim, and Jenny" as her favorite people in the world. Her future plans included "college, job, marriage, good times."

Tim's interests matured and he got a job working at Burger King in Amherst, fourteen miles south of his hometown. There he met a female co-worker named Sarah Hahn. Their relationship developed and it is believed that Sarah was Tim's first girlfriend. They went "steady" and Tim took her to her prom at Sweet Home High School in 1984, the same year that his sister Patty graduated. In his junior and senior years at Starpoint, Tim concentrated on getting good grades. Starpoint classmate, Pam Widmer, recalled how Tim didn't fit into any cliques, but had hospitable traits and was academically competitive at times.

While Mr. Riscile handed back the test he had graded for his honors students, Pam and Tim waited anxiously for theirs. Pam sat next to Tim McVeigh and found him to be awkward, but friendly, someone to talk with before class began. The students received their usual marks, 80 percent to 90 percent, but several times Tim surpassed that average, scoring 92 percent or higher.

"I beat you again," Tim would say, his blue eyes darting from Pam's test paper to his own. "I beat you again." He frequently pulled in such grades and was just a few steps away from being considered a full-time honors student. Widmer said Tim would come alive when he scored well:

> I really got to know him better in senior physics. He was on my left. He never studied at all, and we had this thing going, a competitive thing where we'd get the grades back and he was always comparing his to mine. He was intelligent and told me he never studied, and I used to study like crazy. His score usually beat mine and he'd be gloating about it. I think he com-

pared with others around us, too. His grades . . . could have
been a lot better if he studied.[14]

Even though he may not have hit the books often, Tim was one
of the students known for never missing a day of school. Bill
McVeigh was often at work until the night shift ended at 8 A.M.,
but Tim and his sisters needed to be at school by 7 or 7:30, depending on the grade they were in. After his mother left home,
Tim would have had many opportunities to sleep in or miss the
bus to cut classes. But he didn't. A truant officer from Starpoint
schools, who wished to remain anonymous, said in a taped interview that Tim McVeigh "had a nearly perfect attendance record,
and as far as anyone can determine, never had a discipline refer-
ral turned in on him." Tim was also healthy. His pediatrician, Dr.
Nasser Jafarian of Lockport, said young McVeigh had rare visits
to the office, his last being in 1985.

In addition to shooting and reading, Tim took an early interest in computers. State educational guidelines provided schools in
the 1980s with funding to purchase computer systems and the authority to start classes on programming. They were basic studies,
which turned students on to the future through level-one training.
The movie *WarGames,* about a high school teen and his girlfriend
who tap into government files with the boy's home computer,
was popular at the time. Cable television, with stations like HBO
and Showtime, was booming, and ran movies like *WarGames* and
Red Dawn frequently. Both movies feature students of high
school-age becoming involved in government conspiracies or
problems, and then overcoming the enemy to become heroes. The
WarGames subplot centers on whether the U.S. government
should replace men in nuclear missile silos with computers that
would act on orders, without having "second thoughts" in the
case of an all-out world war. The 1983 PG movie centers on a sev-
enteen-year-old student, played by Matthew Broderick, who is a
computer wiz. He gets the interest of a classmate Jennifer Mack,

played by Ally Sheedy, when his computer skills impress her. Broderick's character eventually breaks into the Pentagon's master computer, NORAD, that controls nuclear silos, and the two running stories are weaved together.

Since Tim lived in such a rural area, there was little to do. Hobbies like shooting, computers, and movies ward off cabin fever, especially during the winter, in places like Pendleton. There's not much else for youths to do but ski or study, both of which Tim apparently disliked. A McVeigh family friend and Starpoint teacher recalled that Tim was known at the school for his computer savvy:

> At that time we used very primitive machines, called the Commodore Pet, which is just first generation. Tim worked out a program to find modems in the 433, 434 calling area. It was an enormously long program. He did it mainly on his own. That was the age when there was no software to speak of and it wasn't user-friendly. Tim and some other kids went out and did this. Why? There were so few modems, how would you find someone else with a computer? Maybe one house in a thousand or a business had one. So, they were looking to hook up with someone else who had a Commodore Pet. In a way, that was fairly advanced. It demonstrates his bright mind.[15]

In the early eighties, the information age of personal computers was just underway. Since the movie *WarGames,* the thought of students changing their own grades by logging into administrative computer systems has been pondered and romanticized by teens. As in *Ferris Bueller's Day Off* where a student alters his absentee days on the school's logs, Tim, seventeen, would have discussed this notion with his friends. One report notes that Tim, many years later, tapped into an air base's computer system to look at some files. Friends say his interest in computers flourished and Tim was later known as a "hacker." In high school, Tim eventually solved the modem problem and was able to talk from his home to friends, all by typing his messages into the keyboard of a modified computer pushed to maximum drive. Justin Genter, a former classmate who now works as a computer specialist, remembered McVeigh as "The Wanderer."

> He had a Commodore 64, which is what I had. We started talking back and forth with a couple of people who also had Commodores. I found out he was running a bulletin board, for maybe a year. I think he went by the handle, "The Wanderer." There were just general messages, teen talk.[16]

Tim said he called himself "The Wanderer" based on the early 1960s song of the same name by Dion and the Belmonts. Western New York is known for radio stations that broadcast "golden oldies," songs that have been popular for decades. Tim McVeigh probably heard "The Wanderer" hundreds of times by the age of sixteen. This song, in a small way, describes Tim's attitude toward social circles; he never stayed in one for too long. His classmate Pam Widmer reinforced this notion when she discussed study hall activities. She would see Tim in the big lobby of the school, where students congregated around benches to go over notes, talk, and play cards.

> People picked on him, in fun, because he was so skinny. He was somebody who would move around out there from group to group. Everyone was sitting in groups of ten or twelve. He'd be talking to us, then he'd go and talk to somebody else. At times it seemed like he had a lot of energy and couldn't sit still. He'd be sitting on a bench, talking to me or someone else, and then he'd be gone.[17]

Tim's interest in sports during those teenage days was remembered as average. He watched Super Bowl football games with friend Keith Maurer and played everything from basketball to hockey in pickup games all around Pendleton and Lockport. McVeigh did not stand out as particularly good in these activities, he was just another player. One track coach said Tim was reliable and that was about it.

I had Tim on the track team in tenth, eleventh, and twelfth grade. Tim was hardworking, no trouble at all. Whatever role we needed, Tim would do his best. But he was never our number one runner in any event. He was our second or third runner. But I never recalled a complaint. He was an uncomplaining kid. The kind that track brings out. Track is really a low-key sport, not intense, not violent.[18]

Maybe "The Wanderer" was a subconscious comment on the habits of Tim's mother. Her reputation in town was shot, and Tim avoided conversation about his family at every opportunity. One classmate said Tim noted once that his parents had "split" but that was all he would say. Mickey McVeigh had been in and out of the home on Meyer Road a number of times for work commitments and apparently because of marital problems. Once, she lived with Jennifer in a mobile home in Lockport. The "park," as the development was called, had small homes made largely of plastic and wood, set on concrete blocks. There were no trees since the land was leveled before the homes were constructed. Some small trees had been planted, but the complex, with hot sun baking the plastic homes all summer, struck an odd contrast to the peaceful country life of Pendleton.

Tim changed in school and seemed to seek more attention than he had in his early years. Pam Widmer remembers her classmate getting a perm in their senior year to make his very straight hair curly. Justin Genter recalls how "ridiculous" Tim looked with the new "do" that didn't seem to serve any purpose. Both said he never dated girls. Some classmates spoke initially with press agencies interested in Tim as a teen. Lynn Miazga, a 1986 graduate of Starpoint, along with McVeigh had been voted "most talkative" by their class.

He was always trying to please other people by doing extra-extra help, being extra funny, anything to please. He went out of his way to make people laugh and to like him. . . . He was always on the outside, trying to fit in.[19]

Bill McVeigh and his estranged wife, Mickey, were drawing up divorce papers by 1986, as Tim's high school years drew to a close. Because of the high costs of the pending divorce, Bill sold the Meyer Road home in June 1985 to Linda and Richard Scruggs. The dream that the McVeigh family would live their lives on Meyer was finished; Bill and Mickey would never grow old together. Bill planned to use his portion of the proceeds from the house to construct a smaller house on nearby Campbell Boulevard. While his parents' marriage was dissolving, Tim tried to maintain a normal life. He earned a five-hundred-dollar Regents scholarship for college because he scored well on the state tests. Tim transferred from the Burger King in Amherst to one in Lockport. None of Tim's classmates who would agree to be interviewed could recall seeing him at his senior prom, usually the biggest event of the school year and attended by many of the 194 students in his graduating class.

The excitement of graduation and the hot spring after the long, cold winter found Tim cruising with his friends to the shores of Lake Ontario and staying out late at graduation parties. Former Van Halen frontman David Lee Roth was on the radio singing the Beach Boys' hit "California Girls," while Sammy Hagar had his own big hit about breaking the law in a red Lamborghini, "I Can't Drive 55!" Both songs were favorites for Tim. He described himself in his graduation bio for the yearbook as hoping to "take life as it comes and buy a Lamborghini." Tim said he enjoyed "losing sleep" and making it up in the classroom. He signed Pam Widmer's yearbook in pencil, saying, "Pam, Gee-zuz! You are quiet! Loosen up woman! It's your senior year. I can't read this. How are you going to?! III-D glasses are the best! Best of luck in the future! Tim."

In September 1987, Tim enrolled in classes at Bryant & Stratton business college in Williamsville, about twenty-five miles from home. He studied advanced COBOL and FORTRAN programming languages, but found that the classes repeated much of his high school experience in computer instruction. It is surprising that McVeigh chose to go to this business school, because during

NIAGARA COUNTY
COUNTY CLERK'S OFFICE
COURTHOUSE
P.O. BOX 461
LOCKPORT, NEW YORK 14095-0461

WAYNE F. JAGOW
County Clerk

WENDY J. ROBERSON
Deputy County Clerk

(716)439-7022
Fax (716)439-7066

CERTIFICATE OF DISPOSITION

SUPREME COURT   NIAGARA COUNTY
INDEX NO 60468

WILLIAM EDWARD McVEIGH

      VS

MILDRED NOREEN McVEIGH

     I, WAYNE F. JAGOW, Niagara County Clerk and Clerk of
the Supreme Court thereof DO HEREBY CERTIFY, that on the 13th
day of June, 1986, a Judgment of Divorce was entered in
this office and the marriage between the parties has been
dissolved.

WITNESS MY HAND and official seal at Lockport, New York, this
15th day of April, 1996.

WAYNE F. JAGOW
Niagara County Clerk

Verification of divorce decree ending the marriage of Bill and Mickey McVeigh.

the 1980s, the college was not viewed as a "destination" by many people his age. It was not necessarily the type of school that would lead to a high-paying executive position; instead it was viewed as a school for future accountants or office assistants. It was also not the type of college for high school students with honors-level intelligence, like McVeigh. Tim became bored with Bryant & Stratton, so he dropped out in December 1987, after only three and a half months of classes. Tim's father was not happy with his son's decision, especially since he helped pay for the tuition.

With little to challenge him, Tim started spending time with friends who went on frequent trips to Niagara Falls, Canada, to buy beer. There, the legal drinking age was nineteen. It was tougher to pass a fake identification in America, where the legal drinking age was twenty-one, but in Canada kids Tim's age were rarely "proofed." Tim could not only buy alcohol from stores and go to taverns, but he could also gain entry to striptease joints.

Instead of studying, Tim read more about weapons in *Guns & Ammo*. He favored the book *To Ride, Shoot Straight and Speak the Truth* by Jeff Cooper, the foremost authority on fighting with a .45 pistol. McVeigh frequently visited local stores that carried military gear, hunting equipment, and guns. Several of these equipment stores existed in the Lockport area where patrons stand and talk for hours about the types of guns they own and their performance. Places like Johnson's Country Store and the Cartridge Corner are very popular among enthusiasts who also belong to gun and hunting organizations called "gun clubs." These are located in the rural towns surrounding Lockport. The right to own and carry a gun is studied at these clubs and members subscribe to literature whose content ranges from information on various weapons to right-wing paranoia pamphlets that claim the federal government's main goal in the future is to disarm America. For example, the Niagara County chapter of the Shooters Committee on Political Education publishes a small quarterly newsletter called the *SCOPE Minuteman*. The publication features local and national (news wire) stories on issues related to the Second Amendment. The local committee for Niagara County boasted 226 members in the group "dedicated to protecting your Second Amendment rights." SCOPE's other publication, *Firing Lines,* features details about state and federal bills aimed at gun control. In addition to SCOPE's front-page plea to "please copy and distribute this newsletter," the group offers telephone numbers of government offices, including the governor, and recommends, "please be polite and calm when speaking to your (government) representatives or their staff." The publication features articles such as "The FBI Wants Ability to Wiretap 1 in 1,000 Americans," "Women Must Stand Up and Join the Fight," and "New Jersey Court Strikes Down Portion of Gun Ban." SCOPE has been in existence for thirty years, according to those in the group itself. Annual dues are $15 while life memberships are $250. The recruitment statement reads: "Our fight is really about LIBERTY, and FREEDOM! We must be ever vigilant to protect our liberty, for there are those whose goal is to steal it from us. One of the best ways you can protect your rights is to help increase our membership."

Weaponry and gun rights became the field that captured Timothy McVeigh's attention. So he decided to leave his fast-food job and look for something in line with his interests. If college wasn't going to work out, why not work in this field, a place where he could excel?

He found an advertisement in a Buffalo newspaper seeking to fill a security position. The hours weren't bad and the starting pay, $6.25 an hour, was better than anything he could get in Lockport without a college education. He applied and was soon on the job. Co-workers at Burke Armour Security of Buffalo in 1987, saw a Timothy McVeigh most high school students never knew—a man influenced by war and weapon literature, angry over his homelife, and living in a survivalist fantasy world. He actually showed up at work wearing camouflage clothing and crossed bandoliers of ammunition on his chest as he and some co-workers played a joke on their supervisor.

McVeigh worked with Jeff Camp at Burke. Jeff told the *Buffalo*

News that his partner was fascinated with guns, an interest that seemed to come from his teen years. "He liked guns and fast cars. He joked around a lot. We had a good time," Camp commented. Jeff also spoke with *Media Bypass* about knowing McVeigh.

> He drove a brand-new Chevy Turbo and always carried two or three guns with him. (He was) really jumpy. He came to work one day wearing a bandolier of shotgun shells and carrying a sawed-off Remington shotgun. He had all sorts of guns, including a .38, a .357, a .45 pistol, and an AR-15 rifle.[20]

Tim's permit to carry a handgun was issued in 1987. He needed the permit to work at Burke because he made money deliveries to banks and stores in the Buffalo area. His co-workers at Burke also carried weapons. But Tim distinguished himself as one of the best shots on the team, as they practiced in the company's weapons range. Around this time, McVeigh purchased a Desert Eagle .44 magnum pistol, which he showed co-workers. Tim later sold the gun because he thought it was "unreliable."

Other than his temper, which rarely showed its face, McVeigh was reportedly only involved in one mishap during his time at Burke. Jeff Camp told *Media Bypass* that during a delivery trip to a shopping center, a woman backed into their armored vehicle. McVeigh leaped out of the truck to see what happened and found a visibly upset woman sitting in shock behind the wheel of her car. Camp recalled that McVeigh felt sorry for the lady: "Our truck wasn't damaged. [Tim] told her we would say the accident was our fault, even though it wasn't. He also told her we would not call the police and report the wreck."[21]

A common sentiment today is that children are not as affected by divorce because it is so common. That's like saying people in California are really unaffected by earthquakes because they happen so frequently there. Divorce often rips the hearts out of the people it touches, and in the case of the McVeighs, it created deep psychological wounds and left permanent emotional scars. In the early 1980s, divorce was not common in western New York's small, rural communities. To suffer the embarrassment and indignity of having a promiscuous mother must have made the situation for Timothy even worse, especially in light of the way rumors spread in gossipy Lockport. An anger grew in Tim the way it grew in the hearts of Niagara taxpayers who condemned their government as riddled with crooks. Today, Timothy declines to speak about his parents and hopes the intimate details of their lives will never be revealed. He did speak of his mother to Army buddy John Kelso, as disclosed to *New York Times* reporter John Kifner.

> I just remember him calling his momma "that no-good whore, a slut," words like that. He never had anything good to say about his mom. He didn't have contact with his mom. I know there was a problem there, but it wasn't discussed much.[22]

Another army friend, Sgt. Albert Warnement, heard of Mickey through Tim. Warnement told Peter Jennings on the April 11, 1996, ABC News special that, "I remember [Tim] kind of held a grudge against his mom. . . . It obviously still upset him. He generally referred to her as a bitch. He was not happy with her at all. He . . . had no love for her I ever saw displayed."[23]

If Mickey was the social light in Tim's early life, then the flame was snuffed out when she left home during his teen years. During this time, Tim also experienced trouble with women. A classmate said Tim would call the pretty girls in class but they would not date him. Tim claims today that he did date and in fact lost his virginity as a high schooler, but no evidence can be found to back up these jailhouse statements.

If encouraged by the rigors of military life, if urged to show its ugly face, Tim McVeigh's anger would be a face not yet seen or understood. Tim's resentment toward his mother's acts just needed to be coaxed out and focused on something big.

Timothy McVeigh was taken to the Noble County jail in Perry, Oklahoma, where he cited his next of kin as James Nichols, and listed 3616 North Van Dyke Road, Decker, Michigan, as his home address. He was photographed and fingerprinted. Jail was a new experience for Tim, but he was used to the orderly, regimented lifestyle that the military had imposed eight years earlier. He only asked one question before he was taken to a holding area: "When's chow?" Once he had a cell, Tim rested. He told jail trustee Herbert Ferguson, who questioned McVeigh's need for sleep, that he hadn't gotten a lot of rest when he was in the army. Later, with jailer Jack Branson, McVeigh talked of army life. He mentioned what it was like at Fort Benning and at Fort Riley. Tim also mentioned his service in Operation Desert Storm.

Chapter 5

Unknown Soldier

Be all that you can be.
> —From a U.S. Army commercial

I could do what needs to be done as a leader.
> —Tim McVeigh on the Special Forces

What he had read in books was out there and he wanted to finally taste it for himself. "I don't understand why. You should stay in college," Tim's father told him. "You don't have to do it."

But Bill McVeigh didn't understand other things his son had done, his interests, or what drove him. Tim grew more distant as time passed. The idea of joining the military had been discussed before at the McVeigh kitchen table, as Bill and a friend pondered how there were no jobs around the area for someone Tim's age. Bill McVeigh didn't think his son took the idea seriously.

Tim let his father remain in the dark, because there was no way to make the old man understand. Tim would soon leave Lockport and join the army to find his way to the top there. Eventually he might become a general, commanding a group of men in a Third World hotspot. Under him, the men would rule the area—a plot of land near a beachhead in Iraq, Iran, Lebanon . . . somewhere. Or maybe he could be in the elite forces, that special breed of man set apart from the rest, a man who is authorized for secret missions.

He could make the army his career, and the travel opportunities would give him the chance to see the world he had only learned about in history classes. A first goal for McVeigh was to try out for the Army Ranger school, which he had learned about from military manuals and other literature available through gun club connections. This advanced infantry group goes through the toughest training of all U.S. forces. The Airborne Rangers, which Tim hoped to join, tackle deserts, swamps, and mountains in training for raids in foreign countries to secure land and free hostages or prisoners of war.

Tim McVeigh had been practicing his shooting with Dave Darlak. Their ten-acre property near Olean, New York, was the perfect spot to get ready. Working part-time at Johnson's Country Store in the town of Lockport during the early months of 1988 gave Tim the money he needed to pool with Dave to buy the land on April 1 of that year. The store, a place where Timothy had met gun enthusiasts, hung out, and shopped at for several years, was woodsmen's modern-day supermarket for hunting equipment and surplus. It gave Tim immediate access to rifles and pistols, to others who shared his interests, and the place at least in his mind to exercise the authority he wanted: being able to instruct over the counter, to tell customers what was what about the available guns for sale. Tim and Dave's undeveloped land comprised nothing but fields with the occasional barn on adjacent land. Nevertheless, it was Tim's "Yellow Brick Road" to his destiny. Located in the town of Humphrey on Cherry Valley Road, the acreage was sold to Tim and his friend Dave by retired police officer Dave Morgan. To Tim, this was the land on which he would train, learn from his own mistakes, and edit errors out of his performance. And then he would be ready when his first master sergeant gave the order, asking him to fire a gun, testing him. Pop, pop, pop. Tim felt the heat of fighting in his heart every time the gun went off. The spring rain came down over him as he reloaded.

"Let's go. I don't want to be out here any longer," Dave said, ready to go home for dinner.

"Just a few more," Tim said. He could stay all night. When he enlisted, he would be known for being the best at shooting, excelling and getting his name around camp immediately, just like the guys in the books. The heroes.

"I need to go a bit more." Tim liked Dave, but his friend was only a player in this deal. He didn't have the same goal. Dave wanted some fun and then it was back to the safety of his North Tonawanda home. Dave didn't have the commitment to train properly, to "survive," like Tim, who was in this for the long haul.

That night, Tim told his father he planned to enlist. Bill McVeigh wanted to know why Tim didn't want to finish college. You start something and then you finish it, Bill told him. Tim stared out the window and heard the wind funneling through the trees. It was a business college. He told his dad he didn't want to be an accountant or a banker, one of those guys who go to work in suits every day, doing the same thing, and go home at night to wives they wind up cheating on because their lives are so boring. Bill McVeigh heard his son say he wanted to enlist and saw failure—an unfinished college education, a dropout. Bill had been in the military as the Vietnam conflict arose, and the romance of fighting for flag and country was finally erased when the true casualties from that war began to mount. Since then, "wars" had become mini-nothings, nothing little political wars over tiny bits of lands. There was no purpose anymore. But Tim saw things very differently; he saw himself serving heroically in battle and then coming home, gaining attention from Mom and Dad, and eventually being validated as a son and a man.

"I don't know," Bill McVeigh told me when I asked why his son enlisted. "Other people have asked me that and I just don't know."

Dave Darlak lost interest in their shooting range and stopped going. Tim had become too obsessed with it, wanting to go every weekend. He would even camp there, and then shoot all the next day. In the rural areas of western New York, about half of the boys growing up are introduced to guns and "conservation clubs," or hunting groups. Fathers, in the tradition of Ernest Hemingway, teach their sons how to shoot and hunt. Each fall, the sounds of gunshot can be heard in areas near woods and bordering Indian reservations.* The average resident in these areas is used to the sound, like residents of New York City have adapted to the sound of sirens and other loud traffic noise. It's commonplace. About 2 percent of those who discover guns on their own, or are introduced to them by family or friends, break away from the whiskey Sunday hunter routine and become another manifestation of that mold, namely the soldier or the survivalist. This was Timothy McVeigh. He devoured books about war and heroes, this man who became obsessed about target practice at the little Olean field.

Neighbors on adjoining properties called the state police once because there was so much shooting from the site. State police logged a complaint in 1988 that it sounded like small bombs were being set off at the property. When an officer investigated the complaint, he found four men at McVeigh's land. The men's names were not recorded in the police report, but the officer asked if they had been using explosives. One of the men claimed they had only been shooting. It is believed that McVeigh and his friends may have been experimenting at this time with explosives, but the report has not been confirmed. Speaking with the *New York Times,* Robert

---

*The Tuscarora Indian Reservation is located in Niagara County, near Lewiston, about twenty miles west of Lockport. The Tonawanda Indian Reservation is located about thirty miles to the east of Lockport. Hunting areas and swampland border these locations.

Morgan of Olean offered this: "One day it sounded like a war out there. Sometimes [McVeigh] would come down during the week, sometimes the weekend. He had on hunting clothes. Camouflage."[1]

McVeigh's best friend from high school, Keith Maurer, was as shocked as Tim's father that his friend wanted to join the army. Like the young McVeigh's father, Keith saw the good in Tim, the side of him that liked to help his dad in the garden, the side that excelled in certain school activities, the side with heart. "The military was not [an option] he needed to take," Maurer said.

Timothy drove up to Buffalo by himself. It was a cool but sunny May 24, 1988, and he was about to take the biggest step of his life. He didn't know it then, but his decision to join the army would one day destroy his fantasies about being a hero, and supply those spaces in his mind with the reality that formed the world outside western New York.

Tim had his birth certificate, Social Security card, a copy of his high school diploma, and a college report card—all the materials he needed to enlist. The recruiter saw a man who looked like he was ready to begin training today. He wondered if the twenty-year-old in front of him was for real.

The recruiter provided some basic introductory information to the young man but McVeigh already seemed to know. The officer then moved on to "the interview," a series of questions that lets the military know if you're someone who's genuinely interested in serving your country.

The recruiter asked questions about McVeigh's education and health. He also asked if McVeigh ever had any trouble with the law.

"Have you ever been arrested?"

The question took Tim by surprise. "No," he said.

"Good." The recruiter hoped McVeigh wasn't lying, because he seemed to be the perfect candidate. McVeigh was telling the truth: his record was as clean as his teeth and always would be as far as Tim was concerned.

McVeigh was given an aptitude test, which he passed, and was assigned May 26 as the date for his physical. That day, Tim received a mental qualification evaluation followed by a medical examination. He passed these tests as well.

The recruiter told McVeigh that he would be able to try out for the Ranger school once he was at Fort Benning, Georgia. But the recruiter allegedly signed Tim up for another program to which the army was pushing to assign new recruits, one in which McVeigh would have no chance of trying out for the Rangers. If the recruiter had told Tim the truth about the program he was headed for, McVeigh probably wouldn't have enlisted.

Tim enlisted for three years of service. A couple of days later, he left on a plane to Fort Benning, where he would meet up with about 288 others who had signed up. Their basic training unit was called Echo Company, Fourth Battalion, Thirty-sixth Infantry Regiment, Second Training Brigade. It was the army's intent to "break" the men, like horses, as soon as possible, so they would obey without question, and forget about the individual pride they had brought with them. The first initiation was the sawdust pit. A drill sergeant met and greeted them on their first day, once the recruits were changed into their stiff new drill uniforms. The leader screamed at the men, calling them "dogs" and "mother-fuckers" and ordered them down to the ground to do push-ups in a pit of sharp, dry sawdust. They were ordered to do sit-ups, run in place, and more push-ups until they fell exhausted into the mess below them. Their sweat caused the dust to cling to their skin—a rough feeling, like sandpaper.

After the first night Tim looked forward to learning new skills and talking with the other men. He slept uneasily. A bunk away was a man named Terry Lynn Nichols, who McVeigh soon learned had enlisted in Detroit. Nichols was a few years older than McVeigh, but had the same liking for guns. They talked and talked, sharing gun stories and other experiences. Soon the two started hanging around together and formed their own tiny clique, long before the others in the barracks.

Tim liked Terry because he was so knowledgeable when it came to the things Tim pondered for years. Tim found in Terry what he never had at home, an older brother. Terry liked Tim because he now had someone to talk to, someone who would listen intently to whatever he had to say. Tim was someone Terry could take under his wing and teach a few lessons.

The son of Joyce and Robert Nichols, Terry was raised on the family farm near Lapeer, Michigan, an area of the country described as isolated, a place where private individuals with guns are the law. In Sanilac County the residents want to be left alone despite their poor economy. *Detroit Free Press* editor Ron Dzwonkowski said on CNN that in this part of Michigan, people distrust the government machine.

> They want basically to be left to do their own thing in their own time, in their own way. The less interference they have from Washington, the better. Where the resentment [for the federal government] comes in a lot for farmers, I think, is when the banks step in and take the farms away. You're not just taking my job away, you're taking away my life. Banks were regulated by the federal government. So the federal government became part of the enemy.[2]

Their isolation from the outside world apparently contributed to the Nichols' naivete, and their ability to try almost anything. James Nichols once kept a "cloud-buster" on the farm in Decker, according to writer Robert Sheaffer. In the March/April 1996 issue of *Skeptical Inquirer* magazine, Sheaffer said cloud-busters are the invention of Austrian biophysicist Wilhelm Reich, who formulated the array of tubes that, if properly grounded and focused on the blue sky, would supposedly bring rain. Sheaffer wrote comically:

> [They] build these implausible contraptions, which they point at the sky, trying to tap the drought away. Typically one or more of the Reicheans will claim credit whenever a drought

ends, although none has yet owned up to being responsible for a destructive flood.[3]

Terry Nichols wanted a new life. Once he realized that the world could offer much more than what was available in his small community, Terry Nichols disliked farm living. He hated getting up before dawn to tend to the animals, then after breakfast it was back to the fields, then lunch and back to the fields, then dinner and back to tidy up for the night. Sundown and bedtime. Terry was too smart for that type of life. He was searching for anything but farming.

About the only aspect of the farm that was interesting to Terry was when his dad blew up the stumps of trees. They would explode the stumps of trees cut in late summer and early fall for firewood, or sometimes trees had to be removed on an area of land that was needed. Terry's father used a bit of fertilizer and oil, placed it inside the stumps, and detonated the mixture. His dad said, "I don't specifically remember instructing them how to do it, but then I don't know that anyone ever specifically instructed me how to do it." Like most things on any farm, that was the way it had always been done. One ingredient in such homemade bombs is ammonium nitrate, which is sometimes used by farmers for blasting to create drainage ditches.

Terry's big brother, James, was more of a leader in school and James's outgoing, gregarious way overshadowed Terry. James and Terry Nichols did not get along well since the elder brother tended to order his sibling around frequently. A thin, willowy boy, Terry was shy in school and bored, unable to concentrate on one thing at a time. As a teen, he rarely dated, apparently unable to commit to a "relationship." Graduating in 1973, Terry Nichols bounced around: he dropped out of a local community college in Michigan after about seven months, tried his hand at other jobs—insurance or real estate—but his demeanor lacked that "love everybody" salesmanship, as well as the "caring, sharing" attitude, which probably caused him to lose his first wife, Lana Padilla. At age thirty-three (the cut-off age for the army is thirty-five), he joined the army, where he met Tim McVeigh.

Others in Echo Company didn't identify with Nichols because he stood out. He was old. But Tim McVeigh clung to Nichols almost immediately, because of that fact. Also, Tim found that he and Terry had plenty in common: both were the product of small-town high schools and broken homes. Terry's mother and father were divorced around the time he graduated from Lapeer West High School. Like Tim's mom, Joyce Nichols had a reputation around town—not for being a man magnet, but for being a drunk. She once trashed her husband's tractor during a domestic argument, had been arrested for drunk driving, and was known as a rowdy, verbally abusive woman.* In those high school days, Terry had been crushed by his parents' separation, just like Tim. And like McVeigh, Nichols had gone to college for a while before dropping out. Terry Nichols had apparently hoped to become a doctor, but his mother was separated and needed help with the crops back in Michigan. Literally ruled by Joyce Nichols, Terry would leave school to enter the farm life again.

McVeigh and Nichols shared another personality trait—bigotry. Their discussions exposed a few things about army life they didn't like. One was working with black people. Both Nichols and McVeigh picked up their racism from the "simple folk" in their hometown areas, where it is not unusual for blacks to be called

---

*In her book, *By Blood Betrayed,* Terry Nichols's ex-wife, Lana Padilla, says Terry was concerned with Joyce Nichols's drinking habits. She says Terry's father spoke of the time when Joyce drove into a field, rammed his tractor, and destroyed her car. Joyce also threatened her ex-husband with a gun on several occasions. *By Blood Betrayed* noted that Joyce is remembered by the Lapeer County law enforcement officials as being intoxicated on a number of instances, including the time she was a hit-and-run suspect trying to resist arrest by Officer Bill Dougherty and trying to attack him with a chain saw. Joyce later pleaded guilty to a reduced charge of drunk driving.

"niggers" by some whites, where blacks are the subjects of jokes, and where they are a people to criticize and foolishly blame for the nation's problems. In Tim's hometown the prejudice was subtle. It came from the teachings of elders passed down through the generations, and a basic fear of the unknown. Parents, grandparents, and great-grandparents in many families in western New York still live with views contrary to the American melting pot. Ask some about what it was like in the early days when Polish immigrants moved into Buffalo and vicious fights broke out. Ask about the Italians or the Irish and the tales are the same.

In eastern Niagara County, where McVeigh was born, there are still only a few black families residing. In Pendleton, there were no black students in Tim's graduating class of 1986. In fact, there was only one black family living in Pendleton when Tim was growing up, and they later moved. McVeigh's classmate Pam Widmer told me, "When I was young, the only place we'd see a black person was in the grocery store. It was weird."[4] She added that the kids at Starpoint played other high schools in sports and sometimes comments were made about blacks on the other teams. In comparison, in nearby Lockport, my graduating class of 1985 had six African Americans. There were no fistfights between the races, but there was tension with a few kids who had been raised in narrow-minded homes. In essence, the area was a breeding ground for people like McVeigh who would carry those distorted beliefs into their adult lives.

Tim McVeigh spent his life, until the age of nineteen, in the cultural wasteland that is Pendleton and its surrounding area. He experienced severe culture shock when he arrived at Fort Benning. Because of his ignorance, McVeigh became a bigot, which helped him get along with Nichols, but not with others in his life outside western New York. His feelings, once sensed and made known, were pounced on. Still, Terry and Tim's bond was fueled by views of "the government" that they picked up from their hometowns. An army friend of Tim's, Dave Dilly, told CNN about McVeigh's right-wing views: "If you said anything about welfare or any government entitlements or anything like that, you'd hear an hour speech from either one of them, you know."[5]

Tim and Terry were assigned to a Cohort unit, defined by the army as a Cohesion Operational Readiness and Training program. In 1980, the army began keeping teams of men together for three years to allow the troops to bond, improving their stability and readiness.

Prior to the establishment of the Cohort unit, those who lost their lives on the battlefield were replaced by lone soldiers who wound up being killed themselves during the fighting because of their own confusion in a new group on the front line.

In a Cohort unit, the men were sent together and replaced other whole units. The idea was not a complete success. It was found that members eventually grew tired of one another. AWOLs and suicides increased. But in the case of McVeigh and Nichols, a lasting bond was formed, which was just what the army wanted in the first place. McVeigh was about the only enlisted man who liked Nichols, other than a later friendship with Michael Fortier. Most called Nichols "Pops," because he was so much older than they were. In time, Fortier fit into their clique well because he also loved guns and weaponry. A year younger than McVeigh, the Arizona native would seek the guidance of a teacher like Nichols.

The son of Irene and Paul Fortier, Michael graduated from Kingman High School in 1987. An attractive, dark-haired man with glasses, Michael Fortier could have walked on to just about any Hollywood set and found a job as an extra. But his small-town views kept him in Kingman after high school, sticking with his sweetheart and future wife, Lori.

Fortier worked for a short time at the local True Value hardware and then enlisted in the army. He was eventually sent to Fort Riley, where he soon met the two men who would change his life forever.

In their first three months of training, McVeigh and Nichols's unit learned marching, barracks rule, weapons handling, and field tactics. They marched about one hundred miles with the unit during basic combat training. McVeigh showed himself to be in good shape. Assistant platoon leader Glen "Tex" Edwards told *Media Bypass* that "McVeigh was really motivated to be a good soldier and performed well at everything expected of him." But Nichols found the regiment more difficult. He was tired, sore, and a bit frayed around the edges at the end of each day. Nichols was given a leadership position by the drill sergeant because of his age and in the hope that he would set an example through maturity. He was named senior platoon leader, but it was later learned he was not the type of character the army would want in charge of its best youth. Glen Edwards told *Media Bypass*:

[Terry] also had some college background and came into the army as a PFC. [But] he hated the United States government. He said the government made it impossible for him to make a living as a farmer. I thought it strange that a thirty-two-year-old man would be complaining about the government, yet was now employed by the government. Nichols told me he signed up to pull his twenty years and get a retirement pension.[6]

Nichols's attitude seemed to parallel McVeigh's on this, in that Tim joined, apparently not to serve his country, but to live out a personal dream of being a "special" soldier on undercover assignment giving himself personal gratification through military achievement.

Both McVeigh and Nichols withdrew from others in the unit in their free time. Tim and Terry traded books and formed a bond that others found strange. They discussed articles in *Soldier of Fortune* magazine and available goods in *Elite Force* and *Uncle Sam's Military Catalogue.* They traded stories about what they wanted to get out of the military experience. Tim told Terry he would one day be a Green Beret or maybe a general. Terry wanted to be "a professional soldier" with a woman in every port. They lived in their military dream worlds while remaining in the army's secure grasp.

Tim was an avid reader from when he was a child collecting comic books. In addition to his magazines and a personal favorite, *97 Confirmed Kills,* the biography of famous Vietnam sniper Charles Haithcock, McVeigh carried and re-read his basic infantry skill handbook, referring to it often. He also liked to read the *Ranger Handbook,* the *Special Forces Handbook,* and a technical manual on homemade explosives, titled *Improvised Munitions.* Around this time, Tim purchased a book he had seen advertised in a gun magazine. The book was titled *The Turner Diaries* and was promoted in the magazine as an educational tome about newly developing gun laws. The advertisement boldly asked, "What are you going to do when they take your guns?" The work of fiction piqued McVeigh's interest because it detailed something to him that in his mind could one day be real. What if the government decided to disarm America for its own purpose—to gain absolute control over its citizens? He found as he read the book that the author, William Pierce, had his own idea of how people would respond if the feds took such action.

But that was not all this book was about. Its author, Dr. William Pierce, is a former physics professor at the University of Oregon. Dr. Pierce wrote the 211-page *Turner Diaries* under the name Andrew Macdonald, and had it published through National Vanguard Books of Hillsboro, West Virginia. The book is supposed to be drawn from the diaries of a revolutionary who lived in the early 1990s in America—a country divided into two categories, the System and the Organization. The System represents a liberal government that sees all men as equal, and the Organization is an underground movement of white supremacists who try to violently cleanse America of the social ills caused by liberal, Jewish, and black leaders in power. The book reveals its racist nature when speaking of the "Cohen Act" to disarm America and how that federal law is enforced:

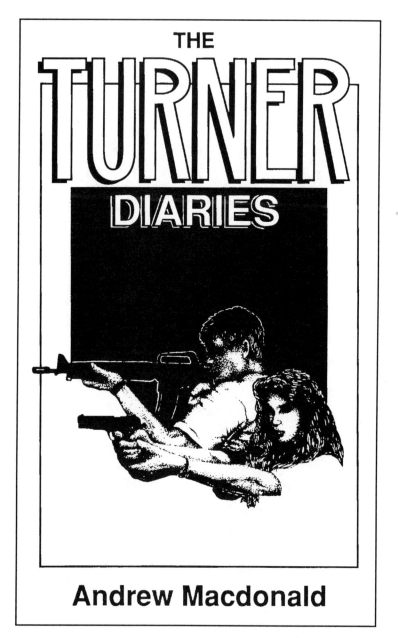

Timothy McVeigh was greatly influenced by *The Turner Diaries,* written by former physics professor William Pierce, using the pseudonym Andrew Macdonald. The fictional book details a bomb strike and other acts of prejudicial rage against the government.

Robberies of this sort had become all too common since the Cohen Act, with groups of Blacks forcing their way into White homes to rob and rape, knowing that even if their victims had guns they probably would not dare use them.[7]

Dr. Pierce's ties to the nonfiction world are as shocking as his book—the book Tim McVeigh began carrying with him along with his army manuals. Pierce founded the National Alliance in 1974, four years before *The Turner Diaries* was published. Pierce was active in George Lincoln Rockwell's American Nazi party and in its successor, the National Socialist White People's party. He was editor of *National Socialist World,* and used a religious front, the Cosmotheist Community Church, to get tax-exempt status in 1978. The status was revoked in 1983 on the basis of the church's white supremacist beliefs. Pierce's National Alliance published the tabloid *Attack,* which became a bimonthly magazine retitled *National Vanguard.* It was not revealed until 1984 that he was the author of *The Turner Diaries.** The book allegedly inspired the neo-Nazi paramilitary group "The Order" that assassinated Jewish talk-show host Alan Berg in 1984.

Earl Turner, the main character in *The Turner Diaries,* details his group's random, violent strikes against the System and, not until page 74, does he "justify" the Organization's killings of innocent people by stating the following:

For the first time I understand the deepest meaning of what we are doing. I understand now why we cannot fail, no matter what we must do to win. . . . Everything that has been and everything that is yet to be depends on us. We are truly instruments of God in the fulfillment of His Grand Design. These may seem like

*John George and Laird Wilcox, *Nazis, Communists, Klansmen and Others on the Fringe* (Amherst, N.Y.: Prometheus Books, 1992), pp. 364–65. George is professor of political science and sociology at the University of Central Oklahoma, and Wilcox is a long-time collector of extremist literature.

strange words to be coming from me, who has never been religious, but they are utterly sincere words.[8]

With no other way to justify his racist thinking, Pierce, through Earl Turner, attempts to explain that bigotry and hate are godly qualities. The violence against Jewish people, African Americans, government officials, and other innocents is, to Turner, justified by God. At the end of *The Turner Diaries*, National Vanguard Books advertises some of its other publications, like *Hunter*, also by Pierce, writing under the name "Andrew Macdonald." *Hunter* is advertised as follows:

> The author of *The Turner Diaries* has produced another blockbuster of patriotic action. When an honorable man is confronted by evil, he must neither submit to it nor ignore it, but take up arms against it. That is what Oscar Yeager, a former combat pilot in Vietnam, now a comfortable yuppie working as a Defense Department consultant in a suburb of the nation's capital, does in response to race mixing, homosexuality, political corruption, and other evils in Washington, D.C., with spectacular results: he becomes a one-man death squad. With rifle, silenced pistol, knife, garotte, and bomb, he dispatches the filthy creatures who are overrunning America.

Other books of a similar nature are also advertised, including *The Saga of the White Will*, a three-dollar racist comic book geared toward fifteen-to-eighteen-year-old high-school-age students. When one orders *The Turner Diaries* through National Vanguard Books, several catalogues arrive along with the book, including Delta Press Ltd. and Delta Force. The press catalogue offers books on how to make homemade bombs, how to be a sniper, and various other how-tos for budding terrorists. Nazi World War II posters, fake police identification patches, and fake I.D. kits are also offered. *Response*, the Simon Wiesenthal Center World Report magazine, said in its summer 1995 issue that *The Turner Diaries* motivated Robert Jay Mathews to found "The

Order," a white supremacist group that intended to start a race war modeled after Pierce's novel. *Response* also said that Dr. Pierce himself in 1995 predicted organized terrorism "on a scale the world has never seen before."[9]

In early September 1988, Tim's unit went to Fort Riley, Kansas, and was separated into two groups, with McVeigh going to Charlie Company and Nichols to Bravo Company.

An early bond was formed between McVeigh, Nichols, and Fortier. The three often went shooting together at the base range and at a farm by the Republican River and Tuttle Creek Lake near Manhatten, Kansas. McVeigh sometimes visited a house Nichols owned off base. Tim showed these friends his collection of guns, which included an H&K 91 with heavy barrel, an AR-15 A2 Sporter, a Desert Eagle pistol, a Taurus 9mm, and a Mossburg shotgun. Nichols was genuinely impressed with McVeigh's expertise at handling guns and with his broad knowledge of such weapons.

But Nichols's military career was short, like most everything else he tried. According to military records, Nichols was discharged in 1989, after only one year of service. A report said he was allowed to leave because of a "family emergency." His wife, Lana Padilla, was apparently preoccupied with some other aspect of her life, and Nichols had to leave the service to care for their son, Josh, who was under ten years of age. Just before leaving the army, a brooding Terry Nichols showed his true colors to Glen Edwards. Edwards told *Media Bypass* that Nichols had big plans if he got the chance to come back to the base. Stressing that McVeigh and Fortier would be recruited, Nichols invited Edwards to join in.

> He told me he would be coming back to Fort Riley to start his own military organization. He said he could get any kind of weapon and any equipment he wanted. I can't remember the name of his organization, but he seemed pretty serious about it.[10]

With Nichols taken away from him, McVeigh had no friend.
Michael Fortier was with a different unit so McVeigh saw him in-
frequently. Tim did not consciously attempt to be liked or disliked
by those in his company, but he never again had an army relationship like the one he had with Terry. McVeigh was now on his
own, and had to prove himself . . . to himself. He would only stay
in contact with Nichols through letters and an occasional call.

In the Charlie assignment, with the Second Battalion, Sixteenth Infantry Regiment, McVeigh became a gunner on a Bradley
fighting vehicle. It was an armored tank-type troop carrier that ran
on tracks. When political leaders and dignitaries visited Fort Riley
and wanted to see what an M2 Bradley Armored Fighting Vehicle
was capable of, McVeigh and Staff Sgt. Albert Warnement would
demonstrate. Warnement told *Media Bypass*: "We kept that vehicle immaculate. McVeigh and I spent our own money to buy
Armor-All and other cleaning materials to make our Bradley look
brand-new." There were four vehicles in the unit; each carried a
commander, a driver, a gunner, and the infantrymen. At last
McVeigh had his first position of authority. He was the vehicle's
shooter. Tim was a happy man, finally secure in the army way; all
the shooting practice back home had paid off, just like he knew it
would. He penned a letter home one night, and held it until he
could mail it out to his dad.

About this time, 1988, the former Mickey McVeigh was back
in the city of Lockport, and had taken up residence with daughter
Jennifer at an apartment on Park Place. The street in the city is
short but wide and lined with many old homes that have been pre-
served and subdivided into multiple rental units. These apart-
ments are home to everyone from welfare recipients to lawyers,
depending on the rent and condition of the building. A former city
court judge lives at one end of the street today, while the opposite
end houses people he would probably have put in jail over the
years. Apartment rents ranged from $260 to $450 a month.

Mickey, Jennifer, and their miniature collie, Lady, lived in

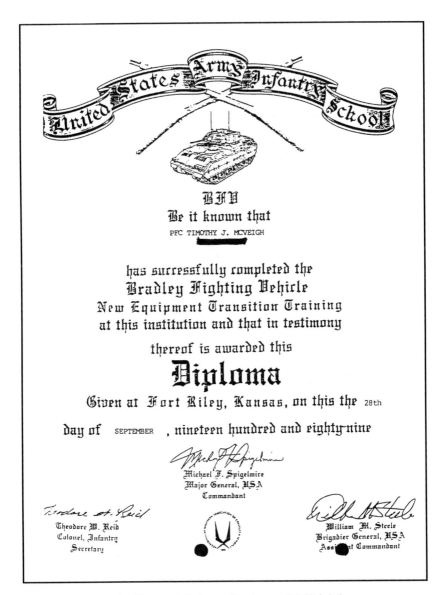

While serving in the Sixteenth Infantry Regiment, McVeigh became a gunner on a Bradley Armored Fighting Vehicle.

one of the nicer apartment houses. For about a year, Mickey was employed at the Basset Travel Agency, before she changed jobs to work at Four Seasons Travel.

Jennifer McVeigh, who was in her mid-teens, made two friends in the neighborhood, Mary and Angela Butler, who lived across the street. Jennifer walked to Emmet Belknap Junior High School each day with Angela, and the girls' friendship grew to the point that Jennifer was practically part of the Butler family. The girls spent many evening hours on the telephone or talking to that "cute" boy from school. Angela was interested in dancing, and Jennifer finally had someone to confide in about her family and the difficulty she had being moved around so much by her mother. Eventually, Jennifer had two mothers, Mickey and Ms. Butler from across the street. A friend explained that Mickey was frequently absent from Jennifer's life on Park Place, due to work or other commitments. In time, because of Mary Butler's supervision and friendship, Jennifer began calling her "Ma." At a time when Tim missed his mother and harbored anger toward her, Jennifer had found herself a substitute mother.

Mary Butler, as it turned out years later, was not only a second mom to Jennifer, but also a strong guardian. Dan Kane, Mary Butler's boyfriend at the time, was managing editor of the *Union-Sun & Journal* in Lockport. Kane lived with Butler for several years and recently recalled that time.

> The first member of the McVeigh family I met was Jennifer when she was thirteen or fourteen years old. She was a very good friend of a lady who was my companion at the time, and her daughter—they were about the same age—Jennifer and Angela. So I got to know Jennifer over a period of several years. [The girls] were best friends.[11]

Jennifer McVeigh spent many nights at the Butler home, Kane noted, and many at his summer cottage in Olcott, New York, about fifteen miles from Lockport. Olcott is a tiny hamlet bordering the skipping-rock shores of Lake Ontario. On a clear day, Toronto, Canada, can be seen thirty miles across the lake from the beach lookout areas. Olcott, now a bit rundown compared to its heyday when Lockport was more prosperous, is frequented by private fishermen and summer tourists. Much of Olcott's prime lakeside property is owned by people from Lockport and surrounding towns. Other than a few small bars, restaurants, and shops, the village is undeveloped. Its major attraction, next to the Niagara County fishing derby, is the annual "Polar Bear Swim" in March, sponsored by the local Lions Club. The fundraising swim features a few brave souls who jump into the frigid, ice-spotted lake waters, while about five thousand people watch. The drunken bash has drawn news cameras from around the world in its decade-long history.

Mickey was otherwise busy in Lockport with work or her social life. Dan Kane remembered Jennifer McVeigh spending long weekends at the cottage. He said something happened to Mickey in those years on Park Place that precipitated a move back to Florida.

> She was living with some guy, some sort of a strange, dark, swarthy kind of guy. I suspect he was married. He came around a lot at night. The guy was sort of a live-in boyfriend whom I suspect was living with somebody else, somewhere else at the same time, maybe two companions. He had a pretty regular schedule. He wasn't a sociable person—pretty much just stayed in the house. . . . Jennifer was home a lot because Mickey was going out. She bowled and was always going out and socializing. So, Jennifer was home alone a lot, too, and she'd stay overnight with Angela. As a matter of fact, Jennifer called my companion "Ma," and still calls her "Ma" to this day. There was some problem later that Mickey had with her boyfriend, either wanting him to get a divorce or he decided to go back to his wife. I think that's the reason [Mickey] decided to move to Florida . . . her older daughter, Patty, was already living there. Jennifer and Angela had gone to visit Patty before, and . . .

>Mickey got disgusted with her relationship here, maybe she
>also wanted to break from Bill [McVeigh] completely and de-
>cided to go.[12]

Many miles away from Fort Riley, Kansas, Timothy McVeigh's
desire for solitude made some fellow soldiers uneasy, while his
dedicated attitude caused everyone to trust him. If they got into a
jam, McVeigh would be the one to have along. He was his own
army, tucked inside of a package that followed orders like a robot.
Marion Curnutte, who served with McVeigh, recalled those early
military days to the *New York Times*: "When they called for down
time, we'd rest. [McVeigh] would throw on a rucksack and walk
around the post with it. He played military twenty-four hours a
day, seven days a week."[13]

With McVeigh guarding the barracks like a junkyard dog, the
others in the unit did what young military guys do. On their time
off, they hit the bars. McVeigh was a main topic of discussion
when others in the regiment were out. What was in his head?
Why didn't he party? Who was he trying to impress? Another
army colleague, Todd Regier, recalled this in a *New York Times* report:

>McVeigh was real different. Kind of cold. He wasn't enemies
>with anyone. He was kind of almost like a robot. He never had
>a date. . . . I never saw him at a club. I never saw him drinking.
>He never had good friends. Everything (McVeigh did) was for
>a purpose.[14]

One of the only methods of socialization for McVeigh was
being the Fort Riley "savings and loan." He hid his money in a tin
box, saving it and counting it over and over, like a lonely king.
While the other budding soldiers left their cash in taverns and
restaurants, McVeigh hoarded it, like he did supply rations later,
during the Desert Storm operation in the Gulf.

When another private was low on cash, McVeigh would lend

him money—not out of the goodness of his heart, but for profit. McVeigh charged interest on the loans, and built quite a reputation. Friend Sheffield Anderson said in the *New York Times,* "He was very cheap with money, very tight." Another soldier stressed to "Dateline NBC," "He was the bank of Fort Riley, Charlie Company. . . . He'd loan it to you at a high interest rate." How high? About five to ten dollars for a "weekend" loan, or sometimes 15 percent, depending on who you were.

Other than reading and watching television, McVeigh went bowling for recreation. He excelled at this family tradition, as some army associates recalled. Those same army brothers found it strange that McVeigh did not seek out women. He didn't really talk about them or go after them when the guys went out for the night. He had no homosexual tendencies, so they wondered further. Sheffield Anderson, now a corrections officer in Florida, had served long hours with McVeigh in the Bradley vehicle. He told the *New York Times* this about Tim: "He was very shy of women, almost embarrassed. It didn't seem [that] he was gay. He was just awkward."

Tim's ignorance toward other cultures was evident to officers on base, including Sgt. Anthony Thigpen, a squadron leader who shared status with McVeigh when Tim became a sergeant. Thigpen told the *New York Times*:

> If we had a company function that was inclusive for all nationalities, McVeigh wasn't too enthused. If it came down to all of us sitting down conversing with one another, McVeigh wasn't in the crowd if there were African Americans there.[15]

Fellow soldier Todd Regier told the same newspaper that he saw problems between Thigpen and McVeigh. "When [McVeigh] talked, he'd mention those words like 'nigger.' You pretty much knew he was a racist." Regier said there was "bad blood" between McVeigh and Thigpen. "I remember they yelled at each other quite a bit."[16] In his first military failure, McVeigh was reprimanded while in a supervisory position for assigning the "dirty" jobs to black soldiers.

Royal Witcher, who McVeigh later lived with, provided the *Times* with similar accounts of McVeigh's bigotry. "He was a very racist person," Witcher said, noting that McVeigh thought of black people as "inferior" and "not as smart as us." Whether they got along or not, McVeigh and the others were stuck with each other for the duration. They finally got a chance to travel, just like the army advertisements say, in April of 1989. Charlie Company went to Heidelberg, West Germany, over Easter Sunday weekend, for orientation with the Bundeswehr, or West German army. During their brief stay, the Americans learned of the soldiers' motivation techniques, and went on a border patrol mission.

Back at Fort Riley, McVeigh was unhappy in the Cohort group. In the summer of 1989, he learned that his only chance to leave the group would be by gaining acceptance into the Special Forces. McVeigh began readying himself by embarking on a rigorous course of physical training and study. He worked at personal training for almost a year and was scheduled for his first fitness test in July 1990.

That spring, McVeigh made a weekend trip home that would alter another man's life forever. Tim was cruising in his Chevy Turbo along Interstate 70, near the Illinois-Indiana border. The sun had gone down and his trained eye, taught in the military to always scan the darkness in search of the enemy, spotted a Blazer off the side of the roadway and a man lying nearby. McVeigh pulled his car to the side, grabbed his army-issued first aid kit, and dashed out in the darkness. He knelt by the crash victim, a male in his thirties, who moaned, seeing McVeigh through blurry eyes from the mild concussion, and holding his right leg that had been mangled in the one-vehicle crash just minutes before.

"You're going to be all right. I'm here," McVeigh said in a soothing tone to the man he had never met. The injured man wondered who this military angel was and how he'd been spotted by him. McVeigh applied a compress to the leg, to slow the bleeding where part of the bone protruded. The soldier worked quickly as the man listened to the sound of eighteen-wheelers passing across the highway.

"You've lost a lot of blood," McVeigh calmly told the victim. He rolled up the man's sleeve and inserted a needle into the right arm, beginning a saline IV. "You risk going into shock. This IV will help stabilize you and keep your fluids going. Relax."

As a siren pierced the distant wind, McVeigh quickly packed his kit, and placed the IV bag under the man's hip. He hopped back into the Turbo and disappeared into the night. As the ambulance finally approached, the injured man grinned and let out a chuckle to greet the emergency medical crew. His life had already been saved.

The next day, McVeigh was at home in Pendleton. He told his sister Jennifer a little about his adventure—then swore her to secrecy. Not only had McVeigh broken the law by being a vigilante savior, he had used his IV bag from the Combat Lifesaver Pack, which is prohibited off base. He had to get a replacement bag, quick, before the 1,200-mile journey back to Fort Riley in two days. Grandpa McVeigh had worked with the South Lockport Volunteer company and Tim had met some of the men. McVeigh made a phone call to a volunteer he knew, and told the acquaintance they should meet for coffee at Friendly's in Lockport.*

Timothy McVeigh was promoted in 1990 from specialist to corporal. Then, after a Primary Leadership Development Course, he jumped to sergeant on February 1, 1991, just prior to the beginning of the Desert Storm operation. His transition from soldier to leader was perceived as rapid among the rank and file. Todd Regier recalled: "It was unusual to have sergeant stripes so soon.

---

*"Lifesaver" story gleaned from Lawrence Myers, who interviewed Tim McVeigh about the incident, and from Jennifer McVeigh, who confirmed the story with me for this biography.

The rest of us in the Cohort were (only) specialists." Regier told "Dateline NBC":

> He blatantly soldiered twenty-four hours a day. He'd be train-ing or reading training manuals. He'd be out drawing road markers by himself or running. Anything to do with the military, he was doing it.[17]

Like his own gun training in the lonely Olean field, McVeigh's early show of dedication to his unit was a smart move. Though he was scheduled to start the Special Forces assessment course on November 17, 1990, at Fort Bragg, a November 8 Pentagon order shelved his plans. All leaves and training assignments were can-celled, and McVeigh's unit was ordered to Saudi Arabia. Tim was not happy. Conflict with "the enemy" was what he had trained for, but he personally felt it was not time for America to intervene. Al-bert Warnement recalls his observations to *Media Bypass*:

> He was against the National Command Authority's decision to go to war. McVeigh did not think the United States had any business or interest in Kuwait, but . . . he knew it was his duty to go where he was told, and he went.[18]

Soldiers don't have much of a choice when our country declares war. As long as they are employed by the U.S. Army, they go where they are told no matter what. This period of anticipation made McVeigh uneasy and he thought of the days years ago that he spent with the McDermott family on Meyer Road. McVeigh wrote a letter to Liz McDermott, Jack's wife. "This is definitely the real stuff," McVeigh scribbled. "And we had an alert yester-day. Everyone had to get into their chemical protective gear and wait. I'll write more later, and send you some sand."[19]

In charge of the men with whom he trained in basic, McVeigh led his unit through ground action in the barren desert. The Sec-ond Brigade of the First Infantry Division, deployed to Saudi Arabia, took up its position along the border of Iraq. The unit was there in a supporting role, avoiding the deadly front-line duty.

In the town of Pendleton, Tim's relatives and others from his home were watching the light show of air to ground and ground to air missiles on televised news programs. This "war" was narrated by America's media personalities. The approximate month-long "war" was an easy victory. Soldiers today recall the "enemy" giving up almost immediately to the U.S. forces and their massive display of power.

It was not the hard-fought war McVeigh had read about. It really wasn't a war at all to many, just a political ploy by the Republican leadership in Washington, hoping to get reelected. It was a vast sham, as Tim's father had envisioned most battles were after World War II. Of course, Bill and Tim's sister Jennifer worried about their Timmy, but soon they realized that he would come back unharmed.

Before knowing the war's purpose, Tim was in action. He described it as one long drive in the desert, but he was still defending what his country thought was right. McVeigh waited with the other ground troops for orders while the airplanes did the work, breaking down Iraqi defenses. He didn't sit idly by playing cards, but cleaned his M-16 and concentrated on what his role would be in this battle. He also cleaned the 25-millimeter cannon. He thought about his role until it scared him. McVeigh was in charge of a group that might not make it out alive. He envisioned his name on a wall like the Vietnam Memorial. "Timothy J. McVeigh, SGT," dead at twenty-one. Sheffield Anderson reflected:

> The night before the ground war kicked off [McVeigh] was saying he was scared because we were going to be part of the first wave. He was scared we weren't going to come out of it. Maybe we would get shot, blown up. . . . He was just concerned. I was feeling the same way, but most people didn't express it.[20]

Anderson told *Playboy* magazine, "We were in the desert, sleeping on the sand, and he really thought we were going to die. He was worried that we would be killed by our own helicopters or tanks."[21] McVeigh's fear was well founded. Just one week earlier, at a post three miles away from Charlie Company's, Col. Ralph Hayes, Jr., mistook a Bradley and another U.S. vehicle for the enemy and fired on both. The friendly-fire incident killed Spec. Jeff Middleton, twenty-three, and PFC Bob Talley, eighteen, when their Bradley was incinerated. McVeigh and the other soldiers heard the incident on their tactical radio. They were horrified.

Most of Charlie Company made the initial drive to Kuwait. McVeigh's unit was held back to handle prisoners, clear mines, and secure bunkers. The platoon was fired on and returned fire, but was never in the thick of the action.

A lot of shooting by the Americans was directed at the enemy's dug-in trenches. The Iraqis, many of them, surrendered when fired at, coming out of their hiding places, looking for food and water.

McVeigh shot an Iraqi soldier on the first day of fighting on the border. It felt bittersweet to him. On the one hand, he took an excellent shot, hitting the "enemy" in the neck from 1,100 meters away. On the other hand, McVeigh knew he had taken a human life, someone he didn't even know. He had killed a man who his government told him was the enemy, someone he should destroy with the weapons he had been given. The rush was not there as McVeigh thought it would be. There was no sound, really, just his gun and then, a millisecond later, the headless body of the man falling and hitting the earth. The feeling was not heroic, but he had to tell the others who fought alongside him that it was.

As remembered by former platoon member Kerry Kling, McVeigh said, "He was proud of that one shot . . . from that distance, it's impressive." And Todd Reiger recalled, "He bragged about his kill a lot. He reveled in it."[22] A former soldier told NBC's "Dateline": "He bragged about it, which didn't bother us.

That was his job. It was a fire situation. He blew [the Iraqi's] head off, too, literally."[23]

But to his aunt Jean (Hill) Zanghi, Tim confided a much different story. Tim wrote letters to her from overseas and met her when he came home. In his heart, he knew the war and the killing were wrong. Zanghi told researcher Julianna Jacoby in a *Union-Sun & Journal* story:

> He came to see us after the Persian Gulf. When he came back he seemed broken. When we talked about it he said it was terrible there. He said he was on the front line and had seen death and caused death. After the first [killing] it got easy.[24]

The pseudowar wound down. Sgt. McVeigh's unit was reassigned to guard Gen. H. Norman Schwarzkopf, the Desert Storm commander. It was a bore, worse than when the troops were waiting to go into battle. At least back then they had some anticipation of what might happen. Now, there was really nothing but a broken country they no longer wanted to be in.

Though it was less than a victory, McVeigh had proven himself and had come through without a mark. A high point for McVeigh after the conflict was when Unit Commander Colonel Anthony Moreno requested that McVeigh receive the Army Commendation Medal for his additional performance on the field during the conflict, which read, "He inspired other members of his platoon by destroying an enemy machine-gun emplacement, killing two Iraqi soldiers, and forcing the surrender of thirty others from dug-in positions."* The Special Forces would take him, and place him in an active role, instead of being a figurehead, like a general.

In April 1991, McVeigh left the Gulf, gathered personal belongings from Fort Riley, Kansas, and headed to Fort Bragg, North

---

*From certificate for Army Commendation Medal, issued June 26, 1991. Information credit: Lawrence Myers, "Biography: McVeigh Part 2," *Media Bypass* (March 1996): 25.

Carolina. He had received orders to report to the Special Forces Selection and Assessment Course located there. He was a little surprised, in part because he felt the harsh desert life had weakened his body, but he looked forward to the chance to try again. Someday, when he returned to his home, he would be a Green Beret, and have proven himself. McVeigh told *Newsweek* reporter Dave "Hack" Hackworth: "After I got through the leadership course, I recognized that I could do what needs to be done as a leader. And there wouldn't be anything I'd really have to fear from that."[25]

An *Amerinoid* is an American who is paranoid. Webster's dictionary lists a *paranoid* as a person suffering from chronic psychosis marked by delusions of persecution or of grandeur. The person defends these illusions with "apparent logic and reason." The typical Amerinoid believes that the American form of government is full of corrupt leaders who have a set agenda, which includes disarming law-abiding citizens, giving tax money to liberals to further their "dangerous" causes, and creating a "New World Order" that will govern the people of the planet with an iron fist, extinguishing creativity and original thought. Like religious war leaders, most Amerinoids feel that what they believe is absolutely correct. Attempts to change their thoughts and bring them back to reality are met with fear that the advocate of reason is working for the government as a spy, or that the person simply "doesn't see the big picture" and will be an eventual victim of the government takeover.

There are harmless Amerinoids like Ross Perot and there are dangerous Amerinoids like James Nichols. Harmless Amerinoids are peaceful and attempt to affect change in government in a positive manner, like creating a third major political party for those unhappy with Republican and Democratic leadership. Dangerous Amerinoids are those who believe violence is needed to change government and the public's thinking. They believe acts of violence against the American people, like the Waco and Ruby Ridge incidents, should be answered with violence. What makes such

Amerinoids a scary group is the fact that, like Hitler and the Nazis, their outlandish ideas, based loosely on unrelated incidents of decades of crime in government from Watergate to Whitewater, are believed by so many. Their answers to America's problems enlist more than one believer willing to carry them out.

Timothy McVeigh was the perfect vessel for dangerous Amerinoid tendencies. He already had the seeds of paranoia planted in his head months earlier by his mentor, Terry Nichols; by his favorite book, *The Turner Diaries*; and by the limited view of America that he cultivated during his youth in rural western New York. Tim told other soldiers and friends how the government would extend its control over the people. One fellow soldier recalled to NBC's "Dateline": "I think he had a certain paranoia that the government was gonna perhaps take his weapons away. He had mentioned that a few times."[26] Now, McVeigh just needed some trigger event in his life to take him over the edge, to make him think that somehow all the disappointments in his life were related. He could then find a common enemy among them and, at the right time, be moved to retaliate for all the previous wrongs done to him.

Fresh out of Persian Gulf service, McVeigh went to Camp McCall, North Carolina, west of Fort Bragg, to the Special Forces headquarters on April 10. "I'm a Green Beret already," McVeigh thought. He excelled in army service, was named a sergeant practically overnight, and had received the Bronze Star, the Army Achievement Medal, the Southwest Asia Service Medal, and the Kuwait Liberation Medal. From his personal preparation and the army's training, McVeigh knew he could outrun, outshoot, and outfight anyone he met from this point forward. He smiled to himself: "I will probably teach the Berets a few things." The Gulf War was somewhat of a setback in his mind, but, if others really believed it to have been a war, then let them! McVeigh had taken home the big honors, and he had some stories to tell of his desert fighting.

For "Dateline," another soldier from Desert Storm remembered McVeigh's demeanor at the time of his departure for North Carolina:

> When he was leaving the Gulf, he was so excited. He packed his rucksack, his duffel bag, he was getting everything ready in a hurry. He was smiling, he was happy. Most of us just wanted to go home, get back to the United States, but he wasn't happy about getting back to the United States. [McVeigh] was happy about going to the Special Forces. That's what got his blood flowing.[27]

McVeigh was told, with the other Special Forces hopefuls at Fort Bragg, that they were to take part in a twenty-one-day assessment and selection course. He was told how difficult the tests would be, but McVeigh shrugged it off even though others in the group seemed worried. The course rigorously tested the mind and the body, and was notorious for leaving more than half the applicants in the dust. One candidate said, "We were subjected to things that tested us mentally, psychologically, and physically. It was tough. Few make it through."

The future Green Berets and those who would never realize that dream marched for hours and were asked to do as many sit-ups and push-ups as they could in two minutes. Then there was the swimming competition, in battle clothing and combat boots.

McVeigh and the other hopefuls were told that one field test included a long walk, with the candidates carrying forty-five pounds of weight in a rucksack. They were to pack what they thought they needed on the foot trip, but no matter what, their sacks had to weigh forty-five pounds. McVeigh packed what he needed and it weighed about twenty pounds, so he made up the difference with some sandbags. New boots he had just purchased were cutting into his feet on the walk and the weight proved to be too much. He met with a member of his unit, Mitch Whitmyers, who was taking the same tests. In their first few hours at the camp, the two had discussed how they felt worn from the war, like they were carrying a permanent case of jet lag. Mitch and Tim stood by a water fountain, filling their canteens. They knew there would be further physical testing, which would be much more difficult. Though he felt mentally prepared, McVeigh told his comrade that this just wasn't the right time for him to try for the Forces. McVeigh went to the field office and filled out a Statement of Voluntary Withdrawal, stating only, "I am not physically ready, and the rucksack march hurt more than it should." That was it. The time that had gone by without field exercises since his departure for Desert Storm had been too long. He'd lost his edge. McVeigh was angry with himself and with the people who had allowed him to get this far without going the distance. In essence, McVeigh was told to go back where he had started, basic army life.

The Special Forces course also included a psychological test. Tim's test went ungraded for years, because it is generally not graded until after the program is in full swing for ten days. Since McVeigh left after only two, there was no reason to grade his test and it was placed into a file with his name on it. McVeigh washed out of the program before it could even be looked at by the government.

Special Operations Command spokesman Lt. Col. Kenneth McGraw mentioned McVeigh's option to *USA Today,* but, in expected bureaucratic form, failed to emphasize McVeigh's detailed reason for leaving: "Students are told they can withdraw at any time, no questions asked, and that's what happened in this case."[28]

It was revealed in confidence to this author in 1995 that answers McVeigh gave on the psychological tests were apparently a bit off-center, not the answers of a man capable of long-term assignments with the exclusive and tight Special Forces.

Undetected at the time, McVeigh may have been suffering from Persian Gulf War Syndrome, reportedly brought on by exposure to harmful chemicals. The federal government has not publicly admitted to using chemical warfare, nor has it confirmed that the Iraqi government employed chemical weapons. But some leaks have hinted that both the United States and Iraq wanted to mix it up in unconventional methods, according to the November

1995 *Life* magazine special investigation. The "testing" of these
chemicals by either side likely had much to do with the mental decline of thousands of soldiers, including possibly Sgt. McVeigh.
The dangerous chemicals used included depleted uranium from
nuclear reactors, nerve and mustard gases, and pyridostigmine
bromide (a pretreatment for exposure to a nerve gas called
soman). The federal Centers for Disease Control found that Gulf
War vets had been unusually susceptible to memory loss, rashes,
hair loss, incontinence, chronic indigestion, chronic pain, and
other problems such as asthma and recurring pneumonia. Many
children of vets, born years after the war, have had serious birth
defects. Iraqis are also suffering from similar problems, which is
ironic since much of that country's chemical stock was made by
companies from the United States. "Studies are still going on in
Washington," said Robert Talluto, supervisor of a Persian Gulf
War clinic at Veterans Hospital in Buffalo, New York. "We've
screened about five hundred veterans in this area since the war,"
Talluto told the *Buffalo News.*[29]

A factor that also worked against McVeigh was the rigid independence he demonstrated in basic training. He could work as
a team player, but not to the degree needed by the Special Forces.
On an NBC "Dateline" program, Northeastern University criminal justice dean James Fox commented: "Serving his country may
not have been an altruistic act. It may have been very self-serving.
It gave him a feeling of structure in life, a feeling of purpose."[30]

So the early tests trimmed the undesirables from the Green
Beret candidate pool. McVeigh was gone after only two days.
The nightmare had continued, but now, he was living one during
the day. His dream of being in the Special Forces was spent, like
a bullet's puff of air. He would not write home to say he had been
accepted. He would never tell stories to his dad, his grandchildren,
or his friends of secret missions that could only be revealed
decades later. Tim McVeigh was now an outcast, unfit to perform
with the best. And he really didn't understand why. He could still

serve his country without anyone knowing of the failure . . . well, no one he would ever see again. But how would he tell the others, especially his dad, why he was not accepted? Fellow Persian Gulf soldier Sgt. Anthony Thigpen told the *New York Times*: "Everybody knew he was upset. We never knew the reason why he didn't make it. We figured, you don't make it, you don't make it. But he was definitely angry. He was upset, very upset."[31]

James Fox echoed Thigpen's sentiments. Fox told "Dateline" that McVeigh's reaction to the failure with the Green Berets was a defining moment in his life that would eventually lead to a mental collapse: "Whether he withdrew or was kicked out, it still was a failure and very easily he could externalize blame."

The frustration McVeigh felt was part rejection and part not knowing how or what to say to all the people he told that he was good enough to be a Green Beret. He sat and thought and then he'd wander the camp. Tim was very embarrassed, but this rejection did not make him want to kill. He was just angry with himself and a bit peeved with the Special Forces leaders for allowing him, an award-winning shooter and soldier, to fall by the wayside. Marion Curnutte, an infantryman who fought with McVeigh, remarked to the *New York Times*, "I think maybe he felt that he should have [been accepted]. I can recall they didn't give him a second chance."[32]

Others who tried were unable to stay in because they had been injured. Blaming the Green Berets for an "injury" would not only give him a reason for leaving, but also get back at them—in a way —showing people that the course itself is unfair and "there are many others out there, like me, who've been let down by a system that tries too hard to sift through its men with brutal force." On the outside, McVeigh was as tough as he wanted to portray himself to be. But on the inside he was just an average Joe who suffered failures from time to time, and he knew it. McVeigh maintains his "injury" story today, but with a twist. In a guarded interview, he told *Newsweek*: "I had gotten new boots and blisters started to break out. Any realist knows that if you develop blisters on the second day . . . you're not going to make it."[33] McVeigh denies failing the psychological test, but he was in no position to know since it hadn't yet been graded.

With his longtime dream of glory shattered, a changed Tim McVeigh went back to Fort Riley, Kansas. Today, reports are being issued on chemicals released in the Gulf War and those who were affected by them. Some of the seven hundred thousand soldiers suffer from paranoia and illness, as well as stonewalling from the government. Their children suffer from birth defects. McVeigh, whose mind was likely affected by those chemicals, was back at his old barracks with renewed fanaticism for guns, the protection of his rights as an American, and ready for the eventual showdown when the agents and liberals in Washington would try to take his country from him. Former army mate Robin Littleton told the *Sunday Times* of London that with the Special Forces failure, McVeigh's paranoia surfaced with a vengeance.

> He got real bitter about everything. He read lots of books about the JFK assassination and he was convinced the government was behind it all. He also started reading a lot of fiction, all of it to do with big business and the military planning to overthrow the government. He started to rant on about the private armies that were springing up inside the federal government, and how the CIA and FBI were out of control.[34]

McVeigh had reenlisted for a few more years, so he was safe and secure in his present position. But he was not the soldier he had been. Now his mind wandered as his sleep became more restless.

To Sheffield Anderson, who'd been in McVeigh's vehicle in the Gulf, Tim talked of home but not about the calm waters of Lake Ontario, his family, a love interest, or the peaceful, rolling fields of Pendleton, New York. Instead, he spoke of his shooting range near Olean. This was a place of solitude where Tim lived out his fantasies and no one could stop them from coming true. Rambo, who would be comfortable here, was not Special Forces material. Rambo's real-life counterpart, Timothy McVeigh, wasn't either.

McVeigh confided in Anderson as if there were secrets to be had, of getting a shelter ready on his Olean refuge and loading it with food and weapons. This, of course, would be a foolish idea for someone preparing for World War III or a government take-over, since western New York and Niagara Falls are great centers of hydroelectric power and would be one of the first to be struck in the event of an attack. On the shore of Lake Ontario, near Barker, New York, is the massive Somerset Power Plant and about thirty miles to the east, the New York Power Authority at Lewis-ton—not to mention all the industrial development in the area— prime targets in a clash. But, even with his military savvy, a now fearful McVeigh apparently believed he would be safe in Olean. "He was going to be ready if the Apocalypse hit," said Anderson.

At this point McVeigh began to flirt with life off the military camp. Barracks living at Fort Riley became irritating to Tim so he exercised his option to move into a residential area. He became the McVeigh who lived from place to place with no set direction or real goal. Our soldier, once a white bread, well-liked, small-town boy, ventured where evil lurked and allowed the specters of angry America to share his soul space. Here his body was as adrift as his thoughts.

John Kelso, another sergeant who McVeigh knew, said Tim could move in with him and Sgt. Richard Cerney at a place owned by Kelso's mother. McVeigh gathered his things and took a bed-room there, staying for two months of a hot summer that helped cause tension among the three. Kelso and Cerney were always in-terested in what McVeigh was doing, not because they admired him, but more likely because they thought he was so strange. McVeigh felt buggered after only a few weeks and silently made plans to get out. He reportedly complained to Sgt. Royal Witcher that John and Rick were getting "into his business too much."[35]

In September 1991, Tim asked Sgt. Witcher if he could share the house Witcher was already renting. Witcher said sure, sharing the rent would be a good way to save money while he waited to get married. Witcher said McVeigh could stay with him for about four months, until Royal's wedding day. Tim was happier now, with an upstairs bedroom at the yellow house on South Broadway in Herington, Kansas. He lived there as if he were in the barracks. Tim had a mattress with green army blankets. He covered the two windows in the large room with camouflage ponchos and used a tiny lamp, even during the day. Here McVeigh finally had privacy, in contrast to Fort Riley and the house he shared with the other two sergeants. Tim was also well armed, reportedly keeping ten guns at the house and two in his car, in addition to the fictitious arsenal he had back in New York, which he bragged of often to some. Witcher told the *New York Times*:

> They were hidden. He had a couple [guns] in the kitchen, a couple in the living room under the couch. I think there was one in the bathroom, behind the towels. Up the steps there was a little ledge and he kept on there a .38 revolver. I don't know if he was paranoid or what . . .[36]

Still a dedicated military man, McVeigh received his second Army Commendation Medal, issued September 27, 1991. It was issued for his work from September 4 through the award date, as a Bradley crew gunner who "fired a perfect score of 1,000 points on the Bradley qualification table."

In addition to his routine barracks duties, Tim relaxed at home, watched television, and read gun/weapon catalogues. He spent hours each week cleaning his guns, taking them apart, and putting them back together. Witcher reported that he would often come home to find McVeigh working with pistols and odd handguns. McVeigh stored other guns at the barracks, and dealt them himself, selling to acquaintances for current, fair prices. Tim had a Glock 19 in a shoulder holster and rarely ventured out without it.

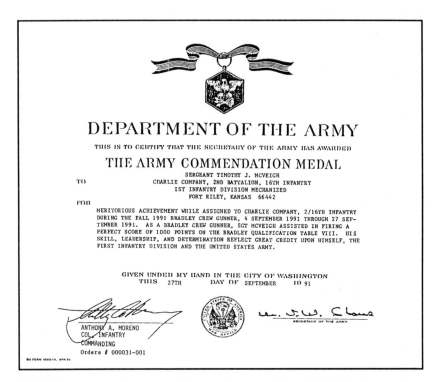

McVeigh was awarded a second Army Commendation Medal for his work as a Bradley crew gunner.

He ordered guns and materials from the catalogues he read and frequented Herington's as well as other gun shops in town, speaking with the owners and workers, impressing them with his wide knowledge of weaponry. McVeigh spent his money on food and weapons. He would cook for Witcher sometimes—usually spaghetti—and take him out to eat at fast-food places. Occasionally the two would take in a movie.

Their conversations consisted of weapons and problems with the government. When McVeigh called home, relatives sometimes informed him of the federal investigation into local politics in his hometown. The FBI was in the newspapers on a daily basis with reports of corruption in Niagara County government, which included politicians in Niagara Falls, Lockport, and nearby North Tonawanda. The Niagara County sheriff, social services commissioner, parks commissioner, and various county legislators were being investigated for theft, bribery, and other crimes. "This is what my local taxes are paying for, crooks" and "We elected these people" were common hometown sentiments. McVeigh was extremely interested in TV reports of politics gone bad on the federal level, his mind filing each new incident for future reference. Tim also read the Herington newspaper, the *Wichita Eagle-Beacon,* and the military's *Stars & Stripes,* a paper that details and praises the achievements of good soldiers. The *Eagle-Beacon* enforced McVeigh's negative feelings about the government by publishing wire stories (or Associated Press and United Press International features) about government problems and corruption. *Stars & Stripes* made him jealous of the achievements of other enlisted men, those in the military who were not rejected, men who had great military careers ahead of them. Witcher noted in the *New York Times*:

> I don't know if there's such a word, but he was ill-political. There was at least one thing in each paper he read each day that the government had something to do with that he took issue

with. Like gays in the military. The government getting involved in things he didn't really think it needed to be involved
in, things dealing with weapons, like raids.[37]

Raids. Common criminals fear them. Illegal weapons collec-
tors, drug dealers, and gamblers have nightmares about such acts
of government power. In McVeigh's mind, one day, the dark-
cloaked agents would be at the door to break it in with a battering
ram, rough him up, and haul him away to jail's eternity, just because he had original thoughts. McVeigh was scared and mad, and
getting madder with each printed story of a sneak attack somewhere or the trampling of the rights of good Americans by their
tax-supported leaders. It was not that McVeigh identified with
common criminals, but he knew the rights of law-abiding citizens
were increasingly at risk from gun-toting feds.

McVeigh heard about a meeting of his fellow soldiers. The
November meeting off the Fort Riley barracks was being held by
people who wanted to form a group opposed to weapons bans and
to all forms of government interference in their own lives. In December, McVeigh attended such a meeting and liked what he
heard. At last he found himself with others who felt as he did, that
there was something wrong with America. Some politicians were
saying it, too. We needed an overhaul, a change. Many changes!

McVeigh briefly dated a girl from a local town around this
time, but he seemed too uptight for their relationship to last.
Catina Lawson met McVeigh at a party given by a friend. Catina
told the *New York Times,* "I've always been attracted to tall,
skinny guys." When McVeigh mentioned politics to her, she recalled that his face would get red and he'd have plenty to say,
echoing some of the anti-Semitic sentiments from his favorite
book, *The Turner Diaries.* Lawson told the *Times:*

> He would talk about the government a lot. Usually the topic was
> brought up by him. He would shoot off his mouth and just bitch
> about the government. He also talked about Hitler; this is what

CAUTION: NOT TO BE USED FOR IDENTIFICATION PURPOSES

THIS IS AN IMPORTANT RECORD.
SAFEGUARD IT.

ANY ALTERATIONS IN SHADED AREAS RENDER FORM VOID

CERTIFICATE OF RELEASE OR DISCHARGE FROM ACTIVE DUTY

1. NAME (Last, First, Middle)	2. DEPARTMENT, COMPONENT AND BRANCH	3. SOCIAL SECURITY NO.
MCVEIGH TIMOTHY JAMES	ARMY/RA	

4.a. GRADE, RATE OR RANK	4.b. PAY GRADE	5. DATE OF BIRTH (YYMMDD)	6. RESERVE OBLIG. TERM. DATE
SGT	E-5	680423	Year 99 Month 05 Day 11

7.a. PLACE OF ENTRY INTO ACTIVE DUTY
BUFFALO, NY

7.b. HOME OF RECORD AT TIME OF ENTRY (City and state, or complete
5289 CAMPBELL BLVD
LOCKPORT, NY 14094

8.a. LAST DUTY ASSIGNMENT AND MAJOR COMMAND
CSC, 2/16TH INF INF 1ST INF DIV
FORSCOM - FC

8.b. STATION WHERE SEPARATED
FORT RILEY, KANSAS

9. COMMAND TO WHICH TRANSFERRED
CSC 1st BN, 174th INF, 79 DELEWARE STREET, TONAWANDA, NY 14150

10. SGLI COVERAGE   None
Amount: $ 100,000

11. PRIMARY SPECIALTY (List number, title and years and months in specialty. List additional specialty numbers and titles involving periods of one or more years.)	12. RECORD OF SERVICE	Year(s)	Month(s)	Day(s)
11M20, FIGHTING VEHICLE INFANTRYMAN, 3 YRS AND 4 MOS//NOTHING FOLLOWS	a. Date Entered AD This Period	88	05	24
	b. Separation Date This Period	91	12	31
	c. Net Active Service This Period	03	07	08
	d. Total Prior Active Service	00	00	00
	e. Total Prior Inactive Service	00	00	00
	f. Foreign Service	00	03	00
	g. Sea Service	00	00	00
	h. Effective Date of Pay Grade	91	02	01

13. DECORATIONS, MEDALS, BADGES, CITATIONS AND CAMPAIGN RIBBONS AWARDED OR AUTHORIZED (All periods of service)
ARMY SERVICE RIBBON//NATIONAL DEFENSE SERVICE MEDAL//ARMY LAPEL BUTTON//
SOUTHWEST ASIA SERVICE MEDAL W/2 BRONZE STARS//BRONZE STAR MEDAL//ARMY
ACHIEVEMENT MEDAL //NOTHING FOLLOWS

14. MILITARY EDUCATION (Course title, number of weeks, and month and year completed)
PRIMARY LEADERSHIP DEVELOPMENT COURSE, 4 WEEKS, 1990//NOTHING FOLLOWS

15.a. MEMBER CONTRIBUTED TO POST-VIETNAM ERA VETERANS' EDUCATIONAL ASSISTANCE PROGRAM	Yes	No	15.b. HIGH SCHOOL GRADUATE OR EQUIVALENT	Yes	No	16. DAYS ACCRUED LEAVE PAID
		X		X		

17. MEMBER WAS PROVIDED COMPLETE DENTAL EXAMINATION AND ALL APPROPRIATE DENTAL SERVICES AND TREATMENT WITHIN 90 DAYS PRIOR TO SEPARATION	Yes	X No

18. REMARKS
BLOCK 6 INCLUDES PERIOD OF DEP: 880512-880523//SUBJECT TO ACTIVE DUTY RECALL
AND/OR ANNUAL SCREENING// NOTHING FOLLOWS

92·12

19.a. MAILING ADDRESS AFTER SEPARATION (Include Zip Code)
5289 CAMPBELL BLVD
LOCKPORT, NY 14094

19.b. NEAREST RELATIVE (Name and address - include Zip Code)
WILLIAM E MCVEIGH
SAME AS 19a

20. MEMBER REQUESTS COPY 6 BE SENT TO NY DIR. OF VET AFFAIRS	X Yes	No	22. OFFICIAL AUTHORIZED TO SIGN (Typed name, grade, title and signature)
21. SIGNATURE OF MEMBER BEING SEPARATED			GARY A. WADSWORTH, GS7, CH, TRANS PT

SPECIAL ADDITIONAL INFORMATION (For use by authorized agencies only)

23. TYPE OF SEPARATION	24. CHARACTER OF SERVICE (Include upgrades)

25. SEPARATION AUTHORITY	26. SEPARATION CODE	27. REENTRY CODE
AR 635-200 PARA 16-3	LCC	2B

28. NARRATIVE REASON FOR SEPARATION
FOR THE CONVENIENCE OF THE GOVERNMENT - FY92 EARLY TRANSITION PROGRAM

29. DATES OF TIME LOST DURING THIS PERIOD	30. MEMBER REQUESTS COPY 4
NONE//NOTHING FOLLOWS	Initials

A wash-out of the Special Forces program, McVeigh opted to leave the military through its Early Transition Program.

made me angry. From what I remember, he didn't necessarily agree with all those Jews being killed, but he said Hitler had the right plan. I think he was talking about when Hitler tried to conquer the world, how he went about it, little pieces at a time. He thought that was admirable. I didn't like him after that.[38]

Other than agreeing with Hitler's goals of world conquest, McVeigh didn't seem to have anything nice to say about anything. In fact, other soldiers from the base who had met him jokingly called Tim "Anti-McVeigh," noting his criticism of just about everything.

Witcher was going to be married in January 1992, so McVeigh made plans to move out. He was still employed by the army, an arm of the government he had grown to dislike. If I'm going to follow this road with people who are making a change in America, I have to join their side, McVeigh thought. Others, those who attended the meetings, found it odd that this new person, Tim, who was working for the government was hanging around with them. McVeigh responded when he learned of a new program the army was involved in that gave him an early release from the service. The Early Transition Program would save money by cutting military forces in the post-Persian Gulf period. McVeigh took the honorable discharge and was soon a free man.

Outside the jail, speculation among news agencies and the nation pointed to international terrorist groups from the Middle East, like the Islamic fundamentalists who had been involved in the World Trade Center bombing.

As mass fear over another possible bombing spread, the country was in an uproar. Not since the slow chase of O. J. Simpson down a California highway had people been so glued to their televisions. Panic among the rescuers in Oklahoma had hit because of a rumor that another blast might occur at the site. Immediately following the blast, the top three television news agencies and right-wing extremist organizations focused their blame on foreign madmen. Even Michigan Militia Commander Norm Olson declared that the bombing had been executed by Japan because the United States was supposedly responsible for the nerve gas attack in Tokyo's subway. (Olson later resigned.) Arab Americans may have suffered most as word spread that authorities were looking for people of Middle Eastern descent.

In little Lockport, New York, the Union-Sun & Journal *newspaper sought to "localize" the Oklahoma tragedy by asking people on the street for their personal reactions. Of course, no one answered that the bombers might be from America.*

Chapter 6

American Psycho

A man's deeds are his life.
                                        —African proverb

A lost soldier named Timothy J. McVeigh had returned to his
Pendleton, New York, home a failure. While some in his family
viewed Tim as a type of war hero and offered proud sentiments,
McVeigh let the congratulations pass over him. What had he really done except participate in a bullshit Gulf War that the president used as a ploy? Tim had been just another one of the pawns.

Back in Fort Riley they were probably on morning break now,
Tim thought. He had to get a job to get back on track. That could
be done at home for the time being. Tim talked to his old friend
Terry Nichols on the phone, telling him he was back at his dad's
place. Terry said the offer was always open if Tim wanted to visit.
There was plenty to do in Michigan, like helping Terry at gun
shows. Tim said he'd consider it. Nichols, now divorced, was
taking care of his young son, Josh, for a while and asked if they

could visit. Josh Nichols had always wanted to see Niagara Falls. McVeigh also said he'd like to show Terry around New York sometime. Tim also kept in touch with Michael Fortier, who was in Kingman, Arizona, working part-time after he left the army because he'd injured his shoulder.

Tim stared around the living room, wondering where his life was going. This place on Campbell Boulevard was not his home. That warm, comfortable place where Christmases included Mom and Dad had disintegrated long before he joined the service. His childhood was a mile away, on Meyer Road, where he had friends and a neighborhood. Tim's childhood band of rebels was just a group of ghosts now, voices in the woods. He recalled hiking with a few of them who had been Boy Scouts. They built small campfires and told stories of "what we'd do if . . ." Those innocent times were gone. Now Tim divided his time between his dad's house and a small apartment he'd rented on Dysinger Road in the town of Lockport. McVeigh picked up the days-old newspaper and sifted through it, stopping at an article about a Niagara County Social Services Department worker involved in illegal dealings with other county employees. The news report stemmed from unnamed FBI sources who said the worker was part of a wide federal probe of county government corruption. Even at home, McVeigh thought, politicians who feel they're above the law use their positions to steal. He threw the newspaper across the room. Thieves in government; talk of the "Brady Bill" that would disarm legal gun owners; the fake Gulf War where Americans senselessly slaughtered surrendering troops all for the pride of a president.

Tim talked with Jennifer about what had been going on. She hadn't heard much about the Niagara County corruption probe, except for what their dad mentioned now and then when he read the newspaper. Jennifer agreed with Tim that problems seemed to be at every level of the American government. Jennifer had pondered these subjects in the past with her brother, but their talks focused mainly on national events and how the Constitution was followed more closely by political leaders years ago. Through telephone conversations and letters, Jennifer and Tim had formed a closer relationship when Tim was thousands of miles away in the Gulf. He often wrote to her from the lonely desert. Now, Jennifer was happy to have her brother home after his time away in the military. He talked of a few of his old army buddies and how he missed them, but they were distant figures to Jennifer. She enjoyed the car rides they took at night, listening to old tapes, just cruising around with no planned destination. Tim said he loved the freedom the road offered; it reminded him of his high school days when he and his friends would hang out together and drive to the lake, stopping to eat at the Seafood Bar in Olcott.

To Jennifer, Tim was still the same person she had known when their parents split up. She thought Tim was a little "pissed" about some of the "crap the government was pulling," but he was right. In fact, if he put his mind to it, maybe her brother could change things someday. She was just a senior in high school, but even then Jennifer knew public office turned good people into slimy politicians. Tim would never let that happen to him. Jennifer listened to him intently. She was just happy that three-fifths of her family was together in one place. She hoped it would last for a long time.

Unlike her brother, Jennifer McVeigh was a bit of a rebel in her later high school years. Someone who laughed in the face of authority, Jennifer was a wild girl, the party type, like her mother had been so many years ago. Classmate and McVeigh family friend Brian Haines said during an interview with me:

> I got closer to Jennifer than I did to Tim. My brother David dated Jennifer. He had graduated in 1989, but he dated her later and took her to her senior prom [in 1992]. She had a lot more friends in school than Tim. She was like in the in crowd. She was very, very outgoing and very friendly, but she was also part biker chick, part rebel. The rebel side of her liked to go smoke in the restroom at Starpoint. She's been like that her whole life, [wearing] tight jeans, guys hitting on her. She'd always leave a

certain school function with somebody different, never had a set boyfriend. She wants the attention. . . . She was smart, though not smart enough to stay out of trouble.[1]

Other former classmates, like Melissa Curtis, have not been as candid as Haines. Curtis told the *New York Times* that Jennifer was not in the "preppy or cheerleader crowd" but still "had a lot of friends." Like Mickey McVeigh, Jennifer "gets along with everyone," according to former classmate Karen Stellrecht, who was also interviewed by the *Times.*[2]

Starpoint school guidance counselor Tamah Alt told a *Times* reporter that Jennifer was "a really nice girl, very bubbly." Alt said Jennifer took a heavier academic load than was expected and passed state Regents exams in English and social studies.

At least two graduates of Starpoint told this author in conversation that one or two administrators at the high school were disliked greatly by members of the student body. Tim likely formed his first dislike for authority figures, during these early years, because of a principal who had a "complex" with leadership and conformity. This was probably one of the reasons why Jennifer was rebellious in her teens.

Since coming back home, Tim had been working part-time at Burns International Security as a guard during special events at the Convention and Civic Center in Niagara Falls. The center hosts activities year-round, from dirt-bike racing to concerts. The job included duty at many places in Niagara and Erie counties. McVeigh was hired because of his good military record, but when he first started the job his supervisor found him to be a little too intense for the public. Linda Haner-Mele, his supervisor at the center, told a *New York Times* reporter of the McVeigh paradox. He was boyish yet fiery.

He seemed more like a child to me than an adult man. He didn't really carry himself like he came out of the military. He didn't

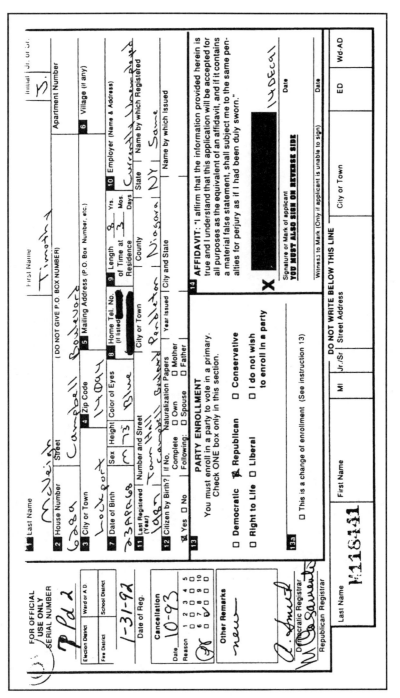

McVeigh enrolled in the Republican party on his voter registration application.

APPLICATION FOR IDENTIFICATION CARD

1. LAST NAME - FIRST NAME - MIDDLE NAME (Print or type)
McVeigh, Timothy J.

2. ADDRESS (Preferably Military Installation)
76 Delaware St.
Tonawanda, NY 14150

DATE OF 9 Feb 92

TO BE FILLED IN BY ISSUING AUTHORITY
EXPIRATION DATE: 11 Apr 95
CARD SERIAL NUMBER: 6125476
5. DATE OF APPLICATION: 9 Feb 92

3. HOME PHONE
4. OFFICE PHONE

6. CHECK TYPE OF CARD DESIRED
DD FORM 2A — X (INITIAL ISSUE)
DD FORM 2A (Res)
DD FORM 2A (Ret)
DD FORM 489
DD FORM 1934
DA FORM 1095
DA FORM 1602
OTHER (Specify)

7. CHECK REASON FOR REQUESTING CARD
INITIAL ISSUE — X
REPLACE LOST CARD
REPLACE MUTILATED CARD
EXPIRATION
REENLISTMENT
CORRECT AN ERROR
ENTRY ON ACTIVE DUTY FOR MORE THAN 30 DAYS
CHANGE OF IDENTIFICATION OR GRADE
TRANSFER TO RESERVE COMPONENTS
RETIREMENT (Specify type)
OTHER (Specify)
IF REPLACING LOST CARD, STATE CIRCUMSTANCES UNDER WHICH CARD WAS LOST (Continue in "Remarks")

8. GRADE (See reverse): SGT
9. SOCIAL SECURITY NO.
10. DATE OF BIRTH: 23 Apr 68
11. WEIGHT: 160
12. HEIGHT: 73"
13. GENEVA CONVENTION CATEGORY

14. COLOR OF HAIR: Brown
15. COLOR OF EYES: Blue
16. BLOOD TYPE: O P'S
17. EXPIRATION TERM OF SERVICE OR OBLIGATION: 11 Apr 95

FOR CARDS OTHER THAN DD FORM 2A, DD FORM 2A (Res) AND DD FORM 2A (Ret)

18. SOCIAL SECURITY NUMBER (DA Form 1602 only)
19. STATUS (DA Form 1602 only)
20. SEX (DA Form 1602 only)
21. CAPACITY (DA Form 1934)
22. RELIGION (DD Form 489 and DD Form 1934)

23. EQUIVALENT RANK (DD Form 489 and DD Form 1934)
24. POSITION TITLE (DD Form 489 and DA Form 1095)
25. UNIT, SECTION, BRANCH OR ACTIVITY/COMMAND OR SERVICE (DD Form 489, DA Form 1602 and DA Form 1095 only)

SIGNATURE OF APPROVING AUTHORITY
Doug J. Reine CPT

SIGNATURE OF APPLICANT

RECEIPT OF CARD IS ACKNOWLEDGED (Signature)
Tim McVeigh

DATE ACKNOWLEDGED: 9 Feb 92

K132

DA FORM 428 REPLACES EDITION JUN 78, & DA FORM 428-R, For use of this form, see AR 606-5; the proponent agency is TAGCEN.

McVeigh filed for an identification card while serving in the New York National Guard.

stand tall with his shoulders back. He kind of slumped. He was a very, very thin man, almost like anorexia. He was the thinnest person I've ever seen. He didn't talk about his home life. He didn't talk about any type of girlfriends. He just wasn't an open type of person. He was a loner, a follower, not a leader. He wasn't a person I could trust to put in a high pressure area. If someone didn't cooperate with him, he would start yelling at them, becoming verbally aggressive. He wouldn't be able to react to that, where he had to think and react in a split second. But he was very good if you said, "Tim, watch this door. Don't let anybody through."[3]

Persian Gulf War Syndrome probably had quite a hold on Tim by this time. He would tell Terry Nichols's brother, James, during one of his visits to their Michigan farm, that he believed the government was keeping tabs on him through a computer chip the army had implanted in his buttocks one night while he slept. McVeigh visited the Nichols farm in Decker, Michigan, several times before coming home to stay with his dad, and he would continue brief guest stints there during the next three years. James didn't fully believe Tim's claim about the computer chip, but if his friend was correct then something had to be done. Nichols made an appointment for X rays, but for some reason, Tim never went. A Nichols neighbor named Phil Morawski has echoed James Nichols's story, in published reports, of McVeigh believing he was being electronically monitored by the army. Tim would also file papers to receive compensation for Gulf War Syndrome, and show a "rash" to doctors at the Veterans Hospital in Buffalo. But his request for compensation was eventually turned down, for unknown reasons.

At home in New York State, Tim registered to vote. He had first registered at the Pendleton Town Hall one year after high school. This time, December 14, 1991, he filled out a form at the Niagara County Board of Elections in Lockport. He wrote that he was seventy-three inches tall, with brown hair and blue eyes. Tim fibbed a bit by stating that he had resided at 6289 Campbell

Boulevard for eight years and three months. He listed his party enrollment as Republican. Once officially registered by the elections commissioners, McVeigh was listed as voter #M118441.

He had needed more to do with his spare time than the sporadic guard work, so he took a second job. He made the natural transition for a soldier by joining the New York Army National Guard. McVeigh was assigned to the Combat Support Unit, First Battalion, 174th Infantry, based in Tonawanda. At $150 a month, he was the leader of a missile squad, which, during wartime, is responsible for knocking out enemy tanks. Tim would spend five months and a day in the guard's employ. The guard may be the only place in his whole life where Tim didn't leave much of an impression. Just about everywhere else McVeigh would travel in his entire twenty-seven years, there are people who remember him in some odd way—something he did or said. For some reason, the guard is the one place where he would be remembered pretty much by name, a uniform tag, and time of employment only. Sgt. Kazmierczak told the *Buffalo News*:

> My impression, which is limited because he was here such a short time, is that he was a squared-away soldier. The one thing that made him stand out was that he had a combat patch, because he served in Desert Storm. His appearance was always good and he was always punctual.[4]

McVeigh had portrayed himself as having a genuine concern for people, their protection, and preservation of their American lifestyles. A writer himself, Tim McVeigh authored possibly hundreds and hundreds of letters to friends, agencies, publications, and, of course, relatives. Jennifer and Tim were close pen pals when Tim entered his twenties; Tim wrote to his aunt Jean and to several friends over the years. He discontinued his National Rifle Association membership with an angry letter when he felt the group's opposition to pending gun bans was not strong enough, and he loudly promoted his views in three 1992 letters—two of which were sent to his hometown newspaper and one to his local congressman, John LaFalce.

Though the world would not know of Tim's interest in writing until three years later, McVeigh used some spare time in February 1992 to pen a note to the *Union-Sun & Journal* in Lockport, the news agency for Niagara County. Tim's mind was a furious jumble over numerous unrelated social and political problems as he sat home typing out the letter to the newspaper editor, Dan Kane, a friend of Jennifer's. He banged away at the keys as he concentrated on stories he had read in newspapers or watched on television. It all seemed to be building up: the problems in America were related to one another in a way that only Tim could understand. Something had to be done to wake everyone up, and maybe his letters would open a few eyes. Tim thought of the reported increases in crime, prisons that were breeding grounds for more problems, the number of racist incidents he had heard of and the militiamen who practiced shooting often to be ready for a real race war, increasing taxes imposed by crooked politicians, new gun laws proposed by government leaders in their reelection campaigns, the fall of Russia, universal health care, and imports that put American workers out on the street. He switched the typewriter key to "caps lock" and hit each letter with force to say "AMERICA IS IN SERIOUS DECLINE" and sat back to look at what was on the page. If America's patriots were alive, they would have organized another Boston Tea Party to protest the way the country is being run today, Tim thought. He continued typing. Why not do the same to the Japanese—why not sink a ship of imports as a statement of our disappointment with the "System"? He brooded a bit and then typed, "Do we have to shed blood to reform the current system?" Earl Turner, the main character in *The Turner Diaries,* came to mind. Tim thought maybe some people would have to get hurt before changes would be made. He genuinely hoped the federal government would see these points before a new revolution began. "I hope it doesn't come to that. But it might," he

typed, hitting the final period with a flourish of his wrist. Then he
reread what he had written, signed his name, and used his name
and address stamp at the bottom of the letter. Tim had a rubber
stamp (it said simply "Tim McVeigh" and listed his dad's address) made because he wrote letters so often that he was actually
sick of writing out the address every single time.

When the letter he had written appeared in the *Union-Sun &
Journal* a couple days later, Tim was unhappy that some of his ex-
clamation points had been edited out, but the letter was there all
the same. He liked seeing it in print. He even received a couple of
calls from friends who had seen it. Even great-aunt Helen
McVeigh of Lockport called. She agreed that imports were getting
out of hand. Why, even at Kmart, there were things on the shelves
that had "Made in Taiwan" labels, a common sentiment among the
locals. What was the country coming to? Tim didn't get the type
of response he had expected, though, but he had warned them—
if changes weren't made soon, there would be a revolution. Someone would pay.

Tim talked to his father about a *Buffalo News* article he saw a
day later that said a man had been arrested for carrying chemical
mace. The notion of a guy carrying mace seemed a little "gay," but
what about a woman? What if Jennifer wanted to protect herself
when she went out at night? She didn't carry a gun, so mace
would be a good alternative if she was ever attacked. There are a
lot of crazy people out there, Tim said to himself, thinking of the
common good. He was personally reminded of a passage in *The
Turner Diaries* where the government wanted to outlaw mace
completely, along with private ownership of guns. In the book,
after his girlfriend Katherine was nearly attacked by a "young de-
generate," hero character Earl Turner reflects, ". . . the same people who agitated so hysterically for gun confiscation before the
Cohen Act are now calling for tear gas to be outlawed, too. There
have even been cases where women who need their tear gas to
fend off would-be rapists have been charged with armed as-

sault!"* Turner says rape is virtually tolerated by the government he lives under. He explains, "Black civil rights spokesmen . . . have had only praise for the Supreme Court's decision. Rape laws, they said, are 'racist,' because a disproportionately large number of blacks have been charged under them." How would Jennifer, or any woman, protect herself? "Tell your congressman," Bill McVeigh said to his son. "He's the one who makes the laws." He may not have known the chemical mace law was drawn up and approved by the state legislature, not the federal government.

Bill McVeigh also liked to write letters now and then. He would write to John LaFalce a year later—once about the North American Free Trade Agreement (NAFTA), a pact signed by the Clinton administration that aggravated union men like Bill, and again in a note on the General Agreement on Tariffs and Trade (GATT).

On his father's advice, Tim clipped out the mace report, grabbed a pen, sat down, and feverishly wrote out a longhand letter to Congressman LaFalce. "I strongly believe in a God-given right to self-defense," Tim stressed. He wanted to tell LaFalce that using mace was just one way a person had to protect his or her life, right? Tim offered a couple options, too:

Should a governing body be able to tell people that they cannot save their own lives, because it would be a violation of the law to do so? If faced with a rapist/murderer, would you choose to (a) die as a law-abiding citizen or (b) live and go to jail?

Tim ended his letter to LaFalce by saying he was "in shock that a law like this would exist that prohibits a woman from protecting herself, as if the police could be everywhere, to protect everyone, at all times." It was bad enough that guns were being restricted. He stamped his name and address on the letter and signed it, leaving his telephone number also, in case the congressman wished to address these concerns in person. Tim placed the Na-

---

*Andrew Macdonald [William Pierce], *The Turner Diaries* (Hillsboro, W.Va.: National Vanguard Books, 1978), p. 59.

FEB 19 1992

16 FEB 92

Dear Mr. LaFalce,

Recently, I saw an article in the Buffalo News that detailed a man's arrest; one of the charges being "possession of a noxious substance" (CS gas). This struck my curiosity, so I went to the New York State Penal Law. Sure enough, section 270 prohibits possession of any noxious substance, and included in section 265 is a ban on the use of "stun guns". Now I am a male, and fully capable of physically defending myself, but how about a female?

I strongly believe in a God-given right to self-defense. Should any other person or a governing body be able to tell another person that he/she cannot save their own life, because it would be a violation of a law? In this case, which is more important: Faced with a rapist/murderer, would you prefer to a.) die, a law-abiding citizen or b.) live, and go to jail?

It is a lie if we tell ourselves that the police can protect us everywhere, at all times.

I am in shock that a law exists which denies a woman's right to self-defense. Firearms restrictions are bad enough, but now a woman can't even carry mace in her purse?!?!.

TIM McVEIGH
6289 CAMPBELL BLVD
LOCKPORT, NY 14094

McVeigh's handwritten letter to Congressman John LaFalce, complaining about New York's chemical mace law.

tional Rifle Association sticker on the back of the envelope and placed it in the mailbox for the next day's pick up. But what was one letter? Would Congressman John LaFalce, an owl-eyed, limp-wristed, liberal Democrat who'd been in office for too long, ever even think of this point of view when a discussion or vote on mace or any other weapon came up in the House of Representatives? He was on *their* side and had said before that the people should be disarmed. What was in this man's head when he spoke of outlawing guns? What country was he living in? LaFalce responded a few weeks later with a one-page letter, detailing the state law that prohibits chemical mace and why it is important. LaFalce would end his letter by saying that if his constituent ever has any other concerns, "Feel free to contact me." But that would be about it. On May 2, 1995, McVeigh's letter to LaFalce received national exposure because the author had become an important part of American history, and an infamous character in his own right. While Rep. LaFalce selfishly promoted himself in newspapers by using the fact that he had received a handwritten letter from Timothy McVeigh, he said Tim's letter was "mild" compared to others he receives from constituents concerned with weapons laws.

McVeigh put his typewriter to use a couple weeks later in early March 1992 to pound out another letter to Dan Kane at the *Union-Sun & Journal.* Tim was upset over a meat industry cow farm he'd recently visited where the animals were slaughtered. While he was not a vegetarian, he thought it was inhumane to slit cows' throats in the slaughtering process. Hunters received a bad reputation from the liberals, but at least a hunter kills his prey immediately, instead of letting it slowly bleed to death while caged in some building. Deer lived normal lives in their natural wooded habitat, while the cows were just treated as if they were already meat before being killed, Tim thought. He wrote, "Would you rather die while living happily or die leading a miserable life?" His letter was published just a couple days later on March 10 in the newspaper. He wasn't sure why the editor at the paper had placed such a title on his letter, but it said "Meat Insured Survival." He hoped it would have said something about hunting being part of man's existence, but at least the letter appeared.

Terry Nichols and his son, Josh Nichols, the only child from his marriage to Lana (Walsh) Padilla, which was dissolved by Lana on December 18, 1989, finally traveled from Michigan to New York for a visit, and Tim felt great to be with his friend again. He took his guests on a tour of Pendleton, and then for a ride north to Niagara Falls. The Nicholses met Bill McVeigh, too. Terry was on vacation that week, and spent a lot of time talking to Tim about his new wife, Marife.

Marife Torres was a mail-order bride he had married in 1990 in the Philippines, a place Terry enjoyed visiting often. She was in her late teens at the time they were married. Terry saw her as someone clean and fresh, "someone to train up," he joked with Tim. She was ready to serve also, unlike Terry's ex-wife, who had been divorced twice before she even met Terry. Tim talked of how he was unhappy back home, and again Terry said that the offer was always open if he wanted to come live with them in Michigan. Marife would wait on him hand and foot, and he could help Terry with work at the gun shows. Terry and Josh left New York after a short stay at Tim's Lockport apartment and went back home to Decker, while Tim continued to ponder just where he was going. He seriously considered living with the Nicholses because it really seemed like there was nothing keeping him in Pendleton. To Tim, living back at home with his dad had been a giant step backward in his life. All the people he knew from the area who had ever made anything of themselves had left town and never come back.

Spring was coming and Jennifer was doing poorly in high school. She had been rebellious at Starpoint, but her grades weren't all that bad. But now Jennifer began failing in her easiest class, Cinema. Her teacher recalled that Bill McVeigh met with him to see what could be done to make sure Jennifer would get the class credit she needed to graduate. The teacher was impressed by Bill's concern and love for his daughter.

> It was three or four years ago. She was obviously a moderately bright girl, and very polite. Cinema is an elective taken by two kinds of people—kids who have an interest in film or the arts, and kids who've got to have a half credit to graduate. This isn't physics. It's watching *Singin' in the Rain* and *Casablanca.* Jennifer took the course and was doing badly. Her dad came in on a "Parents Day." Here's a dad who was truly interested in how Jennifer was doing.[5]

Jennifer did pass the class and graduated from Starpoint in June 1992. Bill McVeigh had a big graduation party at the house for his daughter, with lots of family and friends. There was plenty of music and the festivities continued well into the wee hours of the morning. Grandfather Ed McVeigh was there, along with friend Mary Butler and brother Tim, but Tim seemed to be detached that day, with his mind on other things. Butler's friend Dan Kane said:

> I was at the Campbell Boulevard home once in particular that I can remember. I went to Jennifer's party, and Tim came in at some point and I shook hands with him when we were introduced. He was very aloof. He came into the house and went to his room and didn't really participate. But Bill McVeigh was there with his girlfriend. We sat in the kitchen all night and really had a grand time. We talked quite a bit. Tim just disappeared somewhere.[6]

If he was going to settle into a civilian life, it wouldn't be in New York, Tim thought. The welfare system was entirely out of control. An able-bodied person like himself could actually live in the state and collect benefits for the rest of his life without ever having to work, he thought. That was bullshit. The social services programs in New York were so strong and so well entrenched in bureaucracy under Governor Mario Cuomo that it was costing taxpayers millions. Welfare seekers were actually moving to New York State because of the great benefits, and New York was jokingly called "The Cadillac of Welfare States." It wasn't just welfare though; taxes were insanely out of control, and there was no work for someone who didn't have a college education. At least in Michigan the people were more in control of their lives. Everyone protected themselves and there were groups of people forming that were interested in protecting our rights in the future. Plus, Tim could be back together with Terry.

McVeigh had applied for a job with the border patrol in Niagara Falls. He passed the screening test, but was later informed there were no positions immediately available. He didn't know that most of those jobs went to those with political connections, but such are the politics in the Falls.

Around this time, McVeigh hoped to date a pretty Lockport girl he had first met in his high school years. In an August 18, 1995, story published in the *Union-Sun & Journal,* DeSales High School graduate Marsha Thrall remembered the crush Tim had on her twin sister, Maureen, in 1992. "He didn't know what to do. He kept calling and calling and wouldn't take no for an answer," Marsha said. But the answer remained, "No, but thank you."

McVeigh quit the National Guard in June 1992; shortly thereafter he quit his security guard job as well. He told his father and younger sister that he wanted to go live with Terry. Tim made his own decisions as far as his dad was concerned, but to Jennifer, Tim's news was a shock and a disappointment. She was going to be separated from him again, and it looked like it would be for a long time. That day Tim McVeigh may well have made the worst decision of his entire life. He would reenter the Circus of Losers—the hate-filled group of people in Michigan, in Kansas, and in Arizona who would aid in his progressive mental disintegration: Terry Nichols, the man who was born to lose, dominated by an older brother, a drunken mother, a portly ex-wife, Lana; an unfaithful wife, Marife, with a child by another man; alleged substance-using friend Michael

Fortier; and a ragtag band of other friends and associates who believed in all sorts of "government conspiracies," including one about federal officials attempting to hide alien spaceships that were recovered in America's Southwest desert. It was these people who would nurture and support all the negative views Tim absorbed from books and from his Gulf War experiences. His Amerinoid status was set in stone the day he left Pendleton for the Land of Fools. Political scientist Claude Welch, Jr., of the University of Buffalo, suggests that people like Tim McVeigh need to be around other people who think the way they do. In an interview, he explains.

> Their own perceptions are reinforced, rather than questioned. And this could reinforce their dedication to the cause, to the point of doing something. Tim just got drawn into these circles that got narrower and narrower.[7]

In Decker, Michigan, Tim was a welcome sight. The boys—Tim, Terry, and James—were back together again. Tim and Terry enjoyed shooting together, but mainly this small group of disgruntled men sat together to complain about the state of the nation and to feed each other's anger. They all agreed that the government was hurting the citizens by interfering in their lives. Tim related the stories about New York that he'd learned, and the Nichols brothers were in awe. Welfare alone would break the state, said Tim. Government largesse and laziness on the part of the people would kill the American way of life. James Nichols told CNN in a 1995 interview that his distrust for those in power runs deep.

> When you're out in the open, you start thinking for yourself. The government doesn't make any sense. I don't trust the government because every time they get into something, they muff it up. They screw it up.[8]

Information began trickling in over the shortwave radio and in such right-wing publications as the *Spotlight* that a standoff in-

McVeigh's growing paranoia about the federal government was fed by such right-wing publications as the *Spotlight* and the *Patriot Report*.

volving a man in Idaho was developing. Randy Weaver heard they were coming for him and he was ready. He would do whatever it took to protect his family and his home. Was this Communist Russia? It was certainly not America, he thought, because in America your rights to own weapons and have political views were protected by the Constitution. Weaver knew that those in power now wanted to bend the Constitution and shape it into something new so they could have more control. Once a man's freedom is gone, he is better off dead. Randy was going to fight until the end. He heard his name on the radio and received messages from supporters, so he knew he was not alone in the fight.

The cabin, deep in the Idaho woods, was an eerie sight as the bloodred sun burned that morning. Set at the side of a mountain, the cabin resembled Ernest Hemingway's home, where the sixty-two-year-old author killed himself with a shotgun blast in 1961. Weaver kept one eye on his wife and the other out the window, waiting for the lawmen to approach.

Like a team of black ninjas from hell, the federal agents scaled the hillsides, zeroing in on Weaver's cabin. They were pumped. A wanted man who dealt in illegal weapons needed to be arrested, but he would not go quietly, and may even try to take the life of an agent. It was August 21, 1992—D day for the Weaver family.

Tim was intensely interested and wanted to know more. He hated government "raids." He knew they had happened many times before: agents coming into someone's house, turning it upside down, and dragging the person away, bound and gagged.

Tim monitored the television news and checked the previous day's paper for more information. The TV news offered a brief mention that an agent had been killed in Idaho, trying to arrest an armed man, holed up in a cabin stocked with weapons.

No mention of the boy or the dog being killed. "God damn it," Tim said. "This is America?" He and the Nichols brothers continued to follow the story as the days passed. The mainstream media carried little about the standoff, while "uncensored" radio stations and newspapers told in detail how this man's privacy had been "invaded" by the government. To people like McVeigh, an American family was being treated like a dangerous drug gang, and for what? Exercising their right to bear arms? Nobody really seemed to care. It was no wonder citizens' freedoms were being scraped away little by little—nobody gave a damn, McVeigh thought.

While many opinions, from all sides, were aired about what was going on at the Weavers' mountainside home near Ruby Ridge, the man's story was becoming a rallying cry among the groups and underground news agencies with which McVeigh would associate himself in the next few years. U.S. marshals involved themselves in an eleven-day standoff with Weaver. On the first day, the marshals' approach at the house alerted the family dog. As the animal barked and howled, Randy Weaver, his son, Sam, and their friend Kevin Harris all came out armed. Sam shot at the marshals after a government agent had shot at the dog. Then the gunfight began, claiming the lives of Marshal William Degan and young Sam Weaver, who was shot in the back as he ran away toward the house. Later, FBI agents joined the marshals, and an investigations officer, Lon Horiuchi, shot at Kevin Harris. But that bullet found the head of Randy Weaver's wife, Vicki, who was inside the cabin, and had been holding her baby, Elisheba, in her arms. For days, Weaver refused to surrender, while his wife lay dead in the cabin, and his son's body was outside in a shed. Right-wing radio celebrity Bo Gritz and retired Phoenix police officer and militia hero Jack McLamb eventually convinced Weaver to put down his gun and come out.

To the many thousands of his supporters in Idaho and neighboring states, Randy Weaver had been "hoodwinked" by the government. He was tricked into selling a gun to a government informant, and when the marshals came for him, he just tried to defend his family and home. The "government" senselessly murdered his son and wife. Three people were dead because the "government" invaded the privacy of one of its own citizens. To add insult to injury, the "government" selfishly forgave itself for killing two people by saying the feds, including Horiuchi, were "justified" in their actions. The voice of dissent was growing day by day as publications like the *Spotlight* gave Weaver's story front-page coverage and criticized the "government" heavily for its work at Ruby Ridge, Idaho. Weaver became a symbol to many in the right-wing underground that maybe it was time to teach the government a lesson. But the incident with Randy Weaver was nothing compared to what people like McVeigh would have to get mad about in 1993.

After the fall of 1992, Jennifer McVeigh was still living at home in Pendleton, and had been taking classes at Niagara County Community College in nearby Sanborn. The college has an excellent two-year degree program and is viewed as a springboard to higher education, or a career in law enforcement. She majored in liberal arts and impressed her teachers with a knowledge of politics normally possessed by adults many years her senior. For a twenty-year-old kid, Jennifer McVeigh was well tuned, probably because she maintained such close contact with her brother, who had become as obsessed with politics as he was with guns. Timothy fed Jennifer information from numerous underground publications and recommended that she read the same novels he had. In addition to her school work, during the next couple years Jennifer plowed through such works as *The Turner Diaries, Free Speech, The New World Order,* and *Operation Vampire Killer 2000.* These publications were well-known food for paranoia, written by authors who insist that the government is out to disarm and enslave its people.

Operation Vampire Killer 2000 is by Jack McLamb, a militia hero who writes that the year 2000 is when those in power will try to rule the planet through a system of world government. The idea, promoted by the *Spotlight,* makes the rounds of shortwave radio every time a U.S. president meets with leaders from other countries. *The New World Order* is a vague "big picture" for people who live by the rules of paranoia. In addition to following her brother's reading list, Jennifer allegedly fulfilled one of Tim's requests, one that would place her in legal danger later in life. Timothy called his old employer, Johnson's Country Store, from either Michigan (where the Nichols family home is located) or Kansas (where Terry owns a home), or another location that has not been disclosed. He asked if he could purchase and have the store ship 700 rounds of 7.62mm ammunition to him, but the store refused. Tim likely wanted the thirty-five boxes of pistol ammunition shipped to him because it was either unavailable or too expensive where he lived. He allegedly told Jennifer that Johnson's wouldn't send it to him, so she purchased the bullets herself and shipped them out in the mail, according to published reports. Shipping bullets through the U.S. Postal Service is illegal due to their dangerous nature.

After this period of time in late 1992 and early 1993, McVeigh's life turned into what could only be called a lost crusade. He wandered from the Nichols farm to the homes of other friends and later to places he rented on his own. Today, this part of McVeigh's life would be difficult even for Tim to document, but it was during this odyssey of uncertainty that he became seriously involved in a dangerous world. Tim was now driven by a desire for "citizen action" or a movement by the people to alter the liberal thinking of politicians and officials in power. McVeigh may be only one in a hundred thousand who felt this way, but it is believed that during these lost days, he was frequently exposed to the growing "paramilitary" underworld of Michigan and other states. Groups whose members were upset with taxes, political corruption, and incidents like Ruby Ridge spoke of organizing "militias."

Such militias, more than two hundred years ago, acted like small armies protecting the people of small towns. Now, because of the distaste for the immense power of the American government, men of rural background are organizing their own armies, separate from any government agency. The goal of the militias would be to protect the American way of life as written in the

Constitution and to defend a designated home area in case of attack by government forces, be they American or foreign. The talk of forming such groups was intense in 1993, and underground opposition to a gun-control law dubbed the "Brady Bill" mobilized the National Rifle Association and shortwave radio personalities. Named for James Brady, the White House press secretary who was shot during the March 30, 1981 assassination attempt on President Reagan, the Brady Bill was viewed as a knee-jerk response to one victim's wishes, and was approved by Congress in November of 1993. To powerful liberals in Washington, D.C., the Brady Bill would ban "assault-type" weapons, impose a waiting period for gun permits, and enforce strict punishments on those who broke the law. To a growing undercurrent of right-wing leaders the Brady Bill was Attorney General Janet Reno's first step toward disarming America. The militias would organize to oppose exactly this type of gun control and defend the country against a federal government "conspiring to destroy individual liberty." The goal of these militias was not to take offensive but defensive action. It was precisely this defensive posture that would later keep more radical people like McVeigh and the Nichols brothers from ever being allowed to join.

From Michigan, Tim McVeigh had been in contact with his old buddy Michael Fortier. It was 1993 when McVeigh suggested to Fortier that they should get together to discuss the many problems with the government that had built up—problems that would require citizen action. Fortier was familiar with this type of talk from McVeigh and had followed similar philosophies himself. McVeigh had some money saved and decided he'd go to Kingman, Arizona, and stay near Fortier for a while. In June, Tim moved from Michigan to a home he rented in the Canyon West Mobile & RV trailer park. Park owner Bob Ragin rented him a forty-foot, blue-and-white unit. Tim, who stayed there approximately four months, had his mail sent to a post office box at a place called the Mail Room in Kingman, where he frequently visited, wearing military fatigues.

The valley of Kingman lies in the high desert country of northwest Arizona. Railroad workers founded Kingman in 1880 as a construction camp. Visitors today will find information on the settlement, but will see a sandblown land that howls at night with loneliness and has only bleak opportunities during the day.

At the trailer park Tim was "an ideal tenant." Ragin told the *New York Times* that Tim cleaned up a mess in his trailer that had been left by a previous tenant and brought in all new furniture.

In addition to the steady diet of antigovernment friends and literature, McVeigh's ongoing neurotic suspicions may have been encouraged by the methamphetamines, or speed, he allegedly used. The time he spent with Michael Fortier lends support to this prospect. Tim has admitted experimental use of methamphetamines while visiting Fortier. Speed can be snorted like cocaine and, if strong enough, its effects can be felt for two days or more, keeping the user in an alert, accelerated state until the drug finally wears off and exhaustion is overtaken by sleep, according to sources who have also tried the drug. At least two people have confirmed that Tim McVeigh purchased the drug from them, and Tim actually wrote to his sister once that the high-grade speed made him "remember" his past, according to investigators. Three people who knew McVeigh at the time in Kingman remember him selling the drug, according to a *Los Angeles Times* report. One man who had planned to start an iron salvage business with Tim told the newspaper that McVeigh would go to a house frequented by drug dealers and users. The man said some people at the house liked to discuss the use of explosive devices. During a 1996 interview with Fortier's neighbor Jim Rosencrans, it was alleged by Peter Jennings of ABC News that McVeigh also used marijuana. Jennings said during the interview, "Tim . . . also now smoked marijuana occasionally and dabbled in the drug methamphetamine." Rosencrans responded with, "Not to my knowledge." But Jennings countered, "Well, actually, to your knowledge, I think. I think you told our guys he only took it under pressure."[9]

Fortier and McVeigh allegedly spent many late nights in Tim's trailer, discussing the Ruby Ridge incident. McVeigh seemed overtaken by a sense of urgency, as if something needed to be done right away to prevent more raids by the government, the invasion of innocent people's homes, and the killing of more good people. Tim was already taking preventive measures: he used numerous aliases and never lived in one location for too long. McVeigh kept his double-life well hidden: not even Ragin could see the McVeigh who was ready for the next war. The landlord told *Time* magazine that Tim had only a couple of friends, and he felt sorry for the displaced sergeant. "He struck me as someone just out of the service who was trying to figure out what to do with his life."

* * *

The federal government's next big blunder may have helped sharpen the focus and direction of McVeigh and his brat pack. Agents had been watching Vernon Howell for a long time. Vernon, who changed his name in 1990 to David Koresh, was the religious leader of a cult known as the Branch Davidians. The group had established its base of operation near the town of Waco in west Texas. The dusty, windswept area has been known as a home for odd criminals, deeply religious groups, and weapons enthusiasts. According to author Clifford Linedecker, in 1991, Texas itself was the only state where more people had been killed by guns than traffic accidents. In his book *Massacre at Waco, Texas,* Linedecker states that Koresh's religious commune amassed quite an arsenal of weapons, including pistols, machine guns, rifles, and hand grenades. David Koresh's cult leadership of his flock, which included about one hundred men, women, and children, and the group's weapons and massive home at "Mount Carmel" interested the government law enforcement agents to the point of investigation. Some followers had left the seventy-seven-acre ranch and compound and had spo-

ken to the press. They alleged that Koresh was a child-abuser, a sex-
ual nut, who planned to go to "war" with the people of Waco. As undercover police and government investigations widened, Koresh's
teachings centered more on the end of the world.

On February 28, 1993, heavily armed agents from the Federal
Bureau of Alcohol, Tobacco, and Firearms (BATF) made an unwelcome visit to the compound. They told Koresh they had a
search warrant. A vicious gunfight between the agents and those
inside the compound ensued. Agents and cult members were
killed, but those who lived to tell of the incident would blame each
other for starting the shooting. A standoff between the government
and Koresh lasted for fifty-one days. A BATF raid would end
with the Davidian compound burning to the ground and leaving
about eighty-one devotees dead.

Again, both sides would be blamed for the deaths, but to the
right-wing media, which included radio and news publications,
the federal government had struck with force against its own people. This time, many lives were lost because of the government's
bully tactics. Attorney General Janet Reno, in the barrage of federal red tape and accusations that followed, would say she took
full responsibility for the incident. No tears were shed for the
more than twenty children who were killed at Waco, and Reno offered no remorse for decisions that led not only to her own employees being killed, but also culminated in a raid that would be
a dark blemish on both her career and the Clinton administration.

Koresh was a religious madman to many, but for some observers that didn't mean his "home" should be raided and tear-
gassed by the BATF. It would also be revealed that officials from
the BATF made false statements about exactly what happened
during their raid. The tragedy of Waco, like that of Ruby Ridge,
in the minds of some, was that both were examples of the government arrogantly overstepping its bounds without observing
basic rights. The time had come for the people to act!

Timothy McVeigh left Arizona and allegedly made two pilgrimages to the Davidian compound—once during the standoff and once thereafter. In March 1993, McVeigh was captured on film by Texas television KTVT, a CBS affiliate, sitting on the hood of his car, just outside the Davidian compound. He was part of a group of protesters angry over the government's ongoing raid. McVeigh, according to an Associated Press report of April 19, 1996, was handing out bumper stickers that asked, "Is your church ATF approved?"

Other than TV coverage, McVeigh's information about the raid came in part from the extremist media, through which Koresh's side, or the side he would have offered, was told in lavish detail. The government had made its statements: Koresh killed himself and his followers, the agencies involved in the raid were not to blame in any way. Efforts by the BATF and the FBI to plead innocent enraged McVeigh. He documented his journey to Waco by gathering Koresh's pamphlets, taking photographs at the fire site, and bringing home charred wood that had once been part of the building. "He was very concerned about it," said Stephen Jones, McVeigh's attorney, in a 1995 Associated Press report. McVeigh told *Newsweek* he was "bothered" by the government's actions at Waco and those involved "most definitely" made mistakes.[10] McVeigh's friend James Nichols told CNN that the government was to blame for the Davidians' deaths. "The Waco incident—no wonder people are getting upset. That's outright murder."[11] McVeigh claimed to know the "real truth" about Waco because he had met a Davidian, Paul Fatta, on the gun show circuit. Nichols recalled in the ABC News special with Peter Jennings that, "Tim knew him from the gun shows. . . . So when the raid happened, Tim knew it was all B.S. It was all a lie. And the records show that."[12]

The thinking of the radical right was energized by a video produced and sold by Linda Thompson, the self-proclaimed leader of the Unorganized Militia of the United States of America. Titled *Waco: The Big Lie,* the video claims that the FBI burned the Davidian compound on purpose by shooting flames at the building through a tank. She told the *National Enquirer,* "My tape is the truth." An Indianapolis-based lawyer, Ms. Thompson has also maintained a record of the movements of federal agents who were involved in the Waco standoff, and has forwarded this information to certain right-wing groups, according to a report. That might explain why antigovernment Patriot Movement members watched BATF spokesman Bob Ricks so closely. Timothy McVeigh obtained copies of Thompson's tape and distributed them to friends and associates he hoped would accept his views. Albert Warnement, who had commanded McVeigh's Bradley fighting vehicle, claimed in a *New York Times* interview that he was on Tim's list.

> He sent me a lot of newsletters and stuff from those groups he was involved in. There were newsletters from Bo Gritz's group, some other odd newsletters, some from the Patriots; and then he sent that videotape, *The Big Lie* about Waco.[13]

McVeigh headed back to Michigan later to stay again with the Nichols family. Tim and the Nichols brothers spent a lot of time together, bumming around the house, and treating Terry's wife like a housework slave. Marife Nichols complained to her father in the Philippines that she was sick of waiting on Tim, Terry, and James. The usual general talk of being unhappy with the government changed drastically in these days to action-oriented discussions of what could be done. Paul Izydorek, a Nichols family friend for twenty years, told CNN he remembered the ranting well. James Nichols gave Paul's son an earful of hatred.

> Evidently, James had told him one or two times about how they were going to kill cops and judges and, you know, really clean house on all the local government. I didn't take it serious but I guess maybe that's what the heck they was really talking about, maybe they was a lot more serious, you know, than I realized.[14]

The burgeoning crusade was interrupted on November 22, 1993, when tragedy struck. Terry Nichols and his wife had been planning a move to Las Vegas. Like Tim, Terry hopped around from town to town, never really finding a place where he could settle. Marife had borne a son by a man she had an affair with in the Philippines. The son, Jason Torres, two, had suffocated in a plastic bag and was found dead in the home on that November day. Terry's ex-wife, Lana, who sold her life story to Harper-Collins Publishers in 1995, insinuated in a book titled *By Blood Betrayed* that Tim McVeigh may have had something to do with the child's death. Lana said her son, Josh, told her that Tim "didn't like kids," and the book claimed that Tim found the body. Lana, though, seemed to be the only person with enough gall to accuse Tim. During a taped interview, Jennifer McVeigh responded to Lana's apparent accusation.

> I think it's cruel of her, sick of her to put that in there, because from what I knew about that, Tim found him and tried to save him. Implying he would hurt a little kid like that . . . he has a niece. He likes kids. He would never do anything to intentionally harm a child like that. He would have no reason to.[15]

No charges were ever placed against either man for the death of Jason.

Meanwhile, in Michigan, a real "patriot movement" had begun. Included were people opposed to gun control, unhappy with taxation, angered over the Ruby Ridge and Waco raids, and those on the political fringe who believed in the "New World Order." Many meetings were being held by "grassroots" organizations hoping to form solid groups—armies "of the people." In Michigan, Tim McVeigh was right in the center of it all. James Nichols, who Tim also looked up to and admired as a father figure, spoke at meetings on such topics as taxation and government failings. A Michigan gun dealer and citizen activist, Frank Kieltyka, described their feelings toward the government. Kieltyka said in a *Buffalo News* report that the "New World Order" is backed by the United States and led by the Trilateral Commission and the Council on Foreign

Relations. He said, "We're moving toward the Communists."[16] The right wing gained a foothold in the coming year as leaders in its various media venues preached that mainstream information comes from government lies, as did many of the lessons that were taught in schools. The idea arose that, to preserve American rights, people had to "relearn" the government, or forget known truths to see "the big picture" of government conspiracy and collusion by big business and Jews to control the country's money supply and the population. This fanatical belief, perpetuated by anti-Semitic, antigay publications like the *Spotlight,* only gained more steam when the Waco incident made national headlines.

Baptist minister and gun dealer Norman Olson and former army reservist Mark Koernke formed the official Michigan Militia in April 1994. Olson would declare himself state "commander" and the organization would attract a purported ten thousand members within about a year. Members would come from many counties, including Sanilac, home of the Nichols farm. Olson said the militia's goal was to "defend the Constitution from enemies both foreign and domestic." Shortwave radio carried the message, and meeting dates were announced.

In farm country, where the natives do not benefit from higher education or financial status, the militia was not only something "to do," but something to believe in, when all faith in the current government failed with Waco. Members of the militia, and the militias that began in other states, conducted meetings, established "camps," and even had drills, all in preparation for, as William Pierce stated in promoting *The Turner Diaries,* "when they come to take your guns." Though philosophies differed considerably among the militias in at least thirty states, their memberships were similar: white males between the ages of eighteen and forty-six, many military veterans, predominantly Christian, unemployed or financially distressed, and owning one or more guns. While protecting the American way of life was (and is) their claimed goal, taking offensive action was not. "Our stand in the militia is defensive," said Michigan Militia chief of staff Ray Southwell in a *Toronto Star* report.[17] Still these grown men, looking a tad ridiculous with potbellies in full military garb, were ready to "defend" against but not go out and attack government forces.

McVeigh attended a late fall meeting of the Michigan Militia, where the topic was the BATF. The militia was trying to educate the people by mailing out a catalogue with instructions on how to form paramilitary groups. Included in the package were newsletters on how to store weapons and food. The Nichols brothers also attended the militia's meetings, but Tim, Terry, and James were all too radical to be accepted as members. They were even kicked out of more than one meeting for advocating strong violence, according to reports. Norman Olson said, "These people were told to leave because of that type of talk of destruction and harm and terrorism."[18]

Maybe they wouldn't have the army of the militia on their side, but an attack on the government by McVeigh, Terry Nichols, and others was already being planned. Fueled by a general hatred of the government and the atrocities it perpetrated, Tim and Terry were making calls on their *Spotlight* card, searching for fertilizer companies and making purchases. Storing weapons, accumulating money, and finding recruits had become the order of the day. Nichols's farm neighbor Phil Morawski recalled seeing Tim in Decker at the time. "He said he witnessed part of the siege at Waco and was very upset over it; the government overstepped its bounds. Waco is kind of like the battle cry for Tim and many others."[19]

McVeigh attended many gun shows, actively peddling surplus rations and weapons. Although he sold numerous copies of *The Turner Diaries,* McVeigh didn't profit from the sales. Tim sold the $10 book for $5 each and preached about the book as if it was a survivalist's bible. Terry and Tim continued to save the money they raised, even working gun shows in far-off Las Vegas for their crusade. Nichols's neighbor MariAnn Saenen recalled McVeigh trying hard to raise money. She said he even tried to sell dehydrated army food rations to her husband, Paul Isydorek. Paul,

one of James Nichols's closest friends, told the *Buffalo News,*
"Tim found a market for that kind of stuff at gun shows."[20]

As the money piled up, the focus of the "action" was pondered. It
is strongly believed that the planning of a "bombing" by McVeigh
and Nichols began in July of 1993. It was about this time that
McVeigh used the alias "T. Tuttle" to place an advertisement to
"sell" a military-style antitank launcher replica. The ad in the
Spotlight appeared in the August 16, 1993 issue and in the two issues that followed. The ad offered a light antitank weapon "LAW
launcher replica" that will fire "37mm flares." McVeigh had been
dealing in military surplus and weapons with Terry Nichols, but
this was apparently only an attempt to sell the crusade. According
to one source, McVeigh was looking for recruits, people like himself who read the *Spotlight,* believed in its conspiracies, and harbored anger for the government. In these early months of 1994,
McVeigh used the name Daryl Bridges to purchase a fifty-dollar
prepaid *Spotlight* magazine "calling card." He and Terry Nichols
used the card to make over seven hundred telephone calls during
an eighteen-month period. McVeigh paid for the hundreds of dollars in calls by sending money orders to the *Spotlight* to
"recharge" the card, a 1995 *Media Bypass* report said. To raise
more money, McVeigh and Nichols were also allegedly involved
in a series of robberies, which included banks and a gun dealer's
home, during extended trips to gun fairs in Arizona, New Mexico,
and Texas. McVeigh used the names "Tim Tuttle" and "Terry Tuttle" at various times—likely due to his ever-increasing paranoia
and the growing bombing plot. In McVeigh's mind, Big Brother
was now watching *him.* The government had become the enemy,
and was keeping tabs on him. He even told a friend that he believed a black car was following him when he went out driving.

The "hit," the first act of war by McVeigh, would be to attack
the U.S. government by striking one of its buildings. Throughout
American history, small bombings had been attempted and ac-

Top (left to right): Edward McVeigh (*Union-Sun & Journal* sports file); William (Bill) McVeigh in high school; Mildred (Mickey) Hill in school several years before she married Bill.

Middle (left to right): Mickey and Bill McVeigh's children: Patty, Tim, and Jennifer.

Bottom: The former McVeigh family home on Meyer Road in Pendleton, New York. Author file.

Top: Tim McVeigh (age fourteen) at home with his mother. Photo courtesy of William McVeigh.

Middle: Tim attended Starpoint Central School in Pendleton, New York, graduating in 1986. Author file.

Bottom: Tim on graduation day, June 20, 1986. He is flanked by his maternal grandparents, William and Dorothy Hill. Photo courtesy of William McVeigh.

Right: Tim and Jennifer mug for the camera during the family's celebration of Christmas at home in 1991. Photo courtesy of William McVeigh.

Below: Before joining the army, Timothy McVeigh worked at Johnson's Country Store in Lockport, New York. The store sells guns and hunting equipment. Author file.

Left: McVeigh's army induction photo. *Union-Sun & Journal* military file.

Right: McVeigh is caught on video at Waco, Texas, in 1993 by a film crew from a Texas television station. AP/Wide World.

Below: Sgt. McVeigh stands in line to meet Gen. H. Norman Schwarzkopf after the success of Desert Storm. ©1996 Capital Cities/ABC Inc.

Above: The Dreamland Motel in Arizona where Timothy McVeigh stayed and reportedly parked the Ryder truck used in the bombing. AP/Wide World, Cliff Schiappa.

Right: McVeigh's friend and army mate Michael Fortier, who has admitted to casing the Murrah building with McVeigh before the bombing. AP/Wide World, Cable News Network.

Above: The Alfred P. Murrah Federal Building shortly after the bombing. AP/Wide World.

Right: McVeigh's 1977 Mercury Marquis is shown along Interstate 35 about seventy-five miles from Oklahoma City. The state patrol retrieved the vehicle on April 21, 1995, after McVeigh was charged in connection with the bombing. AP/Wide World, Dale Fulkerson.

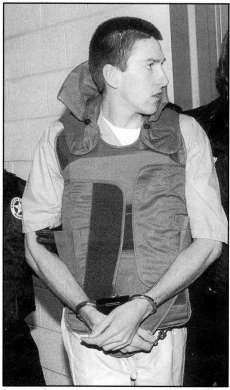

Upper (left): McVeigh is led into federal court in Oklahoma City for a January 1996 venue hearing for the upcoming bombing trial. Not long after being formally charged, McVeigh reportedly voiced concern for his personal safety. AP/Wide World, David Longstreath.

Lower (left): Bombing suspect Terry Nichols, also protected by a bulletproof vest, is led into federal court in Oklahoma City. AP/Wide World, David Longstreath.

Below: *Union-Sun & Journal* Managing Editor Dan Kane speaks to reporters from the world press about the two letters McVeigh sent to the newspaper in 1992. Dennis Stierer photo for the *Union-Sun & Journal*, © 1995.

Lower (right): Federal investigators take evidence out of the Pendleton home of William McVeigh on April 21, 1995, after his son was charged in Oklahoma. Dennis Stierer photo for the *Union-Sun & Journal*, © 1995.

Top: Federal Judge Richard P. Matsch will hear one of the toughest cases in American history when the trial for bombing suspects McVeigh and Nichols begins. AP/Wide World, Joe Mahoney.

Bottom: Respected attorney Stephen Jones serves as McVeigh's lead counsel. Photo courtesy of Stephen Jones.

3 SEPTEMBER 1995

THE SUNDAY TIMES *magazine*

All-American
Monster
Did this small-town charmer
blow a hole in the heart of a nation?

A September 1995 issue of the *Sunday Times* of London featured McVeigh in its cover story "All-American Monster," asking if he was the one who broke the heartland. He noted in a subsequent interview with this magazine that those who govern by the sword will "reckon with protest by the sword."

A memorial for the victims of the Oklahoma City bombing stands in front of Starpoint Central School today. The wood and stone memorial was funded by the Starpoint junior/senior student council. Author file.

IN MEMORIAL
of the
OKLAHOMA TRAGEDY
APRIL 19, 1995
PRESENTED BY
JR.-SR. STUDENT COUNCIL 1995

complished by labor unions and anarchists to show disenchantment with ruling powers in business or government. They were also a spectacular display of power. Traditionally, a bombing had no name attached. The act was carried out by unknown individuals who could later claim themselves a revolutionary force and explain why the act was committed. For angry patriots like McVeigh and Nichols, a bombing was the perfect preemptive strike. A fictional bomb strike against the government had been outlined in *The Turner Diaries*; in fact, its real-life counterpart had already been planned for a site in Oklahoma. Earl Turner's target was in Washington, D.C. (an FBI building), but government agencies in that area were too well guarded. The structures in Washington were either in an enclosed area or secured by terrorist-proof devices. In 1983, a real bombing of the Alfred P. Murrah Federal Building in Oklahoma City had been planned.

Richard Wayne Snell, who would be executed twelve years later for killing a police officer, was an Oklahoman involved with a group called the Covenant, Sword, and Arm of the Lord. Snell was a big troublemaker as far as the government was concerned. He associated himself with members of the radical racist group The Order and was nabbed in a 1987 roundup by federal authorities seeking those involved in a plot with Aryan Nations leader Richard Butler for "seditious conspiracy between July 1983 and March 1985 to overthrow the government." Butler, Snell, and eight others were indicted by a federal grand jury in Fort Smith, Arkansas. In their book *Nazis, Communists, Klansmen, and Others on the Fringe,* John George and Laird Wilcox note that a 1988 jury found Snell and twelve others not guilty.[21] Snell was angry with the government because action by the Internal Revenue Service made him lose his home. The anti-Semitic Covenant group had planned to strike the city building by parking a truck in front of it and setting off a timer that would fire rockets into the government structure. Then, the truck itself would explode. A former member of the Covenant, Steven Snyder, said the 1983 Oklahoma bombing plot was based on the plan fictionalized in *The Turner Diaries* and converted to the group's standards by Covenant founder James Ellison. Oklahoma's Murrah building was an easy target because of its accessibility from the street.

The argument of striking with a bomb that would kill many innocent people had already been won in McVeigh's mind by a passage in *The Turner Diaries*. In the novel, Earl Turner and his group of "patriots," using a fuel oil and fertilizer bomb, strike FBI headquarters in Washington, killing seven hundred people. Turner hopes the bombing will inspire others to lash out at the system for outlawing guns. After his plot is carried out, he forgives himself for murder by calling it "necessary" action to effect change.

> All day yesterday and most of today we watched the TV coverage of rescue crews bringing the dead and injured out of the building. It is a heavy burden of responsibility for us to bear, since most of the victims of our bomb were only pawns who were no more committed to the sick philosophy or the radically destructive goals of the System than we are. But there is no way we can destroy the System without hurting many thousands of innocent people—no way. It is a cancer too deeply rooted in our flesh. And if we don't destroy the System before it destroys us—if we don't cut this cancer out of our living flesh—our whole race will die. We have gone over this before, and we are all completely convinced that what we did is justified, but it is still very hard to see our own people suffering so intensely because of our acts. It is because Americans have for so many years been unwilling to make unpleasant decisions that we are forced to make decisions now which are stern indeed.[22]

Timothy McVeigh now thought that with such a bombing, his views (called right-wing by many) would be taken seriously and a government that had grown too large to serve the people properly would feel the injury and retreat from its plan of disarming and persecuting its own citizens. McVeigh believed this in much the way a brokenhearted lover believes suicide will win the affection of his beloved. But the wheels of revolution were in motion and, despite a dropout here and there, Oklahoma City's fate was set.

From Michigan and other ports of call for McVeigh, it was back to Arizona to finally get Michael Fortier on board. McVeigh's second extended stay in Kingman was later widely publicized by the national press in mid-1995. He was described as a horrible tenant at a mobile home park, according to neighbors and a landlord. McVeigh was the type of person who drank beer all day, often talked of going back into the military, didn't follow rules, blared loud music, had a junk car sitting in the driveway, and lived with a pregnant girlfriend. These stories, published by many top news agencies like the Associated Press and the *New York Times,* were completely wrong. One of the sources quoted even recanted his statements. Timothy McVeigh may have been unstable, but he was never the type to drink a lot of beer, play loud music (he is known for using headphones unless he was in his car), or have a girlfriend, much less a pregnant one.

Instead, when Tim went back to Kingman, he stayed with Fortier. Terry Nichols was living close by in a Las Vegas condo with Marife. Nichols often made trips to Kansas and stayed at the Dreamland Motel in Junction City. While there he reportedly told people he was going to start his own business dealing in military surplus. Terry, Marife, and their daughter, Nicole, moved to a small house in Kansas in March. Terry worked in Marion on Jim Donahue's Hayhook Ranch until September 1, 1994, where he was able to save $12,000.

In Arizona, Fortier helped Tim get a job at True Value Hardware, where he would work from February to April of 1994. Store owner Paul Shuffler was just one of many people in McVeigh's path that year who saw the lost soldier but had no idea of the real plan Tim had in mind. McVeigh passed through the calm waters of life during these days with little to say to those "on the outside," those who did not know and would never understand about the "New World Order" that was afoot, or the underground's response initiative. Passersby, like Shuffler, saw Tim as he was before joining the army; that all-American boy in a T-shirt, camouflage pants, and tennis shoes, wandering through life with no known goal other than to pay the rent. Shuffler told the *Union-Sun & Journal*:

> [Tim] seemed like a well-mannered person. He was well-spoken. That's one of the things I looked at when I hired him, because he had to deal with the public. [He also] worked in the back of the store and handled lumber.[23]

In the summer, Michael Fortier and his girlfriend, Lori, were married in Las Vegas, and Timothy McVeigh served as best man. They had a real party weekend in Nevada, and then headed back to the Fortier home in Kingman. Tim spent time with a friend of Fortier's, Walter "Mac" McCarty, a Korean War vet who had met Michael at the True Value store. Mac had a small home in an isolated mountain canyon, and earned a living by offering shooting lessons. Mac had been known around town for years because of his weekly gun-control protests at the county courthouse. McCarty and McVeigh often pondered the problems with the government. Mac told the *Sunday Times* of London that McVeigh had an undying energy that was focused for a long time on government mismanagement.

> In public, he was quiet and polite and he had this big, easy smile. But when he talked about the country and politics and things, he got real mean and savage. He was one highly strung young man. I don't think I ever saw anybody with such hatred in him. He was bitter about just about everything, and he believed the country was being taken over by big business and organized crime, and they were all tied up with the government. In particular, he hated the BATF boys and the Feds. He used to rant on about how they had become just a big cowboy army who were taking the law into their own hands. I tell you, he was running right on the edge.[24]

McVeigh cried over the Waco incident, according to McCarty, who watched a video of the raid with Tim. Tim shared the touching details of his Texas trip with Mac, who observed, "He really felt for those people. . . . It was a kind of pilgrimage." McCarty, though many years older, also maintained a friendship with Fortier. Mac told the Associated Press:

> We got together many times, usually to talk about things like Waco, Randy Weaver, and other injustices that the big boys at the BATF and FBI got involved in. We liked to discuss guns and the right to carry weapons. I think he was very frustrated with the justice system of this country.[25]

At Michael Fortier's trailer, Tim did his share of chores. Even before entering military service, he had been a stickler for cleanliness, but the Fortiers with their young daughter were genuinely messy. McVeigh often cooked, as he had at the Nichols home, especially for Josh Nichols who enjoyed Tim's specialty, spaghetti with plenty of sauce. At the Fortiers, Tim also washed dishes and sometimes mocked Michael and Lori's lack of energy when it came to tidiness. Tim moved out of the Fortier home for a few months, staying in a small, brown house at 3436 Hunt Street, just outside Kingman, in Golden Valley. Though he was no longer living with his friends, he cherished the bond between himself and Michael, as well as the journey he was about to take them on. As the one-time American symbol of the green rattlesnake on a yellow flag warning "Don't Tread On Me" fluttered in the night wind in front of the Fortier trailer, McVeigh neatly arranged soup cans on the kitchen floor, showing his protégé how to arrange barrels of explosives for a bombing. He pulled out a rough drawing he had of a truck bomb, and displayed a book, page by page, of formulas to make explosives and to shape charges. The purpose for the act was established, but the planning had to be intensive. Everything would have to go just right. Committed to the goal, McVeigh would travel in his vehicle, packed with explosives. He would be involved in transporting the bomb; the duties of the others would be determined in time.

During a three-day period in September 1994, McVeigh made more than two dozen telephone calls to suppliers of bomb components. The calls, from Kingman, were made on a calling card from a company then known as WCT Communications in Santa Barbara, California. A total of 684 calls were made on the card.

In a miscalculation, the 1995 crew of bombers apparently thought the federal building housed the office of Oklahoma Transportation Director Bob Ricks, who had been a lead BATF spokesman at Waco. He was given a cushy DOT job after the Branch Davidian disaster proved embarrassing to Janet Reno and the Clinton administration. The Murrah building did house the Transportation Department, but Ricks's office was in another part of the city.

November 1994 found Tim traveling back to Pendleton, New York. He was ticketed for speeding (just one of many in his driving career) on Arkansas Route 259, ten miles from the far-right Christian Identity camp called Elohim City. His grandfather and early gun mentor, Edward, age eighty-one, had died on the sixteenth in Lockport Memorial Hospital. Family and friends from church and bowling buddies met for a wake at Taylor and Reynolds Funeral Home in Lockport, but Tim was unable to make it back in time for the funeral. Edward W. McVeigh was buried in Cold Spring Cemetery, off Chestnut Ridge Road in the town of Lockport. Tim was back in Lockport to help his dad clear out his grandfather's belongings at the Bear Ridge Road home. An estate sale of Ed McVeigh's belongings was held on November 18, 1994, at his town of Lockport home. Customer Jim Filipertis was quoted in the *Buffalo News* on May 5, 1996, that Tim McVeigh was there, dressed in battle fatigues and combat boots, and addressed Filipertis as "sir." Filipertis said Jennifer McVeigh was also at the event. He said he wound up purchasing a religious print of the Madonna for $1. Tim also spent a few hours alone with Jennifer, driving around the countryside. There was a longing in Tim to go back to the high school days, like the dreams he had about being in class again, the desire to see those innocent friends, the inner feeling that more needed to be learned before he could move on to the next stage in life.

Then, one late night in November, Starpoint High School stared him directly in the face. Former classmate Dave Darlak bumped into McVeigh at a bar late one night, a day or two after election day on the seventh. To McVeigh, the new bosses in government were the same as the old bosses. Darlak, who is now apparently in some type of seclusion, commented to the *New York Times* that the Tim McVeigh he knew was gone forever: "He brought it up . . . something, about the government, that had to be done. He had slowly deteriorated and turned into a paranoid person. He got stranger and stranger . . . he was a troubled person."[26]

McVeigh left Lockport in the first week of December and was reunited with Terry Nichols later in Kansas, and the two would divide their time between Junction City and Fortier's home in Arizona. Bulk orders of ammonium nitrate were being made, and the sacks were stored at various locations. McVeigh and Nichols had become their aliases, but their fingerprints were leaving quite a trail behind. In December, McVeigh and Fortier headed to Oklahoma to poke around the Alfred P. Murrah Federal Building on Harvey Avenue. It was just before Christmas and the two lean young men took their own tour of the nine-story building. It was bustling with activity, from the day-care center with a Christmas tree at ground level to the offices of the BATF on the top floor which they weren't allowed to enter. Their thirty-minute tour ended back on the first floor, where America's Kids Day-Care Center was heavily decorated with lights, a pine tree, and a photo of old St. Nick. They left and got back into the car that had taken them hundreds of miles, just to get to the city. They slowly circled the Murrah building and pondered its fate. Then, McVeigh and Fortier cruised back through Texas and New Mexico, stopping briefly to toast the coming new year, 1995, and back to Kingman. Their trip, preceded by a stop in Kansas, had included an exchange of weapons that had been stolen. The weapons would be sold to raise more money for the bombing. In a 1995 statement to the U.S. attorney, Michael Fortier described part of the journey to the doomed city.

> On December 15th and 16th, I rode with Tim McVeigh from my home in Kingman, Arizona, to Kansas. There I was to receive weapons that Tim McVeigh told me had been stolen by Terry Nichols and himself. While in Kansas, McVeigh and I loaded about twenty-five weapons into a car that I had rented. On December 17th, 1994, I drove the rental car back to Arizona through Oklahoma and Oklahoma City. Later, after returning to Arizona and at the request of Tim McVeigh, I sold some of the weapons and again at the request of Tim McVeigh I gave him some money to give to Terry Nichols.

It is believed that Terry Nichols and Michael Fortier, despite their rage against the government and its partners in evil, may have realized just what was being planned—a *real* bombing that would tear a city to shreds, *killing* hundreds of innocent people. No doubt they realized they could be caught and prosecuted for their involvement, and this would change their lives forever, making them public enemies. Sure, McVeigh and Nichols had declared war on the government for its many faults, but to Terry Nichols "declare war" were just words of protest. They were nonviolent when they were just words. Those words didn't kill anybody. But the planning he was involved in would certainly harm many people. The fuel, fertilizer, blasting caps, and other materials they purchased were real. Maybe this plot was too much.

McVeigh, a trained infantryman who was told by the army he may have to "off" one of his own in battle, apparently sensed that Nichols and Fortier were weakening. Tim reminded the other two of the story in the nonfiction book *Armed and Dangerous: The Rise of the Survivalist Right* by James Coates, which details The

Order's murder of Jewish talk-show host Alan Berg.[27] According to the book, The Order had robbed armored cars, amassed $3 million, and gave a lot of the cash to white supremacist groups. He also reminded Nichols and Fortier of their own cause—to save the America created by the founding fathers from its own conceited, lying, cheating government.

As February cold gripped Lockport, New York, an old hippie sat at his beat-up typewriter, tapping his observations of the national political scene onto a page. He was afraid of people like Newt Gingrich, who seemed to be spewing Christian fundamentalist rhetoric at every turn. The hippie, a poet and prophet named Christopher Shearer, typed out, "Contemporary eugenics could imply our fast and furious Republican concept of a final solution to the unobtainable welfare reform dilemma, or at least a very obscene step nearer to the orphanage." He glanced up at the wall in front of him, decorated with a rejection letter from the *New Yorker* and a small, weathered photograph of Jack Kerouac. Shearer continued with his letter, covering the downward spiral he saw American society in and the dangers of speech containing hatred. A self-described socialist, Shearer ended his letter with, "The fever of America's extreme right is spiking." He set the letter aside and began typing another, this time detailing his extended visit to Denmark during Vietnam. Christopher wrote that America just may survive well under a socialist government, one that would save the people from a strong and dangerous Republican takeover: "we now have a real revolution in the making" by Republican leaders who have no concern for the poor, Shearer wrote. He mailed both letters to the *Union-Sun & Journal,* and they were both published in the March 2 edition. The letters were titled "Beware of Right-Wing Politics" and "Revolution Is Possible."

An avid reader, Jennifer McVeigh, a student attending Niagara County Community College, saw Shearer's letters and was shocked by his beliefs. Jennifer loved to write, and her hobby had gotten her a job at the *Spirit,* the student newspaper. There she mainly wrote about her concerns with the environment. During the day Jennifer toiled at college, but at night she liked to let it all hang out at the Crazy Horse Saloon in Niagara Falls, New York. As a bombing of a federal building was being planned by her brother, Jennifer was hundreds of miles away at a country western bar, working at selling drinks to urban cowboys. The Crazy Horse, nestled between low-rate motels and a greasy spoon restaurant, was a place where you'd walk in and hear Travis Tritt's version of "Take It Easy" blaring through overhead speakers near the dance floor. The door girl, a redhead clad in a cowboy hat, tight T-shirt, and silk shorts, charges you two dollars to get in and hands you an index card to fill out to "Win a 12-gauge shotgun!" The many female employees, dressed like the door girl to accent their breasts and legs, dart about the room, spreading good cheer and four-dollar shots. On Sundays, the Crazy Horse featured Jell-O wrestling in a boxing ring full of one hundred gallons of lemon-flavor Jell-O that doesn't stain. Male volunteers from the audience wrestle two female employees, dressed in one-piece bathing suits. Jennifer participated in the event, and was seen by former classmate Brian Haines. He recalled:

> I saw her a couple times. I line dance, so I went there on a Sunday night, and I didn't even know it was her until she was finished and got out of the ring. The girls try to pin the guy down in the pit. The girls rip the guy's pants off or whatever and try to throw him down. The girls wear full bathing suits, but you may see some tits once in a while.[28]

Meanwhile, Christopher Shearer's letters to the editor set Jennifer to do research on the definitions of socialism, communism, the speeches of Adolf Hitler, and civil disobedience. To Jennifer, it was the thinking of people like Christopher Shearer that would ruin America by turning its citizens into sheep who don't think, but merely obey. Her brother, Tim, would be outraged at such thought. "Maybe socialism does work, but it's certainly not the answer here in America," Jennifer wrote. The people were already being abused by a government that had grown too large to manage even its own affairs. She wrote feverishly, telling Mr. Shearer to research the Waco and Ruby Ridge incidents. She ended her long letter of response with, "Americans are being brainwashed into giving up our rights." Her letter was published on March 9 in the newspaper. She mailed a copy to Tim. He graded it with an "A" and mailed the letter back to his sister.

On March 21, 1995, the Niagara County Sheriff's Department received a 4:20 P.M. visit from Jennifer. She filed a complaint with a deputy, saying that she had been "receiving aggravating phone calls from a Joann Barger [of Lockport]." Jennifer added that, "Mrs. Barger called her residence on 3/21/95 and [Jennifer] advised Mrs. Barger not to call her residence again," according to the aggravated harassment report filed with the department. The report concluded, "Mrs. Barger has continued to call on a daily basis at all hours of the night." Jennifer McVeigh signed the report, which was apparently related to a love triangle involving Barger's husband, according to a source who spoke to this author and advised this author to seek the report filed at the sheriff's department. The department would not hear the McVeigh name again until April 21.

Meanwhile, in Kingman, months passed as the planning of the attack on the U.S. government was in place. Almost two years had gone by since the Branch Davidian holocaust at Waco, Texas. McVeigh, pumped by nervous energy as D-day approached, dashed off a letter to Jennifer, who was at home in Pendleton. He mysteriously used buzz words that one might hear in television detective shows from the 1950s. "Be careful on the phones because the G-men are watching," Tim wrote. "Use the pay phone."[29] He warned her to be wary of Dad because their father should not know of the plot. At a friend's party, Jennifer McVeigh allegedly told someone, "Something big is going to happen and Tim is going to be part of it." Later she would vehemently deny she ever made that statement.

On March 31, Timothy McVeigh rented a room at the Imperial

Motel in Kingman, listing his address on the registry as Fort Riley, Kansas. He rented the movie *Blown Away* and watched it a couple of times. Tim rarely left the motel room, except to eat. He rested and made no telephone calls from the room. On the twelfth, Tim left the motel in his reliable Pontiac and drove to Junction City, Kansas, where he stopped at Elliot's Body Shop to get rid of the Pontiac. Tim was at the height of his paranoia at this point and may have believed federal authorities were tracking him through the Pontiac. Fearing he was being followed by the government, he traded the car, along with two hundred and fifty dollars, for a yellow 1977 Mercury with AM/FM radio. From Elliot's, McVeigh located the Dreamland Motel, where Terry Nichols had stayed in the past, and checked in. A smooth talker and spendthrift, Tim smiled his way into getting the motel's owner, Lea McGown, to lower the room rate to twenty dollars per night. He signed the register "Timothy McVeigh," and gave James Nichols's address at 3616 North Van Dyke Road, Decker, Michigan. Lea gave him room twenty-five. Tim drove the Mercury to Oklahoma City on April 16, Easter Sunday, and parked it, leaving a note as if the vehicle was disabled. He called Terry Nichols, who was at home in Herington, Kansas, and Terry gave Tim a ride all the way back to Junction City. Nichols has claimed that during this trip, McVeigh told him, "Something big is going to happen."

Tim's father, Bill, hoped that night that his son had been to the post office box in Arizona where Tim had his mail sent. Tim's twenty-seventh birthday was approaching, on April 23, and Bill had mailed a $50 money order to Tim's box, just as he had so many times before. Bill didn't hear much from his son, didn't even know where he had been since December 1994. But that didn't matter. Bill knew Timmy would make his way in the world someday. After all, his son was an American.

On April 17, Tim McVeigh and another man rented a Ryder truck from Elliot's in Junction City, Kansas. Tim referred to himself as "Bob Kling" when he rented the vehicle, and used a South Dakota driver's license he had made himself. Instead of the yellow

Mercury, Tim was seen driving the Ryder by Lea McGown, and she wondered about the truck because he parked it far away from his room under the sign for the motel. A day later, the eighteenth, the Ryder truck was seen at Geary State Fishing Lake, fifteen miles south of Junction City. A couple other vehicles were seen at the site. A lot of work needed to be done on the truck. It was packed with blue barrels containing almost five thousand pounds of explosives made from fuel oil and fertilizer. Holes were drilled in the cab under the seat of the Ryder vehicle and through the cargo trailer so fuses could be fed through them into the explosives. The main fuse was crimped to a nonelectric blasting cap inserted into the detonation cord. With the loading work completed, the truck just needed to be placed at the desired target, and the fuse lit.

Tim dialed the number to the CAUSE Foundation, a legal team suing the government over its actions at Waco. Foundation director David Hollaway answered. Tim identified himself as "a patriot" and told Hollaway that suing over Waco would be moot because "justice is corrupt" and the government would beat the lawsuit, just like it had the Davidians.

"You are absolutely right," Hollaway told McVeigh. "But if we win the case, it will put a damper on the government. If we lose it, we will put hypocrisy on trial."

Tim said no, action was needed instead. "These people in government need to be sent a message."

"Watch what you say," Hollaway stressed. "It's not smart to use a telephone to discuss such matters." Hollaway got an odd feeling in the pit of his stomach.[30]

Before dawn on April 19, McVeigh was outside the Dreamland Motel working on something or looking over a map inside the cab of the truck. The door to the cab was open and his face glowed under the dome light. After remaining there a while, Tim shut the door, started the engine, and maneuvered the humming truck out of the parking lot. Waves of light from the sun sneaked into the sky. It was going to be another gorgeous day in the Heartland.

Federal agents were looking for clues locally and internationally, from farming stores in Kansas to airports around the world. Sketches of two John Doe suspects were released to the media Thursday as agents carried the generic drawings from witness to witness.

In Oklahoma City, the truck axle found by Governor Keating proved to be the best piece of evidence for the FBI. The axle had the vehicle identification number, and the FBI traced the number to Ryder rentals of Miami, Florida. It was still Wednesday, April 19, when Ryder employees who had searched their records found that the Miami business owned the truck, but it had been rented to Elliot's Body Shop in Junction City, Kansas. Employees at Elliot's told the FBI agents that the truck had been rented on Monday by two young men, one with a crew cut and another with longer, darker hair. The short-haired man referred to himself as Bob Kling, as his license stated.

Chapter 7

Public Enemy

I've always dreamed of pulling a Guy Fawkes on the Texas Legislature. Just blow the damn thing sky high. I've got maps in my room and I'll do it someday.

—Old Anarchist*

Sketches of the two men were made at Elliot's from the descriptions by the employees. When the sketches were released in Junction City, many people recognized them, including Lea McGown of the Dreamland Motel. In Oklahoma City, several people recognized the sketch of the man who had a crew cut. The witnesses said they saw him hanging around the Alfred P. Murrah Federal Building at 8:55 A.M., Wednesday, before the bomb went off. FBI agents learned the name used to rent the Ryder truck was false,

---

*From the 1990 movie *Slacker,* written, produced, and directed by Richard Linklater. "Old Anarchist" character played by Louis Mackey. "Old Anarchist" refers to Guy Fawkes, who in 1605 attempted to blow up Parliament.

and found a lead at the Dreamland Motel. The address listed by the man who booked into room twenty-five was 3616 North Van Dyke Road, Decker, Michigan. The address was run through Department of Motor Vehicles computers, which turned up a 1991 driver's license issued to Timothy J. McVeigh. To get that license, McVeigh had turned in a Kansas driver's license with the address listed as Fort Riley.

The John Doe sketches had made the rounds of national television. On Friday morning, the FBI received a telephone call from a man who claimed to be a former co-worker of Timothy McVeigh's. FBI agent Henry Gibbons told Gannett News Service that the co-worker had plenty to say about McVeigh.

> He further advised that McVeigh was known to hold extreme right-wing views. [McVeigh] was a military veteran, and was particularly agitated about the conduct of the federal government at Waco, Texas, in 1993.[1]

The reference to the Branch Davidian incident had already been mentioned to the FBI and speculated upon in the media. The Oklahoma bombing was possibly an act of revenge on the American government for the Waco deaths.

It was the night of April 20 and McVeigh needed to sleep. The mission had been completed and now there was time to be alone and rest. His heart had slowed to normal, as the rest of his body regained control of itself. The shakes of anticipation had stopped. The only problem was that a nosy trustee working in Noble County's jail kept watching. "Damn, dude," the male trustee called into the cell. "You sure sleep a lot!"

Timothy McVeigh, the patriot, our Patrick Henry, now had the energy of someone twice his age. But it just seemed that so much had been resolved. Rest Period had arrived. "I'm . . . ," Tim drifted, "catching up on the sleep I lost in the army."

The trustee faded into the clouded mystery that was Tim's dream . . . of a flag in the early morning where men stood tall to salute Old Glory as she snapped at a blue sky. Another day in America where decent men are free.

An FBI computer check Friday morning, April 21, found that Timothy McVeigh was in jail in Perry, Oklahoma. McVeigh was facing an arraignment and was about to make bail on a misdemeanor weapons charge. The FBI placed a call to Perry. In the courtroom, Assistant District Attorney Mark Gibson handed a note to the judge. The note said simply, "I need to talk to you." Gibson later said he informed the judge by handing him a note because he didn't want McVeigh to know the federal government was after him. Gibson added that the FBI was "thrilled" when it found that the Social Security number and birthdate for John Doe #1 matched the Timothy McVeigh who was now in Perry.

Mark Gibson said Timothy McVeigh was not the normal type of man he prosecuted. Gibson told CNN: "It was an eerie calm that McVeigh had. You wouldn't look into his eyes and say, 'There's evil exuding.' You just looked into his eyes and said, 'There's nothing.' "[2]

McVeigh was sent back to jail, where at about noon he was met by federal agents. James Norman, Jr., and Floyd Zimms asked McVeigh if he knew why they wanted to talk to him. McVeigh, who had apparently not been previously briefed, allegedly answered, "Yes. That thing in Oklahoma City, I guess." Norman and Zimms posed a few more questions, but Tim's reply was to tell them he wished to have a lawyer. When Norman told McVeigh that he was to be taken to Oklahoma City, McVeigh said he was concerned about his "safety." When the agents questioned his concern, McVeigh replied, "You remember what happened with Jack Ruby."

Not long after he was formally arrested by the FBI, McVeigh's name was released to the media and a crowd of two hundred and fifty people gathered outside the county courthouse in Perry. Federal authorities had nabbed one of their accused terrorists and the agency certainly wanted the world to know about it. As McVeigh was led out of the courthouse for the return trip to Oklahoma City, the angry crowd shouted at him. The footage of an emotionless young man surrounded by grim-faced agents and deputies set the tone for how the nation would view Timothy James McVeigh: a cold, unfeeling army reject, with eyes glaring straight forward—the hundred-mile stare of the lost soldier—his tall, thin frame draped in orange prison clothing. It was widely reported that the man who'd been arrested only gave his name, rank, and serial number when asked questions, and referred to himself as a "prisoner of war." McVeigh himself has claimed that those reports are incorrect, made up by the media, which he distrusts. "I never, never called myself a prisoner of war," *Newsweek* reported McVeigh as saying. Yet the Tim McVeigh who talked to *Newsweek* had apparently not known when he was first arrested that he could eventually face the death penalty for the Oklahoma City murders. McVeigh's look on the film was cold in the face of what he was accused of doing. Many who saw the tape on the five o'clock news said it appeared he must be guilty: "Look, he feels no remorse" was the feeling conveyed by many people in the Lockport community.

Jennifer McVeigh gets very upset when she recalls what people said about her brother's appearance.

> What would they have said about any look he had? I mean, what do they want? You want him to walk out with a big smile on his face? What would they say about that? What kind of look do they expect from someone who has just been accused of a crime like that? I think the sun was shining in his eyes, first of all. He was squinting. I think that was part of it. . . . How would you like it if a bunch of people were staring at you, screaming, "Baby killer!" I don't think you can assume a reason for everything. You can't assume a reason for the way somebody looks at all times.[3]

At that moment, McVeigh was probably full of fear. He told *Newsweek* that he twice asked jailers for a bulletproof vest because he knew of the crowd outside the courthouse. The jailers "just ignored me," he said. Amid the crowd's shouts of "baby killer" as he walked with the agents, a lone male voice that defined America's anger over Oklahoma City was heard to scream, "Rip his head off!" But voices were the only things shot at McVeigh that day. Even if someone had wanted to shoot him, getting a clear line of fire would have been very difficult, except for a trained sniper or someone shooting from far above the crowd. McVeigh walked from the courthouse to a car, and during that brief journey he was surrounded by at least ten police agents. If he had been shot and killed, he would have been convicted at that moment also. The trial would have likely centered only on Terry Nichols, who, along with Michael Fortier, would place most of the blame on McVeigh. McVeigh's story would never have been heard.

On Friday afternoon, April 21, as America tried to deal with the notion that Oklahoma City had been attacked by *Americans,* federal authorities conducted a search of the Nichols farm in Decker, where, they were led to believe, McVeigh had lived for a while. James Nichols was questioned at the home, and agents recovered explosives materials. In Herington, Kansas, Terry Nichols had heard his name on television and that he was being sought in connection with the probe of the Oklahoma City bombing. Terry turned himself in at the local police station in Herington, where he was held as a material witness.

Friday afternoon, the FBI office in Buffalo, New York, contacted Sheriff Thomas Beilein at the Niagara County Sheriff's Department. Agent Joe Wolfinger asked that the department check its records for anything on Timothy McVeigh. Other than a harassment complaint filed by Jennifer McVeigh against someone in Lockport, there was nothing to report to the FBI. Deputies from Beilein's force and members of the state police met federal agents at 6289 Campbell Boulevard to meet with Tim's father, William

McVeigh. Bill had been preparing for a bowling trip to Reno when federal agents knocked on his door. "It's your son," an agent told him. Less than an hour after the police arrived, local media representatives were at Bill's house. Police were instructed to keep reporters well away from the McVeigh home.

The only other person allowed into the home was Father Paul Belzer from Good Shepherd Church. Bill needed a friend like Father Belzer at his side. But Bill's pain, not so strong since his divorce, was just beginning. The strip of Campbell Boulevard near Lockport Road was sparkled with the setting sun and media vehicles lining the ditch. Every news agency, from the tiny Lockport radio station WLVL to the major networks, was broadcasting from outside the McVeigh home. The American flag in Bill's yard was at full-mast until an observant state policeman lowered it. As Timothy James McVeigh was being arraigned at Tinker Air Force Base outside Oklahoma City (because the federal court building in Oklahoma City had been damaged by the bombing), reporters fanned out along Campbell Boulevard, looking for neighbors and friends of the accused Oklahoma City bomber. Timothy's high school yearbook popped up out of nowhere. While photojournalists and camera operators were getting Tim's 1986 high school yearbook photo on film for the five o'clock news, reporters from Buffalo channels 2, 4, and 7 were checking their appearance, waiting for their own moment on camera with the suspect's father. But Bill wasn't coming out, so the focus of talk among the reporters turned to Jennifer McVeigh. But that lead wasn't likely to pan out either because she was believed to be in Florida for spring break. Then agents walked out of Bill McVeigh's house with a box of evidence labeled "Old Photos," most likely containing letters Tim had sent home during his many years away.

Father Paul Belzer exited the house later and was mobbed by reporters as he made his way slowly to his car. "He wasn't bad. He liked to play basketball," Belzer said, trying to answer all the questions being shouted at him about Tim. To the local priest, Timothy McVeigh was still that boy he knew at the church picnics.

The McVeigh home also attracted rubberneckers, who stared at the ranch structure as if it was an accident scene and they were waiting for bodies to be pulled out. One brown station wagon across the street from 6289 Campbell Boulevard was filled with children, adults gawking out, and an elderly lady in the front seat with a video camera. Just about everyone quoted in the next day's newspapers, other than saying they couldn't believe Tim was a suspect, was shocked that anybody could bomb a building and kill children in a day-care center.

Friday afternoon, Bill McVeigh's friend Leo LaPort, Jr., was at Allie Brandt's bowling alley. Tim's face was on the television news.

> I was bowling against Art Braunscheidel, and I caught a glimpse on TV. When they brought the name up, I went right to Art and said, "Art, that name really rings a bell. I'm almost positive it's one of Bill's kids." He said, "It can't be." It wasn't two minutes after that and Louise [Art's wife] called and told him the FBI was at [Bill's] house. And they flashed the picture up, and I said, "God, that looks just like Bill."[4]

As Bill McVeigh held his head in his hands in Pendleton in total disbelief, Tim McVeigh had just arrived at Tinker Air Base. Jennifer McVeigh's whereabouts remained a mystery and Tim's mother, Mickey (McVeigh) Frazer, had a caravan of reporters headed her way. Jean (Hill) Zanghi, fifty-four, Mildred's sister, was in her car listening to the news on her radio while on her way home from work at Burger King in Geneseo. Jean had seen the John Doe #1 sketch on television during "Good Morning America," the day before. "Oh, God, it looks like Tim," she said to herself that morning. Jean was careful not to tell her husband, Louis, or anyone, that she'd recognized a man who may have killed possibly hundreds of people in faraway Oklahoma City. "I don't know what it was. Something about the sketch struck me," Jean recalled later in a *Union-Sun & Journal* interview. "But I didn't think it was possible." She glanced at the same John Doe #1 suspect pictured in the Rochester *Democrat and Chronicle.* "You know, when you just think there's no way." A feeling hit her in the stomach and she felt dizzy. The road blurred and she had to pull over to the side. As the radio announcer blurted out the news, her worst fears were realized. She discussed her reaction with interviewer Julianna Jacoby: "I said, 'Oh, my God.' I was only three miles away from work but I had to pull over to the side of the road. I couldn't believe it."[5]

In an effort to report the whereabouts of Jennifer McVeigh accurately, numerous news agencies concluded she was in Florida spending spring break with her friend Dennis Sadler, a construction worker she knew. Yet there is reason to believe that Jennifer McVeigh was no longer in Florida. She had apparently returned (or would soon return) to Lockport and was staying with her very close friend Mary Butler, at Butler's Saxton Street apartment in Lockport. A source who knows Mary Butler said in a recorded interview that Jennifer may have been hiding from the press at Mary's home—the place of refuge she had known. The source described Mary's demeanor and suspicious nature in the days that followed the bombing.

> She acted very strange, almost scared out of her mind, and this went on for several days. She was very nervous acting, very evasive, and didn't want to talk about anything. It was just a sense I had about her, from knowing her. She acted quite a bit different. When the McVeigh story was brought up in a conversation with her, she said, "You do not know the whole story." She said it in a way like she knew something was going on. The reason she was nervous right after the bombing was the fact that Jennifer McVeigh was staying at her house and that's why Jennifer had not come forward for several days after the bombing.[6]

Jennifer McVeigh apparently had a lot to hide, so keeping herself away from the media frenzy was wise. She had received incriminating information from her brother just before the bombing in Oklahoma City. Tim had mailed a letter to her stating,

Still waiting on your letter as to when you rcv'd [received] my last letter. That had a lot of sensitive material in it. So it's important to know if you received it, or if it was intercepted. . . . Please respond ASAP, only one letter. If one is already en route, Don't send another. Send no more after 01 APR, and then, even if it's an emergency—watch what you say, because I may not get it in time, and the G-men might get it out of my box, incriminating you.*

Jennifer did appear days later at the Campbell Boulevard home and was captured on film by Rochester *Democrat and Chronicle* photographer Shawn Dowd, leaving her home with her dad on one of several trips they took with federal authorities for questioning. According to the *New York Times,* Jennifer McVeigh was first met by investigators on April 21, at the house of friend Dennis Sadler. Sadler shared the home with two roommates, David Huckaby and John Donne. Donne told the *Times* that the agents took her to a room in the house and he heard Jennifer yell out at one point, "I'm not going to help you kill my brother."

Also on the night of Friday, April 21, Terry Nichols was taken to a federal facility in Abilene, Kansas, for further questioning. The days of his friendship with Tim were over. The war was over. Terry may never see his son, Joshua, again. One hundred sixty-eight people in bombed-out Oklahoma City were dead, like the people who had believed in David Koresh. To Terry, who was led out of a government building for the cameras to see, those who planned the 1995 American Revolution were soon to be dead, too. Later, federal authorities would learn of a man who had befriended McVeigh and Nichols in the army.

Twelve-year-old Joshua Nichols called the FBI and told Agent Debbie Calhoun about a man named Michael Fortier, an Arizona resident who had apparently spent time with Terry and Timothy in

---

*As quoted by *Newsweek,* May 22, 1995, p. 27. The original letter was signed by her brother under the alias "Tim Tuttle," as was Tim McVeigh's practice in the months leading up to the bombing.

the last couple years. Fortier was visited by authorities twice in Kingman, Arizona. They were particularly interested in an incident where a reporter from the local newspaper was met at Fortier's door by the click of a shotgun and the words, "Stay away from here." After that, the FBI was more than happy to offer Fortier the best in government hospitality. Fortier's conspirator status was apparently later diminished when he admitted staking out the Murrah with McVeigh.

Conspiracy freaks ruled the shortwave radio airwaves. McVeigh was a hero and the government had purposely bombed one of its own facilities as an excuse to impose further regulations on gun owners and militia members. Still, some witnesses claimed John Doe #1, Timothy McVeigh, was seen leaving the Murrah building minutes before it exploded. *USA Today* reports said:

- At 8:30 A.M., April 19, 1995, a witness saw two men in a Ryder truck pull into the parking lot of a business on Hudson Street and ask for directions to Fifth and Harvey, the northwest corner of the Murrah building.

- At 8:40 A.M., a meter maid driving north on Robinson Street saw a Ryder truck, driven by a man later identified as McVeigh, coming toward her at a low rate of speed. She thought the driver wished to stop and ask her a question. But instead, the male driver turned west on Park Avenue and kept going. The woman turned and followed the truck. She only saw one person in the truck and did not take note of the license plate.

- At 8:55 A.M., three people leaving the Murrah building saw a Ryder truck parked in front of the building. They had first noticed the truck as they entered the building minutes earlier.

- At 9:00 A.M., a man driving east on Fifth Street was forced to hit his brakes to avoid hitting a man crossing Fifth Street.

The man crossing the street is later identified as McVeigh, who was moving away from a Ryder truck.

- Also at 9:00 A.M., a witness on the opposite side of Fifth Street saw a man later identified as McVeigh leaving the scene shortly before the bomb went off. The witness saw a yellow Mercury leave the scene with two men inside.[7]

In the days that followed Tim's arrest, James Douglas Nichols was taken into custody as a material witness and then released because of insufficient evidence. But McVeigh would remain incarcerated in El Reno Federal Correctional Facility because, as U.S. Magistrate Roland Howland put it at the hearing in a converted courtroom at Tinker Air Base, there was "an indelible trail of evidence" leading to McVeigh in association with the bombing. McVeigh was provided with a copy of the criminal complaint against him, before he faced the judge. Magistrate Howland asked McVeigh if he understood the complaint and McVeigh replied, "Yes, sir, I do."

As they had sought out William McVeigh, reporters from all over the country tracked down Tim's mother, Mildred McVeigh Frazer, and his sisters, Patricia and Jennifer, for comments about the bombing and Timothy's arrest. After seven days, William, through his attorney, Morgan Jones, sent a fax to newspapers:

I would like to express my deepest sympathy for the people and families of those involved in the Oklahoma City explosion. I am very sorry for what happened and feel terrible about it. My prayers are with the victims, families, and people of Oklahoma. I would also like to thank my friends and neighbors for their kind words of support. This is the only statement I am making to anyone in the news media, and I will make no further statement.

Of course, Bill McVeigh did speak later with reporters. He told the *Buffalo News* that he still loved his son. Shedding tears and holding his squeezed fist against his chest, Bill told *News* reporter Lou Michel, "You still have feelings for your children."[8] Terry Nichols's ex-wife, Lana Padilla, went so far as to call herself and her son, Josh, victims #170 and #171 of the bombing. It's likely that the families of the 168 people who died in the blast are outraged by Lana referring to herself as one of the numbers, especially since she admitted finding but failing to immediately report some incriminating items in a storage locker Terry Nichols rented and a note to Tim McVeigh from Terry that said, "You're on your own. Go for it!"

Bill McVeigh handled the tragedy in a different way. He didn't run out and get a book deal. Bill remained isolated at his home and out of reach of reporters for many days, missing work at Harrison Radiator. He changed his telephone number to a new, unlisted one, and spoke only briefly with a few newspaper reporters and other visitors. In his comments, Bill sounded like the character Chauncey Gardiner in Jerzy Kosinski's book *Being There.* Asked about how he was handling all the attention, McVeigh told the *Buffalo News,* "A friend of mine said I needed to get out, so I golfed nine holes." He also worked in his garden, as always. "I've planted peas, corn, and onions and if the corn doesn't come up, I'll plant it over again. That's the way corn is. Sometimes it comes up. Sometimes it doesn't." But privately, the pain must have been almost too much to bear for William McVeigh, being told by the federal government that his son was accused of the worst mass murder in U.S. history. But despite the initial crush of reporters, and the visits by CNN, the *Sunday Times* of London, and network reporter Diane Sawyer, Bill McVeigh maintained his calm nature, never once telling a media person to leave his property. Though a small No Trespassing sign was placed at the end of the driveway, the yard remained filled in the summer of 1995 with inviting flowers and shrubbery. "I can't talk about Tim," Bill said

I just want to say I feel deep sympathy for the victims and families involved in the Oklahoma City bombing. I have had only brief contact with my son the past 10 years and only know details from what I have been watching on TV the past few days. That is all I wish to say at this time.

Tim's Mom

p.s. Please leave our family alone!

Mickey McVeigh Frazer's note of condolence.

to the occasional person at his doorstep. And other than a couple of interviews, Bill McVeigh has maintained his life as it had been before the Oklahoma tragedy.

Bill's ex-wife, Mildred (Mickey), was remarried and living in Fort Pierce, Florida. Mickey left Lockport, New York, for good in the summer of 1989 and wed Harlan Frazer, who had served in the military in Texas and Florida. The former Mrs. William McVeigh spoke with *Union-Sun & Journal* managing editor Dan Kane on April 25, when he called her at her Florida home. She expressed deep compassion for the victims of the bombing. When located by federal officials and the media, she handed a note to a sheriff's deputy to give to reporters. The note began with, "I just want to say I am deeply" but she had crossed that out and began the note over again.

> I just want to say I feel deep sympathy for the victims and families involved in the Oklahoma City bombing. I have had only brief contact with my son the past ten years and only know details from what I have been watching on TV the past few days. That is all I wish to say at this time.

Mrs. Frazer signed the note one way and then crossed that out. She finally signed the note "Tim's Mom," and ended it with "p.s. Please leave our family alone." Later, in a letter to her local newspaper, the *Fort Pierce Tribune,* Mickey wrote in part, "He could be any of our children." Mickey and Harlan reportedly made a trip to Pendleton in late April, but lived in some type of seclusion for months.

Bill McVeigh's oldest daughter, Patricia Davis, was located by reporters on April 24 at her home in Fort Lauderdale, Florida. The nurse and mother of one girl released a statement, much like her mother's, to the media.

> I have not been involved in my brother's life for the last nine years since I left the Buffalo area. The only information I have regarding this tragedy is what I've learned like the rest of the American public through the news media.

Jennifer McVeigh surfaced days later. Her friend Dennis Sadler told the *Pensacola News Journal* [9] that the FBI had searched the room Jennifer had stayed in when she visited him on spring break. Sadler had met Jennifer when she lived with her mother; they had attended Woodham High School together for a couple years. When Tim was arrested, Jennifer was "in shock," Sadler said. "She really didn't say nothing." Jennifer McVeigh's March letter to the editor at the *Union-Sun & Journal* made headlines when it was revealed just days after the bombing.

As the federal paperwork was completed, Timothy McVeigh and Terry Nichols, who was initially held at Dickinson County Jail in Abilene before being moved to El Reno, were finally indicted by a grand jury on August 10, 1995. The indictment states that the two men committed and caused to be committed the following acts:

- On September 30, 1994, McVeigh and Nichols purchased forty fifty-pound bags of ammonium nitrate in McPherson, Kansas, under the name "Mike Havens."

- On October 1, 1994, McVeigh and Nichols stole explosives from a storage locker in Marion, Kansas.

- On October 3 and 4, 1994, McVeigh and Nichols transported the stolen explosives to Kingman, Arizona, and rented a storage unit for them.

- On October 18, 1994, McVeigh and Nichols again purchased forty fifty-pound bags of ammonium nitrate in McPherson, Kansas, under the name "Mike Havens."

- In October 1994, McVeigh and Nichols planned a robbery of a firearms dealer in Arkansas as a means to obtain money to help finance their planned act of violence. (A report said there were thirteen unsolved robberies in the Midwest that newspapers reported McVeigh and Nichols possibly being involved in.)

- On November 5, 1994, McVeigh and Nichols caused firearms, ammunition, coins, United States currency, precious metals, and other property to be stolen from a firearms dealer in Arkansas. (Victim Roger Moore, a gun and coin dealer who had met McVeigh previously, had been met at his rear door by a man wearing camouflage and a black ski mask. The victim was bound with duct tape and blindfolded while possibly two robbers tore his house apart, and stole more than $60,000 in goods. A 1995 search of Terry Nichols's home in Herington turned up a safety deposit box key of Moore's that had been stolen, according to federal authorities. Lana Padilla has admitted she found wigs, masks, panty hose, gold coins, and about $60,000 in precious metals in an AAAABCO storage locker rented by Terry Nichols. On Saturday, November 5, 1994, Timothy McVeigh was at a gun show in Kent, Ohio, so he could not have actually been directly involved in the robbery itself, according to a source. Whether McVeigh was aware that the Moore robbery was going to occur on that date has not been revealed.)

- On December 16, 1994, while en route to Kansas to take possession of firearms stolen in the Arkansas robbery, McVeigh drove with Michael Fortier to the Alfred P. Murrah Building and identified the building as the target.

- In March 1995, McVeigh obtained a driver's license in the name of "Robert Kling," bearing a date of birth of April 19, 1972.

- On April 14, 1995, McVeigh purchased a 1977 Mercury Marquis in Junction City, Kansas; called the Nichols residence in Herington, Kansas; called a business in Junction City and, using the name of "Bob Kling," inquired about renting a truck capable of carrying five thousand pounds of cargo and rented a motel room in Junction City.

- On April 15, 1995, McVeigh made a deposit for a rental truck in the name of "Robert Kling."

- On April 17, 1995, McVeigh took possession of a twenty-foot rental truck in Junction City, Kansas.

- On April 18, 1995, at Geary Lake State Park in Kansas, McVeigh and Nichols constructed an explosive truck bomb with barrels filled with a mixture of ammonium nitrate, fuel, and other explosives and placed the cargo in the compartment of the rental truck.

- On April 19, 1995, McVeigh parked the truck bomb directly outside the Alfred P. Murrah Federal Building, located within the western district of Oklahoma, during regular business hours.

- On April 19, 1995, McVeigh caused the truck bomb to explode.

The FBI's search for evidence against Timothy McVeigh would include Noble County jail, where McVeigh stayed after his initial speeding and weapons arrest. His possessions at the time included $650, a knife, a gun, a pack of Tums, and earplugs, all of which were seized. The business card for Paulsen's Military Supply was also found in the back of Trooper Hanger's patrol car. Noble County Sheriff Jerry Cook said federal agents seized the film of McVeigh's mug shot, his fingerprint card, booking receipts, clothing, and the mattress McVeigh slept on in the cell. Sheriff Cook said agents needed the fingerprint card to "determine if any explosive residue was removed from McVeigh's hands when he was fingerprinted by our officers." FBI Special Agent David Jarnigan would later testify to the grand jury. It is believed McVeigh watched the bombing from a safe distance. Agent Jarnigan said explosive compounds were found on McVeigh's hands, the knife, clothing, and earplugs, according to grand jury testimony. The bomb itself likely had a ten-minute fuse, so some witness accounts of McVeigh at the scene at 9 A.M. are probably false, since he would have been about two to three miles away from the Murrah building to see the blast.

Though they had pieced together information on the attack that would likely convict McVeigh, Nichols, and Fortier, federal investigators made several mistakes. Apprehending McVeigh and Nichols had been relatively easy. Because of his own errors, McVeigh was in jail and found by a computer. Nichols turned himself in, and Fortier was turned in by a telephone call to the feds by Josh Nichols, who hoped his father, Terry Nichols, would not face the death penalty, according to Lana Padilla in her book *By Blood Betrayed.* It couldn't have been easier for the FBI, especially since McVeigh left so many clues behind: his fingerprints were found, and he gave the motel desk the address of James Nichols. McVeigh also allowed himself to be seen by a great many witnesses in Oklahoma.

Trooper Charlie Hanger was praised by President Clinton for arresting McVeigh, but the officer had no idea who McVeigh was. All the trooper really did was haul in a speeder on a weapons transportation charge. It was McVeigh's own fault that he got caught. Hanger said of Timothy, "I talked to him a lot before we were told he was the [alleged] Oklahoma bomber. I guess I kind of warmed to him. He didn't seem a bad kid. He had a nice easy manner and a real nice smile."[10] Hanger was the last person to think that.

After the McVeigh arrest, the ensuing roundup of the usual suspects was an embarrassment to the federal government. At least three people were arrested and had their names dragged through the press mud—men who, it turned out, had nothing to do with the bombing. Steven Garrett Colbern, dubbed "a gun-toting fugitive" by *Newsweek,* was arrested on May 12 in Arizona. Colbern knew McVeigh through sales of military surplus, but he only knew him as "Tim Tuttle." A UCLA chemistry graduate, Colbern had been employed at Cedars/Sinai Medical Center. His failure to show up at a trial for illegal weapons possession made him a sought man by federal marshals. He had no role in the bombing, but, according to a "senior official" in Washington, he might help the government "clear up the mystery of John Doe #2" though "we are not saying he is John Doe #2."

The saddest cases of FBI bungling were drifters Gary Alan Land, thirty-five, and Robert Jacks, sixty, arrested by heavily armed agents on May 2 at the Kel-Lake Motel in Carthage, Missouri. When the agents arrived, one yelled in at the two men, "Come out with your hands up. Make any sudden moves and we'll blow your heads off." Land and Jacks were released eighteen hours after their dramatic capture, though it was never made known why they were nabbed in the first place, other than that they may have had a "connection" to the bombing and they had stayed in hotels in the same towns at the same time as Timothy McVeigh. Reports detailed that both men, who took polygraph tests, said they didn't even know McVeigh or the Nichols brothers. That didn't stop *USA Today* from placing their color photos on its front page, above the fold, as if the FBI had completely solved the bombing case with the arrests of Land and Jacks. After he was released, Jacks told reporters, "We didn't do it. We're clean. We just got questioned. That's it." Twelve-year-old Josh Nichols was suspected as John Doe #2, as was another young man, David John Ruth of Oklahoma, who was actually arrested and then released. James Nichols was also held as a material witness, and later arrested for "conspiring to make bombs," but was later released.

The mentalities of Nichols's and McVeigh's hometown neighbors is similar in attitude toward guns, but radically different when the subject of the federal probe of the Oklahoma bombing is discussed. When he was released, James Nichols was received as a hero in his native Decker, Michigan, where many believe the government was involved in bombing its own building as an excuse for further persecution. But in Pendleton, New York, and its surrounding municipalities, the reaction to the name Timothy McVeigh is anger. Many residents are upset that he could have been involved in such a cowardly act of violence. People feel sorry for Bill McVeigh, who, they say, has always walked away from a fight. Tim is no hero at home.

Possibly hundreds of other people, including "army deserter" David Iniguez, were taken in for questioning and let go. Processing from seven to eleven thousand possible leads, the FBI was bound to make a few mistakes, but people like Land and Jacks will wind up carrying the scars of their arrests around for the rest of their lives.

Tim McVeigh had an isolated cell at El Reno Federal Correctional Facility as he awaited trial. Since the Oklahoma bombing was declared the top news story of 1995, McVeigh is viewed as American public enemy number one. U.S. marshals guard him twenty-four hours a day to be sure that he cannot be harmed, or harm himself. There are 1,065 prisoners in the medium security portion of the facility, near where McVeigh was housed. The warden's executive assistant, Leon Crawford, said McVeigh was allowed to receive and send mail, read newspapers, and also receive visitors. He could use a radio but was not permitted television.[11] McVeigh apparently has better luck with women in prison than he ever did as a free man; he has received at least four marriage proposals since being sent to El Reno. He still tried to stay in shape in his nine-by-five-foot cell by doing sit-ups and push-ups. Tim met with his lawyers almost daily, and saw his father twice during visits. Tim spent most of his time reading. He still receives right-wing publications and reading materials like Jack McLamb's *Aid and Abet* newsletter, Bo Gritz's *Center For Action* newsletter, the John Birch Society's *New American,* and Chuck Harder's *For the People* newsletter. In addition to the many letters he receives each day, Tim reads the *Dallas Morning News* and the *Washington Times.* McVeigh was in the same prison as Terry Nichols.

Chapter 8

Right-Wing Diary

But how often is the natural propensity to society disturbed or destroyed by the operations of government!

—Thomas Paine*

Only the Thought Police mattered.

—George Orwell†

The first look into Timothy McVeigh's mind did not come from an interview by a top news agency. It did not come from the trial, and was not revealed through initial comments made by relatives, friends, and associates that appeared in every newspaper in the country. The glimpse came from Tim himself, from two letters he wrote to the *Union-Sun & Journal.* The letters, published in 1992, three years before the Oklahoma City bombing, were authored by

---

*Thomas Paine, as quoted by Daniel Boorstin, *The Lost World of Thomas Jefferson* (University of Chicago Press, 1981).

†George Orwell, *1984* (Harcourt, Brace and Company, Inc., 1949).

someone with concern for the people who wish to maintain their American lifestyles while protecting themselves from dangerous outside forces. It's not too broad an editorial leap to say that thousands of people are upset with the United States government. The reasons are infinite, but most center on laws that benefit a select group, a time period, or that are ultimately viewed as infringements on personal rights established by leaders long since dead.

The concept of independence lies in freedom of thought. That point may come strongly into play when Timothy McVeigh faces trial. One letter he wrote suggests that violence may be needed to change the thinking of political leaders on the national level. This could mean an assassination, a coup, or some other drastic act where people and property are viewed as objects for rage. Criminologist Robert Ressler said in a speech at Niagara County Community College, near McVeigh's hometown, that, in his experience, the murderers he has studied (John Wayne Gacy, Ted Bundy, Charles Manson, and Jeffrey Dahmer) viewed other people not as "humans" but as "objects" for their own uses.[1] A connection can be drawn to this and the horrific thinking of McVeigh's fictional hero, Earl Turner of *The Turner Diaries*. In the Andrew Macdonald novel, Turner says the victims of his political bombing are "pawns," and "there is no way we can destroy the System without hurting many thousands of innocent people." Maybe to McVeigh, a change in the way people like President Bill Clinton and Attorney General Janet Reno think could have only been effected by an act of war on the part of citizens hurt by Clinton philosophy, a group which today seems to change with popular opinion on Capitol Hill. If so, then we can believe Timothy McVeigh's mind was already focused on an act such as the Oklahoma bombing when he wrote his letters.

The *Union-Sun & Journal*'s "Letters to the Editor" column is generally quite full. In fact, Managing Editor Dan Kane has said he knows of no other small-town newspaper with such an active letters column. In the Lockport area, residents who write to the newspaper really do believe in the freedom of speech and that words can change or enlighten others. Taxes and government are the two hottest topics among the letter writers. Sometimes, older folks will recall days past, or the religious right will flood the editor with pulp letters on the abortion issue. Gun rights advocates write to the paper many times a year, as do those who urge more participation in government. But local and national political developments are still the most frequent topics.

Timothy McVeigh's letters to the editor fit right in: He questioned the way things are and pondered the way things should be. What sets his most important letter apart from the rest is that it was penned by someone who seems to have lost all faith in current political leaders. He makes reference to politicians' salaries (a major general complaint), and the Los Angeles riots of the early 1990s that mirror the riots seen by Charles Manson in the 1960s, with emphasis on racial tension which he perceived as "growing." McVeigh's suggestion of violence at the letter's end is not as common. "Civil war" and the Boston Tea Party are mentioned from time to time by disgruntled taxpayers, but the actual mention of shedding "blood" is highly unusual. Tim McVeigh would appear to be on the radical end of a spectrum describing people who are truly angry about politics. Those willing to engage in violence often think that the government is intentionally wrong and evil; that it is watching them, and that citizens should not comply with the government's laws. People with such extreme views would try an act of revenge on their target of anger: for example, shooting at the White House, sending a threatening letter to the president, or sending a mail bomb. McVeigh, in his own words of general unhappiness with the "system," wants others to see "the big picture" as he thinks he does. This letter is being reprinted from the February 11, 1992, issue of the *Union-Sun & Journal.*

America Faces Problems

Crime is out of control. Criminals have no fear of punishment. Prisons are overcrowded so they know they will not be imprisoned long. This breeds more crime, in an escalating cyclic pattern.

Taxes are a joke. Regardless of what a political candidate "promises," they will increase. More taxes are always the answer to government mismanagement. They mess up, we suffer. Taxes are reaching cataclysmic levels, with no slowdown in sight.

The "American Dream" of the middle class has all but disappeared, substituted with people struggling just to buy next week's groceries. Heaven forbid the car breaks down!

Politicians are further eroding the "American Dream" by passing laws which are supposed to be a "quick fix," when all they really are designed for is to get the official reelected. These laws tend to "dilute" a problem for a while, until the problem comes roaring back in a worsened form (much like a strain of bacteria will alter itself to defeat a known medication).

Politicians are out of control. Their yearly salaries are more than an average person will see in a lifetime. They have been entrusted with the power to regulate their own salaries, and have grossly violated that trust to live in their own luxury.

Racism on the rise? You had better believe it! Is this America's frustrations venting themselves? Is it a valid frustration? Who is to blame for the mess? At a point when the world has seen communism falter as an imperfect system to manage people; democracy seems to be headed down the same road. No one is seeing the "big" picture.

Maybe we have to combine ideologies to achieve the perfect utopian government. Remember, government-sponsored health care was a communist idea. Should only the rich be allowed to live long? Does that say that because a person is poor, he is a lesser human being, and doesn't deserve to live as long because he doesn't wear a tie to work?

What is it going to take to open up the eyes of our elected officials? AMERICA IS IN SERIOUS DECLINE.

We have no proverbial tea to dump; should we instead sink a ship full of Japanese imports? Is a Civil War imminent? Do we have to shed blood to reform the current system? I hope it doesn't come to that! But it might.

Tim McVeigh
6289 Campbell Boulevard

Another letter from McVeigh was published March 10, 1992. He seems to have a genuine concern for animals, is upset with the way he understands beef is processed, and favors a "hunt" for meat instead, though Tim was never interested in hunting game himself. His method of communication in this letter seems to be that of a professor, instructing a class on decency in survival. Here is the letter as it appeared:

Meat Insured Survival

Since the beginning of his existence, man has been a hunter, a predator. He has hunted and eaten meat to ensure his survival. To deny this is to deny your past, your religion, even your existence.

Since we have now established that about every human being on this planet consumes meat, we in America are left with two choices, buy your meat from a supermarket, or harvest it yourself.

We will, for now, discuss the fact that in many areas of the world, there is no "supermarket." We know the choice these people make; their lives, or the lives of meat. A good hunter enters the woods and kills a deer with a clean, merciful shot. The deer dies in his own environment, quick and unexpected.

To buy your meat in a store seems so innocent, but have you ever seen or thought how it comes to be wrapped up so neatly in cellophane?

First, the cattle live their entire lives penned up in crampt [sic] quarters, never allowed to roam freely, bred for one purpose when their time has come.

The technique I have personally seen is to take cattle, line them up side by side with their heads and necks protruding over a low fence, and walk from one end to the other, slitting their throats with either a machete or power saw. Unable to run or move, they are left there to bleed to death, standing up.

Would you rather die while living happily or die while leading a miserable life? You tell me which is more "humane." Does a "growing percentage of the public" have any pity or respect for any of the animals which are butchered and then sold in the store?

Or is it just so conveniently "clean" that a double standard is allowed?

Tim McVeigh
6289 Campbell Boulevard

The bombing in Oklahoma City occurred on April 19, 1995. Timothy McVeigh was charged with the crime on April 21, 1995, and the world press scrambled to learn more about this nobody who looked like a U.S. soldier. It was widely reported that McVeigh called himself a prisoner of war after his arrest and refused to talk to anyone. Within hours, *Newsweek, Time,* ABC, NBC, CBS, the *Washington Post,* the *New York Times,* the *Los Angeles Times,* the *Detroit Free Press,* the *Boston Globe,* the *New York Post,* and every other agency with the money to send a correspondent descended on Tim's hometown. On Monday morning, the press came to the offices of the *Union-Sun & Journal,* circulation eighteen thousand, looking for information on the local boy gone bad.

A letter, ripe with political complaint, from Jennifer McVeigh had been published in the paper on March 9. The FBI and the *New York Post* called the newspaper on Saturday and asked for copies of the March 9 newspaper. Reports said Timothy McVeigh was angry over Waco and that led to the bombing in Oklahoma. Jennifer mentioned Waco in her letter, published one month before the bombing occurred. Jennifer opened her letter with, "This is a response to Mr. Shearer's letter." Jennifer was responding to a letter from local resident Christopher Shearer, published March 2, discussing his feelings on socialism. On Sunday, an FBI agent told a newspaper executive that the agency intended to subpoena the original letters penned by Ms. McVeigh and Mr. Shearer. On Monday, the paper ran a story by Managing Editor Dan Kane about these letters, which then made national headlines and television shows. The news agency representatives who filled local hotels from Friday to the next Saturday sought more information on the McVeighs. The newspaper had not had a librarian in many years after job cuts reduced personnel, so articles having anything to do with the family (e.g., Bill McVeigh's years in local baseball, Tim's military clippings) were only available on microfilm, which is filed by month and year.

No one currently employed at the newspaper could recall any stories about the McVeighs. Managing Editor Kane knew the family and conducted a couple of interviews, one brief talk with Bill McVeigh and one with Mickey Frazer. Then, an anonymous reader telephoned Richard Pixley, a social studies teacher in Newfane, New York, and told him that Tim McVeigh had written a couple letters to the *Union-Sun & Journal* and that they had been published in 1992. At the time, the barrage of news reports on the bombing centered on the search for victims and the notion that McVeigh was not talking to anyone. Richard Pixley told his wife, *Union-Sun & Journal* city editor Kathleen Ganz, about the call he'd received, and the search was on. Social Page Editor Cindy Meal was pulled from her normal work to secretly search the newspaper's microfilm from 1992. Word spread in the newsroom that she was searching for letters written by McVeigh, and as the Tuesday morning work progressed, under the 11 A.M. deadline, the reporters and editors in the small room cast glances at Cindy, looking to see if she had found anything. At about 10:30 A.M., Cindy gasped, and several people dashed over to the microfilm machine. "I got one," she whispered. There was his name, Tim McVeigh, the man accused of one of the most notorious crimes in American history, on page two of the March 10, 1992 newspaper.

Despite the excitement, the letter was no great find. It wasn't the political manifesto we had been tipped to look for. The March 10 letter just showed he cared about cows, but was not a vegetarian. No insights there. Cindy kept looking. Of course, on older microfilm machines like that at the *Union-Sun & Journal,* the film scrolls backward, so Cindy ended up in February. Eventually, she found another letter, dated February 11, and read it. Cindy announced to whoever was listening that the main letter had been found. But it was almost 11 A.M., too late to run in that day's newspaper. Nerves were tingling. With so many top news agencies in town, we had to wait one more day to break the biggest story the *Union-Sun & Journal* ever had in its 174 years of publishing.

On Tuesday evening, I was working alone in the newsroom on a city council piece. My line rang and it was John Block, a producer from "Dateline NBC." By now he knew me by name, since I had helped him with various background items during that day. "You have anything else?" he asked. Oh, how I wanted to tell him of the letter from Tim McVeigh. If I told NBC of the letter, they would have had it first, beating every top news agency in the world. Finally, Americans would know a little bit about the mindset of Timothy McVeigh, of Public Enemy Number One. "Dateline" would have the story and I would be a part of it. Of course, I would no longer have a job at the paper, but who cared? NBC would find a job for me. Or would they? What if Block took all the credit somehow? Or what if another reporter for the paper was already giving Tim's letter to one of the big news boys? It was too much to worry about, and why should I fool myself into thinking NBC would have given me anything more than a cup of coffee. Maybe it was just my small-town foolishness, but I held my breath.

"No, John, I can't help you with anything more today," I said. "But stop in tomorrow. I think we may have a good story going. Dan Kane is going to have a good story ready." It took me an extra two hours and an extra beer to get to sleep that night because I had probably made the biggest mistake of my life. But I had remained loyal. And that's important, right? Though the context of the

McVeigh story itself was overwhelmingly negative and sad (even our managing editor pointed out in press reports that Space Shuttle pilot Bill Gregory was also from our hometown), the next day, Wednesday, April 26, would be the highlight in the newspaper career of Daniel V. Kane, a twenty-five-year journalist who claimed he once taught himself how to type by blindly typing out the dictionary.

At 7 A.M., the newsroom was packed with reporters, local and national. Church page editor Marilyn Lewis offered everyone (about thirty-five people) coffee and cookies, and Dan sat over at his desk, writing the news story of his life. He had organized the event very well, saving the Tim McVeigh letters for one day, and notifying each news agency that called or stopped in that on Wednesday, the *Union-Sun & Journal* would be running a "big" story about Tim. So each news crew showed up at the paper that morning. Most weren't too happy when they learned they'd have to wait until the newspaper was actually run off the press—no advance copies for anyone. In fact, they would have to wait four hours. Marilyn made more coffee, and they all waited. The cameramen worked on "background shots" most of that time. It was all I could do to keep my eyes on my terminal, as if I was actually getting some work done. A small-town writer with just five years on the paper, this was an exciting moment for me. The excitement was also mixed with an overwhelming feeling of sickness. On the tiny black-and-white television by the wire desk, the rescuers were pulling out more bodies in Oklahoma City, and one desk away, Dan Kane was writing about a person who was an alleged madman, child killer, anarchist. My desk telephone rang and the woman on the line identified herself as Alexandria Horowitz from the *New Yorker* magazine. I was relieved the phone had rung so it looked like I was doing something.

Alexandria told me she was a researcher for the magazine, working on a piece by Joyce Carol Oates about alleged Oklahoma bomber Timothy McVeigh. Both McVeigh and Oates were raised

in the same area and had attended Good Shepherd Church in
Pendleton in their respective youths, which were decades apart.
Horowitz told me Oates had recommended me to assist in the research for the piece. I was honored (I had sent Oates some of my
stories over the years). After speaking with her, a local grocer called
to tell me that a man named Larry McEvoy was a good friend of
Bill McVeigh's and I should call him to do a story. This was the
strange part about this breaking news—the story couldn't have
been any more local, but Dan gave few assignments to the reporters
regarding the McVeigh saga. Out of respect for the McVeighs, and
since Tim had not lived in town for a few years, Dan probably
wanted to leave them alone, relying instead on developing news released by the Associated Press and other wire services. But that was
not this day. He continued to labor over his piece and finally sent
it through to Kathleen Ganz to read. It was 10 A.M., and Oklahoma
Governor Keating had asked for silence at 9:02 (Oklahoma time)
in observance of what had happened just one week before.

We all stopped working and glanced at the television. I don't
remember what was said but the tension that morning was building in the newsroom. The reporters were getting anxious and
began asking again for advance proofs of our front page. Everyone got the same answer, except for CNN producer Bell Adler,
who'd spoken to Dan several times over the past thirty-eight
hours. Shortly before deadline, Kane met with Adler and her cam-
eraman in a separate back room, away from the other reporters.
When the proofs of the front page were finally sent to the type-
setter, wire editor Anne Calos and I grabbed the copies and went
all the way out to the composing room to read them in secret. It
seemed a bit much, to be hiding the story in this manner. But we
had been told to keep quiet. We read Dan's story in silence and
made our corrections.

> "Do we have to shed blood to reform the current system? I
> hope it doesn't come to that! But it might." This stern warning

about the abuses of the U.S. government was issued by Timothy McVeigh in 1992, shortly after he left military service. McVeigh . . . was responding to his own questions that he raised. The letters provide the first clear insight into McVeigh's thought process. The FBI said it views the Timothy McVeigh letters as a major development in the case since it is McVeigh's only known public comment on relevant issues.[2]

Kane's story and the mass publicity it received did not sit well with the FBI, which chooses to silence some of its stories and leak oceans on others. As the paper finally came off the presses and Kane was mobbed by cameramen and microphones, an FBI agent, he says, entered the circle of reporters, displayed a gun at his waist, and handed a subpoena to Kane. That event became the second big news of the day: "McVeigh Sent Letters to *US&J*," and "*US&J* Editor Subpoenaed." FBI Special Agent Steve Skinner was not happy that Kane alleged he displayed a gun at the news offices, but the subpoena for a May 2 Oklahoma District Court date stood. In part, it stated:

> You are commanded to bring with you the following documents . . . any and all original letters . . . to the *Union-Sun & Journal* in the name of, or by Jennifer McVeigh, Timothy McVeigh, William McVeigh, Christopher Shearer, and any other letters referenced or to which the above letters were written in response.

Through the newspaper's attorney, George V. C. Muscato of Lockport, the subpoena was satisfied by mailing the requested letters to Vicki Zemp Behenna at the U.S. Attorney's Office in Oklahoma. Kane recalled the incident with the FBI agent in an interview for this book:

> I think it's our responsibility to cooperate with law enforcement agencies and to help throw any light on such a terrible tragedy as we possibly can. . . . The day we broke the story in the news-

paper ... during the middle of the press conference this FBI man came in and sort of barged through the room, kicking wires and pushing lights aside, and he said, "Are you Kane?" And I said, "Yes, I am." He said, "I have a subpoena for you." I said, "I think you got the wrong guy." He says, "No, you're the guy I want. Here's your subpoena. We'll see you in Oklahoma City." I refused to take the subpoena and he pulled open his coat and in the front of his pants—pointed down toward his penis—was a .45. My immediate reaction was that I should reach over and pull the trigger. If the guy wants to be so obnoxious and abrasive, let's see if the thing is loaded and let the consequences fall. But being a newspaper man of longstanding, my cooler side prevailed and I walked over to [General Manager] Tom Ceravolo's office and that's where I was served with the subpoena, which I told the man I would refuse to [comply with], and that he could take me in handcuffs and shackles, but that I would not go willingly to Oklahoma City and testify. I never did hear again from the FBI.[3]

For the next three days, Dan Kane appeared on CNN and other television news shows. Kane appeared on "Good Morning America" and the "Today" show on Thursday, and that night he talked via satellite with Larry King. The "Larry King Live" limousine picked Kane up at his house and dropped him off at the Radisson Hotel in Buffalo where the hookup was made.

Timothy McVeigh's letters were published (and republished) everywhere. He was indeed very angry with the government, as federal authorities had alleged, and he looked more guilty than ever. Because she was also a writer and has similar political views, the media heat was turned up on Jennifer McVeigh. The revelation of Tim and Jennifer's letters showed that their views toward government and politics were similar. Both harbored great distrust for the United States government, and political leadership on the whole. As was mentioned earlier, Jennifer McVeigh's responses were to letters by Christopher Shearer, another person who disliked the American leadership, particularly the Republicans. While he suggested a socialist cure for America's ills, Jennifer McVeigh merely noted that problems needed to be weeded from the current system. A broad change in overall philosophy was not needed, she said. Here are both of Christopher Shearer's letters, reprinted from the March 2, 1995 edition of the *Union-Sun & Journal*:

Beware of Right-Wing Politics

Not all too long ago, even in this decade, government sanctioned sterilization was and is being practiced within some structures of the American state. The European Nazi, not surprisingly, was not the first to initiate this very delicate ideal of a "neat and orderly society."

If one were to merely take more than just a passing glance at the philosophy of Newt Gingrich and his cronies, he just may see that "applying the pruning knife with vigor" may develop into not just a vulgar, unspeakable analogy, but a sadly off-centered visualization of reality.

Contemporary eugenics could imply our fast and furious Republican concept of a final solution to the unobtainable welfare reform dilemma, or at least a very obscene step nearer to the orphanage.

I find it quite ironic that Oliver Wendell Holmes once stated that, "Three generations of imbeciles is enough." Interesting term, imbecile . . .

Newt, another one of our many self-appointed moralists, if given the green light which he and a few other irritants so desire, could quietly but sincerely take a few giant steps backward in the guise of progress close enough to the "Lynchburg Colony" mentality of the '30s and '40s. Absurdity once again resembles reality.

The moral imbecile, the physically disabled, the unwed mother, the pet food-eating elderly, the confused and homeless mental patient—all of this humanity are not simply wandering abstractions.

Remember, do you or your neighbor meet the criteria? The fever of America's extreme right is spiking.

Christopher Shearer
141 Elmwood Avenue

In light of the Oklahoma bombing and its purported connections to "the right"—those angry about Waco, those advocating violence in the face of gun-control measures, and those insisting that Bill Clinton is a Constitution bender—the final line of Christopher Shearer's letter was prophetic, as was the title placed on it in the newspaper by an editor. Though Shearer mainly addressed the "orphanage" thinking of House Speaker Gingrich, his warnings were appropriate nonetheless. Shearer seemed to say we don't have to fear foreign forces anymore, we have to fear ourselves. His second letter to the editor, published the same day, follows:

Revolution Is Possible

A number of years ago, I prided myself as being apolitical. I left America in the early '70s so as to escape the foolishness of hypocrisy, tension, and the obvious government adversity.

I was then introduced to the working concept of socialism. I learned from living in Denmark and interacting with their system that some governments do work.

Because of money, I was forced to return. To what? The same lies and deceit, and friends still dying in Vietnam. Nothing changes in America, but now I truly believe that some "thing" is about to.

Forget about Clinton's pitiful militant attempts at humanitarianism. That's merely an economy boosting saving face which aids only industry. Where's the money going to come from, and most importantly, where's it going to go? Being a genius is easy, but to attempt to guess about America is nearly futile.

What we shouldn't forget is our past insanity. Realize the fact that we may have a real revolution in the making.

Even the children of the poor are frightened by this absurd Republican takeover.

Please be a little bit aware and read your books.

Christopher Shearer
141 Elmwood Avenue

Of course, Shearer could not have known about the underground movement of people like Timothy McVeigh, who view themselves as patriots, and the plans they had for far away Oklahoma City. But a parallel can be drawn between his line ". . . I now truly believe that some 'thing' is about to" and McVeigh's alleged statement to Terry Nichols, "Something big is going to happen." While both men are obviously upset with their government, Tim McVeigh and Mr. Shearer hope for change at opposite ends of the spectrum—McVeigh to "arm and protect," and Shearer to "disarm and feed the world." As we've learned, Tim often sent literature to Jennifer McVeigh, and their beliefs are still close today. If Tim were living at home at the time, he may have also responded to Shearer's letters with one of his own to the newspaper. But it was Jennifer who met the task, with a letter much longer than the newspaper generally receives. She told me once she really enjoys writing, and as evidenced by her letter, she must also favor intensive fact-finding. As reprinted from the March 9, 1995 *Union-Sun & Journal,* here is Jennifer's letter:

Socialism Isn't Answer

This is a response to Mr. Shearer's letter. I will admit, there are many problems in America today, and maybe socialism does work, but it's certainly not the answer here in America. Let's define socialism.

Socialism is "A political and economic theory based on collective governmental ownership and democratic management of the essential means for the production and distribution of goods; a policy or practice based on this theory." One such practice based on this theory is Communism.

The definition of Communism is almost synonymous with that of socialism, in fact the very word "socialism" even appears in the definition.

Communism is, "A doctrine and program based on revolutionary Marxism socialism as developed by Lenin and the Bolshevik party, which interprets history as a relentless class war eventually to result everywhere in the victory of the proletariat in all countries so as to achieve its ultimate objectives, a classless society and establishment of a world union of socialist soviet republics."

America was founded as a republic, not as a communist nation, and not even as a democracy.

In a republic, "authority is derived through the election by the people of public officials best fitted to represent them." America was not meant to be ruled by a "single authoritarian dictatorship."

Yes, there are many problems in America today, but perhaps our given "form" of government is not the cause. The cause lies in our current form, and the perversion of the Constitution, the document which founded this great nation.

We need not change our form of government, we need only to return to practicing the form of government originally set forth by our founding fathers. If you don't think the Constitution is being perverted, I suggest you open your eyes and take a good look around. (Research constitutional rights violated in Weaver, Waco. Also "Gun Control").

For those of you who favor gun control, just remember the words of one great person, "This year will go down in history. For the first time, a civilized nation has full gun registration. Our streets will be safer, our police more efficient, and the world will follow our lead into the future!"

Who is the great person with such profound wisdom to profess? Adolph Hitler—1935. Enough said? I think it's about time for all of us to step back and ask ourselves—what is gun control really about? Crime? Think again.

It's theories like yours, Mr. Shearer, (if indeed I did interpret your letter correctly) that Americans need to fear, because America is so fast on its way to your so-called "working concept of socialism." Not only socialism, but communism.

I leave you with one last bit of evidence to ponder: Communist Rules for Revolution (captured at Dusseldorf in May 1919, by Allied Forces).

1. Corrupt the young; get them away from religion. Get them interested in sex. Make them superficial; destroy their ruggedness.

2. By specious argument, cause the breakdown of the old moral virtues: honesty, sobriety, continence, faith in the pledged word, ruggedness.

3. Encourage civil disorder and foster a lenient and soft attitude on the part of the government toward such disorders (L.A. riots)?

4. Divide the people into hostile groups by constantly harping on controversial matters of no importance. (race)?

5. Get the people's mind off their government by focusing their attention on athletics, sexy books, plays, and other trivialities.

6. Get control of all means of publicity. (media)?

7. Destroy the people's faith in their natural leaders by holding the latter up to contempt, ridicule, and obloquy. (disgrace)

8. Cause the registration of all firearms on some pretext with a view to confiscation and leaving the population helpless. (gun control)?

Americans, are we being brainwashed into giving up our rights.

Jennifer McVeigh
6289 Campbell Boulevard

Jennifer cares about society as a whole, and does not want to see her country make the mistakes of others in history. But other than her debatable gun-control concerns, Jennifer follows the same paranoid belief that the government has a hand in every aspect of people's lives, and forces them to behave in such manners. She lists unrelated occurrences and perceived controls as being a part of the American government's agenda to rule. Jennifer suggests that the Los Angeles riots (a time period her brother was upset about, as detailed in a letter to military buddy Albert Warnement) were encouraged or tolerated by the U.S. government, when in reality they rose from the initial jury verdict in the Rodney King beating case. Obviously, the government had nothing to do with the decisions of a twelve-person jury in California. Jennifer also suggests that the federal government is involved in racial tension among its citizens, and that the government is using the issue to divide and conquer the people. Federal and state governments and schools, if anything, try to encourage racial harmony. A good example of that is the Million Man March, organized by Nation of Islam leader Louis Farrakhan. Though there weren't a million men in attendance, several hundred thousand people marched on Washington, D.C., to hear a rambling, yet historically significant speech by Farrakhan. The event was held without any major problems. The federal government did not prohibit or criticize the event. The march; programs like busing and affirmative action, which encourages minorities to enter college and the work place; and new curriculums that teach histories of the many races and highlight achievements of people who had been forgotten in the past are all evidence of a government and school system that has come a long way from the foolhardy days of "separate but equal." Racism and racial tensions are handed down through generations of familial bigotry. While many politicians may be prejudiced toward race or religions, the American government itself does not, as a matter of policy, teach or encourage conflict between the races.

Jennifer further implies that the press and media in America are somehow controlled by the government. Many extreme right-wing groups often complain that the press and Hollywood are "controlled" by the government and top-level Jewish business people, not unlike the claims once promoted by Hitler himself. Though an idea encouraged by "alternative" publications such as the *Spotlight,* nothing could be further from the truth. The "press" is run by private organizations that demand the freedom to gather and publish information, and openness among agencies of government and school. In fact, states themselves have established committees on open government that argue in favor of the press when news agencies have difficulty obtaining government information. To believe that America's press is controlled by the government is to subscribe to the highest level of paranoia. This thought is encouraged by alternative presses that, like the "mainstream" presses, are just trying to sell issues and boost subscriptions.

Yet Jennifer McVeigh's views have been distorted by the misinformation used by those on the right. According to University of Central Oklahoma political science professor John George, the "Communist Rules for Revolution," which Jennifer quotes in her letter, is a fabricated document. George read the letter and contacted me to say Jennifer used phony evidence to back up her arguments. He said the "rules" were not "captured" in 1919. Instead, the "rules" were manufactured in 1946 by the British publication *New World News.*

I wrote an April 25, 1996, story for the *Union-Sun & Journal,* quoting George regarding the "rules." He said, "These people would love for the document to be real. But it has been exposed again and again as a phony."

George, and Laird Wilcox, his coauthor of *Nazis, Communists, Klansmen and Others on the Fringe,* wrote that the "rules" are a tool used by those on the right who try to gain support for their crusades. "Widely distributed since the mid-forties, the 'rules' have been trundled out at various times when they 'fit' or 'explain' the issues of the day, especially to argue against firearms control and sex education."[4]

In addition to George and Wilcox, conservative commentators like William Buckley and James Kilpatrick have said the "rules" are a forgery. During his reign, FBI Director J. Edgar Hoover even commented that the "rules" document "is spurious."

Jennifer told me after my article was published that she could not recall where she obtained the "rules." She also said that if she believed the "rules" were fake, she would not have quoted them as a source in her letter to the *Union-Sun & Journal.*

Regardless of its accuracy or absurdity, Jennifer's letter gained national attention because she was the sister of the accused bomber, and had some strong antiestablishment views. Her letter was even displayed by a western New York high school teacher to his students. They read the letter, discussed the points presented, and then the teacher revealed to students who the author was. Newspapers probed Jennifer's life and found she was a top student at a local college and she enjoyed Jell-O wrestling at a country western bar in Niagara Falls. The interest level in Jennifer's life story was high and she received financial offers from talk shows seeking interviews. She declined the offers and talked only with the *Buffalo News,* the *Union-Sun & Journal,* and *Time* magazine, among a few others.

Christopher Shearer did not handle his newfound fame as well as Jennifer McVeigh. He contacted Jennifer (before the McVeighs changed their telephone number) and talked with her briefly. But as word spread about the letters in relation to the bombing, Shearer's problems began. Shearer wrote to me:

> I spoke with Jennifer on the evening of the 25th, I believe it was. I think that I woke her up as it was around 11:30 or so. I identified myself and told her to try not to worry too much about our letters, as there could be some repercussions sometime down the road. She didn't have a clue as to what I was talking about, or so she said, as she hadn't read the *US&J* that day. It's entirely possible that she didn't, but I rather doubt it. In any event, I'm just one person who's been around this country quite a bit from the sixties through the eighties, experiencing both the good and the bad of what there was to offer. I'm reluctant to say that the bad sometimes overshadowed the positive. As you've read in some of my poems and previous letters to the editor, I'm not all that fond of the American way of life, or the American Dream as it were. The irony of all this is that I love my country. The oxymoron is that I hate what America stands for. I love money and all the rest of it more than god, yet I detest the "rules of the road" of achievement. . . . I feel as though you're hip to the fact that our country is one of the most racist, religiously intolerant institutions in the West. I was brought up correctly within the WASP environment, or should I say the privileged white American cocoon! Everything America spewed forth during the sixties, my "normal" family would at-

tempt to emulate to the letter, except for me, of course. I needn't expound on civil disobedience, Vietnam, consumerism, and on and on and on. All that "stuff" wasn't the fault of any one segment of the American family in particular, it was merely the culmination as a whole. Therefore, I just kept close with my books, refused the Draft, left the country for a while, and continued to become more and more aware and embittered with the atmosphere which continued to fester all around me. Dare I mention the Constitution, the Bill of Rights, or Communist Manifesto in the same breath? I intimidate people with my true Marxist ways and Socialist "drivel." Those who write to the "mail bag" are rather indicative of the "small town, small mind" mentality, it seems to me. So what, then, is my point? To be succinct, I believe people like me, the McVeigh family, sans Timothy, and all other innocent people involved in and around this bombing horror show might consider themselves as victims, reminiscent of the old movie adage, "round up the usual suspects," no matter who gets affected by all this guilt by association. The fact will almost always expose itself to the truth. I've had all three of my sisters phone me near tears, wondering just what the hell I did to get myself into this mess this time. I've had two anonymous crank phone calls late at night, screaming cute little expletives only to hang up on me before I could even yell one back. I've had one taxi cab sent to my house very early in the morning, which neither my girlfriend nor I summoned. I've had an "inspector" knock on my door at 8 in the morning, stating that he was to check out my apartment. I refused and called my landlord to validate this guy. He didn't have any idea, as he at no time authorized any so-called building inspector to look into my apartment for any type of violation. I've also had two friends, on two different occasions, call me from south Florida, stating that they read my name in the *Miami Herald* and on the local news. Oh well, what price fame? I feel for Kane—he's getting it from all sides. What did he do to piss off the local Gestapo FBI? Being objective can be a curse.[5]

The shock of having his name associated with the Oklahoma bombing wore heavily on Shearer, who even called me late one

night and left a message on the answering machine. He said he had
nothing to do with the blast, he had only written a letter to the
newspaper. Shearer had a point. He had presented his opinion, and
because Jennifer McVeigh mentioned him in her subsequent letter
and her brother was arrested, Shearer had been harassed and had
his name "all over" the news for a couple days. Which brings another point to light—it's likely that Tim and Jennifer's letters will
be part of Tim McVeigh's trial. His widely read thoughts will be
used in an attempt to convict him on murder charges—not to mention that his signature will be compared to the documents he signed
that were associated with the bomb. "Do we have to shed blood to
reform the current system?" is an incriminating question, surely, in
association with the terrorist act of which he's accused. Tim's opinions, which allegedly drew him to plan such an act of violence
against the government, will be used in court to find him guilty.
Since the allegation has been made that Jennifer McVeigh knew
"something" or that the bombing itself was going to happen, it's
odd that her letter to the editor arrived the month, about thirty-eight
days, before the bombing. She mentioned the Ruby Ridge and
Waco incidents, complaining of them the same way Tim had. Tim
and Jennifer's political opinions have already played a role in the
case, as Jennifer explained. She said the grand jury investigating
the bombing looked for more than just facts from her.

> Toward the end of my time [before] the grand jury, I felt like I
> was on trial. They weren't even asking me about Tim anymore.
> They were asking me my opinion on this, my opinion on that.
> . . . Now what does my opinion have to do with the facts about
> the bombing or the facts about my brother?[6]

Apparently a great deal. It was radical right opinions that pre-
sumably led to the bombing—a violent act of rage against the government in response to its "Constitution perverting" actions
against the Randy Weaver family in Idaho and the Branch Davidians in Waco, Texas.

In late April, a letter from Timothy McVeigh to New York's Democratic congressman, John LaFalce, was discovered during a records search at LaFalce's office in Niagara Falls. The letter was copied and the original was forwarded to the FBI. Because it was not typed like the previous letters, it's an excellent example of McVeigh's handwriting that the agency was happy to receive. Tim wrote the letter about "CS gas" or a chemical form of mace on February 16, 1992, and LaFalce received the letter on the nineteenth. McVeigh said in the letter that he had seen a story in the *Buffalo News* about a man who had been charged for carrying the illegal CS gas. He had apparently seen a February 9, 1992, *News* article about the arrest of the man who's apartment had been searched by police. Officers found a rocket launcher, pipe bombs, fireworks, gun powder, fuses, homemade hand grenades, and homemade explosives. Instructions on how to make explosives were also found. The man, accused of building an illegal arsenal, eventually pleaded guilty to a lesser charge and was fined $200 in Niagara Falls City Court. The man's name is close to one of the names McVeigh and Terry Nichols allegedly used as an alias in September and October of 1994 when they bought fifty-pound bags of ammonium nitrate. The grand jury says the two used the false name "Mike Havens" to purchase the bomb-making materials. Here is the complete text of the letter:

16FEB92

Dear Mr. LaFalce,

Recently, I saw an article in the *Buffalo News* that detailed a man's arrest; one of the charges being "possession of a noxious substance" (CS gas).

This struck my curiosity, so I went to the New York State penal law. Sure enough, section 270 prohibits possession of any noxious substance, and included in section 265 is a ban on the use of "stun guns."

Now I am male, and fully capable of physically defending myself, but how about a female?

I strongly believe in a God-given right to self-defense. Should any other person or a governing body be able to tell another person that he/she cannot save their own life, because it would be a violation of a law?

In this case, which is more important! Faced with a rapist/murderer, would you pick to

(a) die, a law-abiding citizen or

(b) live, and go to jail?

It is a lie if we tell ourselves that the police can protect us everywhere, at all times.

I am in shock that a law exists which denies a woman's right to self-defense. Firearms restrictions are bad enough, but now a woman can't even carry mace in her purse?!?!

> Tim McVeigh
> 6289 Campbell Boulevard
> Lockport, N.Y.
> 14094

In a slick move to gather some local and national press, Rep. LaFalce released the letter to newspapers on May 2, 1995. It was widely published, not necessarily because of the content (McVeigh by now was known for his opposition to gun control), but instead because it clearly showed McVeigh's printed handwriting. And again, he showed concern for the protection of his fellow man. LaFalce, a zealous gun-restriction advocate, claimed some other letters he receives from those opposed to weapons control are more "threatening." The congressman told the *Buffalo News*:

> Frequently, the letters I get are obnoxious or somewhat threatening. This letter (from McVeigh) was neither. (It does) show a number of interesting things about McVeigh, such as his preoccupation with the right to bear arms and noxious substances. [It's] tame compared to some of the letters I get. Some are threatening. They threaten the lives of individuals who would pass some legislation regarding gun control.[7]

Psychologists who studied McVeigh's other letters saw a man with a paranoid distrust of authority and—a macabre suggestion—that the writer, McVeigh, had an ability to rationalize his actions, any action, to meet a goal. Dr. N. G. Berrill is a forensic psychologist and a professor at John Jay College of Criminal Justice in New York. Dr. Berrill told Reuters news service that the man who wrote "Do we have to shed blood to reform the current system?" is somebody who "is capable of considering events and working things out so he can justify his behavior." Reuters quoted another psychologist, speaking on condition of anonymity, that the letters by McVeigh show "a paranoid distrust of all authority figures. He has to gird himself against authorities, [he] literally arms himself."[8] Perhaps the most observant and insightful views of the content of McVeigh's letters came from two authorities quoted by Susan Schulman of the *Buffalo News*. Jay Albanese, criminal justice director at Niagara University, said McVeigh is lost in a right-wing tunnel.

> It sounds like a young person looking for a philosophy. One letter reads like a typical call to Rush Limbaugh. This is a young guy. He probably never had to pay taxes, except withholding taxes, and he hasn't had many jobs in his life. It's unusual for someone at that age to get excited about economic concerns, and political concerns to the extent that the letters suggest. He's not a college student, and Niagara County is not a hotbed of radical thought. The question is what was he doing to get those ideas? What went on in his military experience? Who was he hanging out with?

The *Buffalo News* also quoted University of Buffalo political science professor Claude Welch, Jr., who has specialized in the study of terrorism. He said McVeigh supports "a litany of widespread complaints about the political system" and has a sense that "politics is the problem" that cannot be repaired by its own, tainted conductors. "[McVeigh] seems unwilling to allow politicians any benefit of [the] doubt because he's concerned by what he considers their self-serving nature."[9] In that accusation, McVeigh is not far off, when congressmen bring home $100,000 a year and have a million-dollar war chest in the bank courtesy of political action committees. McVeigh's father is likely paid about $55,000 a year, almost half of which goes to taxes to pay people like Congressman John LaFalce.

Three days after Timothy McVeigh's letters were revealed, the national media deserted the western New York area, with destinations like Arizona, Michigan, and Kansas, trying to grab each detail of the lives of the men allegedly involved in the Oklahoma massacre. The BBC and a second reporter from the *Washington Post* followed the media's caboose in visits to Lockport, New York. The media scrutiny had ended for one year until April 19, 1996, when the one-year anniversary of the bombing would inspire news directors to follow up the many stories they'd gained from Tim's hometown.

Chapter 9

Before the Trial

It was the United States that gave him the uniform he wore, and the sword by his side. I only explain to the reader why he damned his country, and wished he might never hear her name again.

—Edward Everett Hale*

For a weary month and a half in 1995, Oklahoma City was the city of funerals. The Murrah monolith stood as a ghostlike reminder of a time when residents felt safe in America, before their faith in humanity was replaced with doubt and fear. Wind, memories, and specters from the past whistled through the half walls and twisted floors of the structure. The evidence of what had destroyed the building, golf ball-sized remains of the Ryder truck and pieces of blue barrels that housed the explosives, had all been removed by federal investigators for use in the trials of Timothy McVeigh and

---

*Edward Everett Hale, *The Man Without a Country* (New York City Board of Education, 1951).

221

Terry Nichols. Shards of the barrels had even been found in some victims' bodies as they symbolically told the tale of their fate and pointed at their killers.

On May 21, a group of people hired by McVeigh's defense team trooped through the Murrah ruins. An explosives expert, an architect, and a camera crew, all wearing gray hard hats and long clothing, quietly peered into the rubble through massive holes in the building's walls. They took pictures of the damaged structure that was for now a tomb for possibly three victims who could not easily be removed. The bodies of Christy Rosas, twenty-two, of Moore, Oklahoma, and Virginia Thompson, forty, of El Reno, were believed to be entombed in an area of the building marked with orange paint. Both women were Federal Credit Union employees. Alvin Justes, fifty-four, who frequented the credit union, was also believed to be trapped at the site. The defense inspection team was not alone at the site. Adults, people with video cameras and children, accompanied by dogs, clustered around the looming shell of a building, taking a final long look. A memorial service had been held May 6 as rescue workers had completed their search. The service had attracted three thousand people, many of whom had already attended the funerals of their relatives. Federal, state, and local officials at the base of the structure were greeted by standing ovations that lasted up to fifteen minutes. At the building's west end a temporary memorial to the dead was decorated by hundreds of floral wreaths, cards, plaques, letters, and teddy bears. On a slab of displaced concrete someone had spray painted "Bless the Children and the Innocent." Governor Keating stood on a piece of plywood, near the site where the bomb had been placed seventeen days ago. He looked toward the sky to say:

> We know that those who died behind us are with you. We ask that the lessons of the last two weeks not be forgotten. The magnitude of the loss and the madness cannot be described with words. We cannot imagine that one human being could do this to another human being.[1]

On May 21, lawyer Stephen Jones's inspection team took its final look at the building. Federal prosecutors had agreed to give Jones and his researchers until midnight Sunday to inspect the ruins. Jones said the inspection was to understand "the dynamics of the bomb" and "understand the physics of the explosion." Jones told the *Tulsa World* newspaper:

> There needs to be a separate record from that of the government. There is a criminal litigation and civil litigation. All sides will need a record, and the government's record wouldn't necessarily be available.[2]

The remainder of the Alfred P. Murrah Building would be torn down on Tuesday, May 23, relieving the city of its constant reminder that an attack had occurred, its family members died, and a man who many considered a "cold monster" sat in a local jail waiting for his American right to a trial by a jury of his peers. While the long journey into night would end for Oklahoma's citizens at 7:01 A.M. central time, May 23, Timothy McVeigh's walk toward meeting some survivors in a courtroom was just beginning.

In late April, McVeigh's first court-appointed attorneys had asked that they be removed from the case. Prior to the entrance of Stephen Jones to the case, John W. Coyle, III, had been asked by his assistant, federal public defender Susan Otto, to take on the role of defending the man at whom every Oklahoman was seemingly mad. Without fully considering it, Coyle agreed. He even met with McVeigh in jail just days after the suspect was arrested. McVeigh was initially housed in a cell that had thick glass walls eight feet high, and Coyle had to shout through the glass so McVeigh could hear him.

There were many reasons why Coyle asked to withdraw: his friend, golfing buddy, and law partner, Gloyd McCoy, had been one of the five hundred injured in the blast; Coyle knew federal agents and court workers still listed as "missing"; and Coyle's own family had been threatened. During a press conference on April 24 in his Oklahoma City office, Coyle sat before any questions were asked while his aides took two framed photos of his wife and children off the walls and turned away family photos on his bookshelves so the television cameras could not capture those who'd been threatened. Plainclothes security officers even accompanied John Coyle at the conference. He said any Oklahoma lawyer or judge would have difficulty taking on the case, due to the circumstances. He was right. McVeigh and any others arrested with him had touched a whole city, with ties that bled out through the entire state. Otto and Coyle also asked that a U.S. Court of Appeals judge in Denver move the case to another court. Coyle said at the press conference:

> We are not concerned about the fairness of Oklahomans. We have fair judges, fair jurors. But this is too much to ask of any grand juror, any trial juror. I've never seen anyone in my legal lifetime—I've been a lawyer twenty-one years—(who) needs a lawyer more than this young man [McVeigh] does now.[3]

John Coyle's request was denied initially. So he accompanied McVeigh to a Thursday, April 27 preliminary hearing at the Federal Correctional Facility near El Reno. McVeigh, wearing a wrinkled white T-shirt, khaki drawstring pants, and canvas slippers, sat with his hands shackled to his waist. He sat closely between Susan Otto and John Coyle as the three faced U.S. Magistrate Ronald L. Howland. FBI Agent John Hersley testified that the agency had a witness who saw McVeigh and another man speeding away in a car from the Murrah building on April 19, "obviously in an effort to avoid the bomb blast."[4] Hersley said the witness claimed McVeigh, identified from a composite drawing, and another man were in a yellow Mercury Marquis, which sped from an alley north of the building, prior to the explosion. Another witness,

Hersley said, saw McVeigh driving a yellow Ryder truck and stopping to ask for directions to Fifth Street and Harvey sometime after 8:30 A.M. April 19. Hersley continued that McVeigh was suspected of being involved in the lighting of the fuse because chemical traces, commonly used in detonator cord, were found on a shirt seized from McVeigh that was later tested in a Washington, D.C., lab.

McVeigh was calm during the four-hour hearing. He actively conferred with Mr. Coyle and co-counsel Otto at times, and once laughed along with many spectators when a court reporter returned late from a break. Otto, an older woman with glasses, restated her and Coyle's request to be removed from the case. She emphasized her point by reading a list of ten people she'd known who perished in the blast and another who was listed as "missing." Otto pleaded, "We heard it; we smelled it; we lived through it." Otto and Coyle had also asked for a change of venue, but federal prosecutor Merrick Garland argued that it was too early to move the case as the grand jury proceedings would need to be in the city. Garland was quoted in the *Daily Oklahoman*:

> At least at this time, it is inappropriate to transfer venue. Rules of change of venue apply to change of venue for purposes of trial. It did not apply to change of venue for purposes of the grand jury. We are having a grand jury here, which is the locale of the crime.[5]

At the end of the hearing, U.S. Magistrate Howland agreed with the prosecutor, declining a change of venue and ordering Otto and Coyle to continue their service for McVeigh—he would need them. Howland ordered McVeigh held for trial as there was an "indelible trail" of evidence placing McVeigh in Junction City, Kansas, where the truck was rented, and ending up "at the front door of the Murrah building." Howland wrote the following in a portion of his decision:

It is true that an extensive amount of media coverage has accompanied the bombing of the Murrah building. This circum-
stance alone, however, is insufficient to warrant a change of
venue, especially at this preliminary, and narrowly focused,
stage of the proceedings.

Meanwhile, the FBI was still combing the country for more
clues, evidence, and other suspects. Soldiers at Fort Riley, Kansas,
found themselves the subjects of the probe because McVeigh had
spent so much of his short life there. Charlie Company found its
reputation tarnished by the bad press surrounding Public Enemy
Number One. McVeigh's arrest and the media's biographical
frenzy was the third major hit to the regiment in seven weeks. On
March 2, Private First Class Maurice Wilford, a twenty-year-old
Cleveland native, shot three officers before turning a shotgun on
himself. In the end, three soldiers were dead and one wounded.
Wilford had reportedly been angry with his supervisor. On April
6, tragedy struck again. Soldier Brian Stoutenburg, a twenty-four-
year-old from Grand Blanc, Michigan, was found dead in his
quarters after an apparent suicide. And now the ordeal of Timothy
McVeigh.

Kingman, Arizona, and Pendleton, New York, were invaded
by groups of agents followed by the press. Reporters with camera
crews attended services at the Good Shepherd Church, as well as
bingo games and a picnic. Journalists went door-to-door and to
Starpoint School to ask questions like, "How do you feel knowing that the accused Oklahoma bomber is from your hometown?"
A tireless worker and respected leader, Pendleton Town Supervisor Shirley Conner said the media crush on the town was almost
too much for the plain folk to handle. Conner was quoted in the
Union-Sun & Journal:

Everywhere we went, someone was shoving a microphone into
your face. I was ashamed that the Pendleton name was brought
into it. The residents of Pendleton are innocent. Our hearts went

out to the people of Oklahoma. This is a good town, a growing town. We don't need this.[6]

Like many communities directly affected by the bombing, groups rallied in Pendleton to raise money for the victims' funds established in Oklahoma. A run was conducted by Starpoint athletes; 1969 Starpoint graduate Rickie Moje conducted an alumni fundraiser; and in Lockport the YMCA, U-Save, and the Surplus Center joined for a car wash and athletic demonstration for the Oklahoma Relief Fund. DeSales Catholic School, where Bill McVeigh and Mickey Hill graduated years ago, began an elementary student letter-writing campaign and donated their ice-cream money to the victims. Third-grade student Brian Shipley wrote the following letter, which was published in the *Union-Sun & Journal*:

> Dear Mayor of Oklahoma City,
>
> I feel so sorry for you because you had so much on your mind even before the bomb. You also had to see a lot of people lose their lives. Our class has been praying for everyone who lost their lives. I hope there are more survivors. I hope the city will get back together.[7]

The FBI and media attention given to Jennifer McVeigh increased during the month when it was learned that agents who located her either in Florida or Pendleton (the locale was not revealed) found her burning papers on a barbecue grill. Of course, the report was leaked to the *Dallas Morning News* by an unnamed law enforcement source. At this early date in the investigation, lawmen were unsure how credible Jennifer McVeigh would be as a witness. The source was quoted as saying, "You're talking about a woman who burned her papers on the first day we met her." The *Dallas Morning News* did not reveal what type of papers Jennifer was allegedly burning. Later, grand jury testimony from Jennifer's

Florida friend Dennis Sadler would note that after the bombing Jennifer burned a letter or letters in his garage. Jennifer testified that on April 21, she gave thirty-six letters from Timothy to her friend Rose Francis Woods. In the post-bombing madness, Jennifer McVeigh apparently tried her best to erase the close relationship she had with her brother. She also testified that Tim had once written to her that "something big is going to happen in the month of the bull," or April as identified by the mythical zodiac calendar year. Agents also said Timothy confided in Jennifer that he had been experimenting with explosives and had transported them in his car, once nearly getting into an accident. Worried that the FBI was building a case against her also, Jennifer requested help from two top lawyers in Buffalo, Joel Daniels and Andrew LoTempio. Daniels told the *Buffalo News* on May 8 that he and LoTempio agreed to defend her, if necessary.

> She definitely has some concerns about where the investigation is going. She has been cooperating with the FBI since her brother was arrested. She has talked to them extensively. But at this time, she felt it was best she consult an attorney. Since being retained by her on Sunday, I have spoken to the FBI and also to the deputy attorney general in Oklahoma City, who is in charge of the investigation. We're hopeful there will be no charges, but I don't think they've ruled it out entirely. We have to wait and see. It doesn't appear to me that she will be caught up in the web of this thing.[8]

On May 9, one hundred teachers, employees, and students gathered for a forum at Niagara County Community College to discuss the Oklahoma City tragedy. Jennifer McVeigh's enrollment in classes there forced the college into the international spotlight. The forum focused on many issues, including the initial sentiment that the bombing culprits were from a foreign country. NCCC Dean of Institutional Advancement Jane Haenle, a former reporter for the *Union-Sun & Journal* and a graduate of Kent

State, said she fielded calls from the media about Jennifer once her political "letter to the editor" was made public. Haenle said the forum was to talk about the bombing itself, not NCCC's distant connection.

> It was not about NCCC. It wasn't really about the McVeigh family or Jennifer McVeigh. It was a much broader picture than that. The college holds numerous forums each year on national issues and international issues. With this subject, we talked about how we as a country had looked immediately to a foreign influence and not that the bomber could be from America.[9]

On May 15, investigators speaking on the condition of anonymity told the *Buffalo News* that Jennifer McVeigh's status was somewhere between being considered a witness and that of a conspiracy suspect. How much she knew was unknown. Federal authorities were looking at more than twenty letters Tim had sent to Jennifer; some included incriminating information. Of Jennifer, the unidentified source told the *Buffalo News*:

> The FBI believes she knew ahead of time that something big was going to happen. But whether she knew a bomb was going to be exploded in Oklahoma City . . . that's an open question. She's a 'tweener. Is she a suspect or just a witness? Right now, I don't think the feds know what to do with her.[10]

On Thursday, May 25, Jennifer was fingerprinted to comply with a request by the grand jury. A *Buffalo News* report two days later about the fingerprinting quoted the source as saying that Jennifer had made defiant remarks to investigators after her brother was charged. The source claimed Jennifer "even told that, in her opinion, there might be another bombing someday, because of Waco." But the source was noncommittal about the fingerprints. "Prints can be standard investigative technique."

*   *   *

Requests by John Coyle and Susan Otto to be removed from the
McVeigh case were finally granted in May because both attorneys
knew those who had been injured or died. In addition to the hearing tying McVeigh to the bombing, his friend Michael Fortier had
been subpoenaed to appear before the grand jury. To avoid the
death penalty, Fortier agreed to testify against McVeigh. Now the
government had a witness who had known McVeigh for many
years, a man who would likely be believed by the jury in the upcoming trial, because he knew McVeigh so well. During the May
plea bargain negotiations, Fortier gave federal authorities the
smoking gun they were looking for. He said that he and McVeigh
went to Oklahoma city to case the Murrah building as a target for
the bombing. That statement, in addition to testimony from people who claimed they saw McVeigh on April 19, tied the main suspect directly to the building. But the trial was months away, and
this piece of prosecution information had been directly leaked to
the media on or near May 30. The leaks were making the job of
the defense even harder because with each disclosure of information potential defense witnesses were likely to shy from defending McVeigh and Nichols, who were looking more guilty with
each prosecution "source" story that appeared in the newspapers.
Nichols's lawyer, Michael Tigar, filed a motion in June asking that
the leaks stop. He said in part:

> In this case, one abuse has bred another. The government claims
> the right to inquire at leisure and leak at will. The leaks are
> timed and spaced to poison the well of justice in every poten-
> tial venue from Michigan, to Kansas, to Nevada, to Oklahoma.

Now that Coyle and Otto were gone, U.S. District Judge
David Russell appointed well-known criminal attorney Stephen
Jones of Enid, Oklahoma, to represent McVeigh. A longtime

ACLU lawyer, Jones is respected in top legal circles, according to Morris Dees from the Southern Poverty Law Center of Montgomery, Alabama. Dees called Jones a "brilliant defense lawyer." Jones, fifty-four, agreed to take a taxpayer-funded fee of $125 an hour to defend the most hated man in America, a rate well below his usual fee. A Republican, Stephen Jones ran against Oklahoma Senator David Boren in 1990, but lost by a large margin. Jones's office, located in the tallest building in Enid, is decorated with photographs of such prominent Republicans as Abraham Lincoln and Richard Nixon. He has also worked as special counsel to Governor Frank Keating in Oklahoma. A father of four children, Jones has said he likes to spend his free time reading and plans to return to his normal practice in Enid after the Oklahoma bombing trial is completed.

To aid him in effectively researching the case, Jones brought on Richard Burr—another high-profile attorney—to the McVeigh case. Burr, who visited me in Lockport as part of his McVeigh research, has an office in Houston, Texas. He had devoted much of his career to death row inmate appeals. Burr has been a federal public defender and, at one time, directed the Capital Punishment Project of the NAACP legal defense fund, before being named litigation director of the Texas Resource Center, a now-defunct organization that was federally funded to gather information, review cases, and provide assistance to federal court reviews of state-imposed death sentences. He was familiar with McVeigh's home area since he worked for a few years at a law firm handling civil cases in Rochester, New York, about two hours away from Pendleton. Burr also practiced in Florida.

In an Associated Press report, Burr said of the McVeigh case, "From the very beginning, you have to plan the defense as if there were two parts of the trial—the guilt and innocence phase and the penalty phase." There was no question of Burr's ability as a lawyer to work on such a case as McVeigh's. On April 20, the day after the bombing, Attorney General Janet Reno said the United

States would seek the death penalty for those responsible for the bombing. A similar statement from President Clinton followed shortly thereafter. "Justice will be swift, certain, and severe," Clinton said. In July, Burr blasted the government's initial call for the death penalty, saying both Reno and Clinton had violated McVeigh's constitutional right to due process by making "the premature decision" to seek such a punishment.

In a July 4, 1995, letter to me, Richard Burr said the McVeigh defense team had hired private investigator Lee Norton to help develop a life history of Timothy McVeigh by interviewing his friends and associates. Burr asked that I share the biographical information on McVeigh that I had compiled. So, as a responsible journalist, I requested an exchange: I would provide information they needed if I was granted an interview with their client. I was not a friend of Tim McVeigh's and he didn't know me. I certainly had an interest in his life story, but no interest in aiding his defense. That was why an exchange of information between our two parties would be an honest way for me to obtain the interview I needed and for the defense to gather the additional information it certainly needed. This mutually beneficial exchange was not meant to be. My literary agent's attorney forwarded my formal request for an interview to Richard Burr on July 13, 1995. Burr finally responded on September 12, saying in a brief letter that the case was too sensitive to allow the access to McVeigh that I needed. From that date, this book became an unauthorized biography.

Jones and Burr were joined early on by former Tulsa public defender Rob Nigh, also of Enid. Nigh worked for several years as a Tulsa County public defender and for three years as an assistant federal public defender. In 1994, Nigh became the chief federal defender in Lincoln, Nebraska.

Jones told the Associated Press in late May that his defense of McVeigh was a calling.

I didn't take it for the money, and I didn't take it to have fifteen minutes of fame. Lawyers have a duty to represent clients who are unpopular. This is a call to duty, and I didn't know anyone who was in the [Murrah] building.[11]

From the start, Stephen Jones actively attempted to change McVeigh's public image. The original perception of McVeigh was that gleaned only from the tape of him being led from the courthouse in Oklahoma, when his face held no expression and his big blue eyes squinted in perceived defiance, but were apparently just blinded by the sunlight. His personality, according to the federal authorities quoted in initial reports, was that of a man who gave only his rank and serial number and considered himself a prisoner of war. As an efficient lawyer, Jones knew he had to change that image if anyone in the country was ever going to look at McVeigh objectively.

After numerous El Reno jail meetings with McVeigh, Jones began telling the press that McVeigh was a victim of mistreatment by his captors. Jones told *Newsweek* magazine in May 1995 that officials who transferred McVeigh from Noble County Courthouse had disconnected telephone lines when Tim tried to call a lawyer. This odd claim was accompanied by another allegation from Jones that McVeigh had requested a bulletproof vest before being transferred, but the request was denied. "It was like they were hoping Jack Ruby would come out," Jones was quoted as saying. Noble County Undersheriff Raymond Henry was quick to insist that both of Jones's claims were untrue.[12] Jones also criticized his client's living quarters at El Reno, where a twenty-four-hour surveillance camera was set up. Jones testified at a hearing to ask that the camera be removed.

I see the camera as simply an attempt to engage in a kind of psychological warfare and I think, ultimately, perhaps, would have an effect on [McVeigh's] mental stability, which might in turn affect the trial.[13]

Jones also told the U.S. magistrate that he would have Timothy's mental and physical health examined to be sure McVeigh was competent to stand trial. He said he had no reason to doubt McVeigh's mental health because the inmate had not been unruly or threatened suicide. The camera was later turned off for four hours a day, partially complying with Jones's wishes.

As Jones pondered ways to make Timothy McVeigh shine, and the families of the bombing victims continued grieving the loss of their loved ones, the announcement came that the time had come for the damaged Alfred P. Murrah building to be demolished. The date to tear down the remainder of the structure was set for Tuesday, May 23. The federal court in Oklahoma allowed Jones to send in a group of experts to inspect the building and film the site so he could have his own record of the Murrah's remains. On Monday, one day before the planned implosion of the federal building, Terry Nichols's brother, James, was released from custody in Detroit. U.S. District Judge Paul Borman said at the hearing for Nichols, "There is not one iota of evidence that he is a danger to others." Nichols had been held since April 22 on charges that he had made small bombs at his home in Decker. But, the judge ordered James Nichols to limit his travel to the vicinity of his hometown and barred him from obtaining a passport.

At 7:01 A.M. central time, Tuesday, May 25, the Murrah Federal Building was finally leveled by explosives strategically placed in its shell by Controlled Demolition. Relatives of victims watched at a safe distance from the site or on television at their homes. The building collapsed into itself in a cloud of gray dust. Over a hundred pounds of dynamite was used (much less than the 4,800-pound bomb that had killed 168 people a month earlier) and the structure was turned to a heap of rubble. The crowd left the area quickly. In silence, staffers at the *Union-Sun & Journal* watched the network news coverage of the implosion at 8:01 A.M. eastern standard time. Memories of the terror in the faces of those at the site on April 19 were clear, as were the visions of Timothy

McVeigh being marched from the courthouse in Perry; the media camped out at Bill McVeigh's Pendleton house; Terry Nichols being led away in Kansas, wearing a bulletproof vest and handcuffs; and the discovery of Tim's letter about shedding blood to "reform the current system." Each of these images accompanied our recollections of the victims, their faces streaming with blood like tears in the sunny Oklahoma morning.

As part of projecting a better image of McVeigh, it is strongly suspected that Stephen Jones was the one who informed Gannett News Service, owners of *USA Today,* that McVeigh had been receiving a lot of mail in El Reno since he was placed there. On June 9, it was made known that McVeigh had received two marriage proposals, cash, and religious artifacts as part of his large stream of letters. Jones told Gannett that fifty cards and letters arrived for Tim at El Reno each day, from all over the country. He also claimed that "half" the correspondence was supportive, with indications of contempt for government bureaucracy. Jones said:

> The marriage proposals are kind of strange, but people have sent Bibles and other mementoes along with notes of support. Some of these people have very antigovernment views. They will write and say they believe the feds were responsible. One of the more radical said something like, "If you did it, right on." Others either wish him the worst or don't indicate their preferences one way or another, except to say they hope he is able to get a fair trial.[14]

A few weeks later, *Harper's* magazine picked up the story on marriage proposals and listed the fact in its renowned "Index." *Harper's* said that by that time, McVeigh had received four proposals. Like McVeigh, the *Union-Sun & Journal* began getting all kinds of strange letters from around the country, an obvious response to the news stories about McVeigh writing to the Lockport newspaper. A great many of the letters and much of the information we received came from people who believed there was some type of conspiracy by the government to blow up one of its own buildings in Oklahoma. One man said the U.S. intelligence community employs "provocateurs" who meet people like McVeigh and encourage them to commit acts of violence against America. Then politicians have reason to impose stricter laws against the people to protect them from terrorists and ultimately to disarm the citizens. This same individual also forwarded a copy of the children's book *Chicken Little* to the newspaper to somehow illustrate his point. Other Amerinoids who wrote to the *Union-Sun & Journal* made various claims about the identity of John Doe #2: he was from Lyndonville, New York, a small town forty miles from Pendleton; he was actually a Kentucky federal prisoner claiming the FBI was responsible for the Los Angeles riots; or a Montana woman claiming that the government wishes to execute white Anglo-Saxon Protestants lawfully.

Stephen Jones's next effort in his campaign to polish McVeigh's public image was to release a different view of the twenty-seven-year-old by having professional photographers highlight his boyish charm on film. In late May, Eddie Adams of *Newsweek* was permitted to meet with McVeigh at El Reno. Some of the photographs captured a young, innocent-looking McVeigh, while others were eerie, haunting portraits that invite the viewer to gaze into McVeigh's deep blue eyes and wonder, "How could you do it?" In many of the photos, McVeigh is smiling or laughing. David Hackworth, a reporter from *Newsweek* and a former military colonel, was permitted to interview McVeigh at length, also in May. The July 3 story contained only a few sparse quotes from McVeigh and basically rehashed a lot of previously released information about the case. In fact, the story Hackworth wrote and the ensuing publicity seemed to be more of a *Newsweek*/Hackworth promotional campaign than an exclusive story about McVeigh.

Jones said in the opening of the story, titled "The Suspect Speaks Out," that his client is "the boy next door. A boy wonder."

He was also quoted as saying in regard to Tim, "He's innocent." The article did not specify exactly what McVeigh is innocent of, but the reader was left to believe that McVeigh was innocent of the charge of being the Oklahoma bomber. Yet Tim himself did not say that, and if Jones's statement was indeed true, wouldn't McVeigh want to back it up in his own words? When asked if he bombed the building, McVeigh offered merely, "The only way we can answer that is that we are going to plead not guilty." Other than that, the article revealed few if any facts about McVeigh's life. Instead, it allowed Tim to cover up the hurtful and controversial facts about his life. About his parents' bitter divorce, Tim claimed, "There's nothing there"; and about his failure to gain entrance into the Army Special Forces, he claimed, "It wasn't the straw that broke anything."[15] From the research gathered for this biography, both of these innocuous quotes seem to stray far from the truth. But Hackworth apparently took the statements at face value and *Newsweek* printed them, allowing suspect number one to recede into the murky shadows a few months more. On the public relations campaign, Stephen Jones hoped the masses would believe what he told the Associated Press:

> The FBI wants to present [Timothy McVeigh] as they see him. I want to present him as he really is. The public is entitled to know more about Mr. McVeigh than the government has released anonymously.[16]

Reaction to the story and photographs was not good, especially in Oklahoma City. The Associated Press quoted at least two people uninterested in McVeigh's "good" army record and whether he was a friendly person. A June 27 report from the Associated Press said many were "insulted" by the photos of McVeigh smiling. Janet Walker's husband, David, a Housing and Urban Development environmental specialist, was killed in the blast. Mrs. Walker said of the McVeigh image promotion:

They can't make him innocent by putting a smile on his face, and they can't make him guilty until they convict him. It's nothing more than a ploy. I know that. He'll get his in the end, if he's guilty.[17]

Glenn Wilburn lost his two grandsons, Chase and Colton Smith, in the bombing. The two-year-old and three-year-old boys had been in the day-care center when the bomb exploded. Wilburn first saw Tim on television as McVeigh was being led from the Oklahoma courthouse. "The image I hold is the image of him in Perry. There was evil in that boy's eyes. Pure evil. It's clear that this is just posturing."[18]

Stephen Jones attempted to block a July grand jury request that McVeigh provide a handwriting sample in cursive (script). Special Assistant U.S. Attorney Sean Connelly said cursive and print handwriting samples were needed for a "full handwriting analysis." The grand jury wanted to compare McVeigh's handwriting in his letters to the *Union-Sun & Journal* and to Congressman LaFalce with the writing on other, unidentified documents believed to have been penned by McVeigh. The grand jury directive asked that McVeigh write in cursive, three or four sentences; fill out a handwriting specimen form; and copy a list of fifteen undisclosed names. Jones suggested that the prosecution hoped to compare the samples with the rental agreement for the Ryder truck, and with other materials. Jones argued that McVeigh normally printed his words (as evidenced in the letter to Congressman LaFalce) and refused to provide the sample. He claimed that to comply with the prosecution's request would make McVeigh perform "an act that requires a thinking process," which could make him incriminate himself in violation of his Fifth Amendment rights.[19] In response to Jones's argument, Chief U.S. District Judge David Russell ordered the attorneys to submit briefs in preparation for a contempt hearing, apparently regarding McVeigh's refusal.

In line with something McVeigh might believe, Jones further complained that federal officials were listening in on talks attorneys had with McVeigh at El Reno. Jones also said in filed papers that his own telephones at his Enid office were tapped by the government. Prosecutor Sean Connelly denied any illegal surveillance by federal officials.

A *Washington Post* report that day said Jennifer McVeigh provided two lengthy statements to the FBI. She reportedly said her brother had been in Pendleton in November 1994 and asked her to exchange two $100 bills from a bank robbery that had occurred that year, according to the report.

Attorney General Janet Reno's premature statement about seeking the death penalty still hung over her head as July drew to a close. It was a media thorn in the side of U.S. Attorney Patrick Ryan, who eventually had to make the recommendation on whether to seek that punishment for McVeigh and Nichols, before the two men went to trial. Ryan's penalty recommendation would be reviewed by a committee that reports to Reno, who has the final say. Ryan attempted to stand his ground when the question was raised despite the nation's top prosecutor forecasting an outcome of the charges before the trial was even held; despite defense attorneys questioning Reno's objectivity in the case; and in the face of heavy media scrutiny that the case—far more touching and heinous than the Simpson murders—had attracted. (Terry Nichols's lawyer, Michael Tigar, had even called for Reno and Ryan to step aside.) Ryan, claiming he felt no pressure at all, was quoted by the Associated Press: "The fact of the matter is that I haven't been pressured by anyone on this issue and don't anticipate that I will be. I'm going to make my decision based on what is just and right."[20]

Janet Reno's April 20 statement, the enormity of the crime itself, and the amount of people affected illustrated just how precedent-setting the case would eventually be. Never before had Americans allegedly waged such an attack on their own soil, an attack that had killed so many and affected the future of the city and the U.S. legal statutes on how similar crimes would be treated in the future. Each development in the Oklahoma bombing case was history in the making. Prosecutors were waving their arms in the air, trying to figure out what to do, while trying to maintain a veil of calm at the same time.

The massive scale of the crime and the ensuing government action gave defense attorneys many opportunities to poke holes in the investigation and the case. For example, the question of where the eventual trial would be held hovered over the investigation. The Oklahoma City courthouse was right across the street from the Murrah building and had also been rocked in the blast, and the defendants might not get a fair trial in the city where the crime occurred because an objective jury could not be chosen from Oklahoma residents. But, if the trial were to be moved out of Oklahoma City, then many family members of the victims might not be able to attend the proceedings to watch or to testify. Stephen Jones suggested Charleston, West Virginia; Portland, Oregon; and other places for the trial, while Patrick Ryan said survivors of the bombing could not travel that far. The venue questions would remain for at least seven more months.

The defense for McVeigh took another punch at the prosecution on July 24. Richard Burr said that Janet Reno's remarks about seeking the death penalty "made a charade of justice," according to the Associated Press. Burr made a motion to bar Reno from making the final decision on the death penalty, since she had already announced, three months earlier and two days before suspects were arrested, what her decision would be. U.S. Attorney Patrick Ryan iterated that he felt no pressure from Attorney General Reno. Burr countered by writing to the court, "There is no way any subordinate (Ryan) in the Justice Department can defy the attorney general and the president after they have said they would seek the death penalty over and over again." Burr further suggested that the government should form an independent authority to consider what punishment McVeigh should face.[21] But Reno would soon stand firm, refusing to step down from the bombing case.

Meanwhile, in Pendleton, Jennifer McVeigh was anticipating that she'd be called to Oklahoma to testify before the grand jury and federal prosecutors. With her classes at the community college completed, Jennifer was attempting to live a normal life.* On the twenty-second and twenty-third of July, she had attended the Lollapalooza traveling rock 'n' roll show in Toronto, Canada. She even participated in the "mosh pit"† at the alternative band concert. "I got knocked around and hit in the head a couple of times, but it was fun," she told me. Jennifer had pierced her navel and inserted a gold ring, and had a lot of dirt on her pickup truck and under her fingernails from the concert. She told me that day, July 24, her future plans included classes at Buffalo State College so she could obtain a teaching degree. On July 27, her attorney Joel Daniels received a subpoena for Jennifer to testify the next week in Oklahoma. The subpoena meant Jennifer would answer grand jury questions, but was now viewed as a "friendly witness" who would not face charges like her brother. By this date, Jennifer had already been subjected to forty hours of FBI questioning. She said she was once placed in a room with photographs of dead and burned bodies from the bombing. She was threatened with the death penalty, and her mother, Mickey (McVeigh) Frazer, was subjected to similar treatment. Jennifer told *Time* magazine:

> They [the FBI] played a lot of games with me, a lot of things to get me talking. They totally broke me down. I thought I could handle it on my own. I guess I couldn't. I didn't have time to

---

*Jennifer earned four As and a D—the latter because she could not participate in a public speaking exercise as a result of the media attention she'd gained.

†A "mosh pit" is a dirt area near the front of the stage where attendees dance and bounce off each other.

think things out. It was constant pressure altogether. They put me and my mother in this room with all these huge posters with my name and a picture all blown up with all these possible charges against me . . . like life imprisonment, the death penalty, and things like that. My mother was in tears when we walked away. They just crushed her.[22]

Before testifying in Oklahoma, Jennifer was granted immunity from prosecution. With Joel Daniels at her side, Jennifer spent several hours in Special Assistant U.S. Attorney Joseph Hartzler's office. During an August 3 hearing, Chief U.S. District Judge David Russell told Jennifer she would not be indicted by the grand jury that was expected to indict her brother. "She is extremely relieved," Daniels told the *Daily Oklahoman.* Later, during a break in the grand jury proceedings, Jennifer ran into the courtroom hallway, visibly upset, and then dashed into a restroom. Reporters were held back by federal agents and Jennifer was careful to avoid their questions. Her hometown friend, Mary Butler, told me Jennifer hoped she would get to visit Tim in jail while she was in Oklahoma. But she never had the time, according to Stephen Jones. "She wanted to see him and he wanted to see her, but it was just impossible to arrange," Jones said in an Associated Press report. Jennifer was escorted by the FBI to an airport and left Oklahoma on a commercial flight, making a stop at O'Hare International Airport in Chicago, and then heading on to Buffalo.

In early August, the legal situation worsened for McVeigh and Nichols when their former friend and army associate Michael Fortier formally agreed to plead guilty to lesser charges in exchange for testifying as a government witness. Fortier's court-appointed attorney, Michael McGuire, told the *Daily Oklahoman* on August 9 that Fortier was "an important witness." The prosecution's star witness agreed to plead guilty to lying to a federal agent (when first asked, Fortier claimed no foreknowledge of the bombing plot), knowing about a felony but doing nothing to stop it, and interstate transportation of stolen weapons. McGuire said also that Fortier would admit helping to plan the April 19 bombing and that he would face twenty-three years in prison, but his sentence, under federal guidelines, was expected to be shorter. After four hours of grilling by the grand jury on August 8, Fortier completed his testimony and voluntarily agreed to be taken to a holding facility to wait for the eventual trial, thus avoiding would-be assassins and the media. A newspaper reporter from Fortier's hometown in Arizona said the government's number-one witness "virtually disappeared" after that week. Lori Fortier, Michael's wife, was granted immunity from prosecution and testified before the grand jury that Timothy McVeigh made statements regarding plans to bomb the Murrah building. Her attorney, Mack Martin, told the *Daily Oklahoman* of her status before the grand jury.

About the same time that the Fortier report was aired, claims by McVeigh attorney Stephen Jones against the government and the prosecution became more pronounced—even more so than the time he alleged that the telephone wires in his office were tapped. Jones said that a leg, found in the Murrah rubble May 30 and revealed August 7, may have been the remains of the "real bomber." It was apparent to close observers of the case that by making this statement, Jones was reaching for the kind of scenario that might lessen the charges against his client or in some odd way get McVeigh out from under the public spotlight, thereby diverting people's attention. But Jones forged on. Ray Blakeney, Chief of Operations at the Oklahoma State Medical Examiner's Office, said the limb, clad in a military-style boot, two socks, and an olive drab strap used to tuck the pants into the boot, had not been matched to any of the victims or survivors of the blast. The Associated Press first reported on August 8 that the leg was wearing "olive drab fatigues." It corrected that report on August 31, saying the fatigues were merely a "strap." The leg's existence was not actually confirmed until Jones spoke of it to reporters. Responding to questions, he attempted to tie the limb to someone involved with the bombing plot.

Once again, an agency of the government is not being candid and withholding information. Fortunately, I found out about it because of an honest cop. It certainly raises that possibility [that another culprit exists]. It just doesn't fit into the government's neat theory that they are packaging that three people, with little or no formal training in explosives, carried this off.[23]

Chief Medical Examiner Fred Jordan issued a press statement on August 7, saying that more tests needed to be conducted on the limb, but it initially appeared to be from a white male, under the age of thirty. On August 18, Roberta Bennett of Oklahoma City told KWTV-Channel 9 that the leg belonged to her son, Aaron Mc-Callum, a twenty-nine-year-old regular at the city soup kitchen. A Reuters news service report said Aaron had been dropped off at the Murrah's Social Security office just before the explosion. After a DNA test was conducted on the limb, the death toll was officially listed as 169. Both Dr. Jordan and Ms. Bennett were originally wrong in their estimations. Dr. Jordan said in a report issued near August 31 that the test on the badly decomposed leg determined that it did not match any of the seven known victims who were missing left legs. He also stated that it belonged to an unidentified black woman, between the ages of sixteen and thirty, five-feet-five-inches tall. According to Jordan's report: "An analysis by the FBI lab has shown Negroid characteristics. We believe, therefore, that the leg originates from an individual with some African ancestry." Stephen Jones told the Associated Press that he doubted the results. He also brought up the national controversy over DNA testing in the O. J. Simpson double-murder case: "With this contradictory disclosure, no one can have confidence in any of the forensic work in this case. A white male becomes a black female. No wonder DNA testing has been discredited."[24]

On August 10, U.S. officials announced that there was no broad conspiracy in the planning of the bombing, just three former army buddies who hated the government enough to take action through terrorism. As the August 11 indictment date loomed, an

FACTUAL STATEMENT IN SUPPORT OF PLEA PETITION

On December 15th and 16th I rode with Tim McVeigh from my home in Kingman, Az. to Kansas. There I was to receive weapons that Tim McVeigh told me had been stolen by Terry Nichols and himself. While in Kansas, McVeigh and I loaded about twenty-five weapons into a car that I had rented. On December 17th, 1994, I drove the rental car back to Arizona through Oklahoma and Oklahoma City. Later, after returning to Arizona and at the request of Tim McVeigh, I sold some of the weapons and again at the request of Tim McVeigh I gave him some money to give to Terry Nichols.

Prior to April 1995, McVeigh told me about the plans that he and Terry Nichols had to blow up the Federal Building in Oklahoma City, Oklahoma. I did not as soon as possible make known my knowledge of the McVeigh and Nichols plot to any judge or other persons in civil authority. When FBI agents questioned me later, about two days after the bombing and during the next three days, I lied about my knowledge and concealed information. For example, I falsely stated that I had no knowledge of plans to bomb the federal building. I also gave certain items that I had received from McVeigh, including a bag of ammonium nitrate fertilizer, to a neighbor of mine so the items would not be found by law enforcement officers in a search of my residence.

Michael Joseph Fortier

Appendage to the plea petition of Michael Fortier.

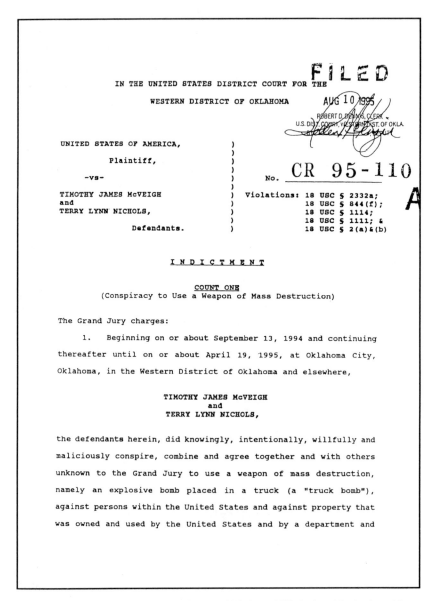

IN THE UNITED STATES DISTRICT COURT FOR THE

WESTERN DISTRICT OF OKLAHOMA   AUG 10 1995

ROBERT D. DENNIS, CLERK
U.S. DIST. COURT, WESTERN DIST. OF OKLA.
BY

UNITED STATES OF AMERICA,   )
)
          Plaintiff,   )
)
     -vs-   )   No. CR 95-110
)
TIMOTHY JAMES McVEIGH   )   Violations: 18 USC § 2332a;
and   )   18 USC § 844(f);
TERRY LYNN NICHOLS,   )   18 USC § 1114;
)   18 USC § 1111; &
          Defendants.   )   18 USC § 2(a)&(b)

A

I N D I C T M E N T

COUNT ONE
(Conspiracy to Use a Weapon of Mass Destruction)

The Grand Jury charges:

     1.   Beginning on or about September 13, 1994 and continuing

thereafter until on or about April 19, 1995, at Oklahoma City,

Oklahoma, in the Western District of Oklahoma and elsewhere,

TIMOTHY JAMES McVEIGH
and
TERRY LYNN NICHOLS,

the defendants herein, did knowingly, intentionally, willfully and

maliciously conspire, combine and agree together and with others

unknown to the Grand Jury to use a weapon of mass destruction,

namely an explosive bomb placed in a truck (a "truck bomb"),

against persons within the United States and against property that

was owned and used by the United States and by a department and

Page one of the indictment charging McVeigh and Nichols with the bombing.

anonymous federal official told Associated Press reporter Paul Queary that "there's no sense or evidence they were helped by a large conspiracy of militia types. What shaped up was just a common philosophy." The source said two men "could have accomplished" the Murrah bombing, with a materials cost of only four thousand dollars or less.

Many members of militia groups were interviewed in the probe, were chastised by President Clinton for their political views, and were finally off the hook with the federal official's announcement that few connections were found between militias and the three primary suspects. The official added that while a total of five people may have been involved in the bombing, only two did the "heavy lifting." The case would remain open-ended, he said, as the United States has five years to still bring charges in the case. And John Doe #2, if he existed, was still out there, somewhere.

Ironically, one of the 1960s icons, who'd stood for peace and love in America, died the day before. Grateful Dead singer Jerry Garcia passed away in a drug rehabilitation clinic in California. The band still had a following of many hundreds of thousands, including President Clinton, and a new cult of devotees in the twenty-something generation. McVeigh, a man from that age group, sat in an Oklahoma jail for allegedly plotting a bombing in the country that had, at one time, prided itself on seeking an inner peace. In the 1960s, civil unrest was rampant and a madman named Charles Manson thought a race war was imminent. That decade was now being mirrored in the Los Angeles riots, which upset McVeigh, and in the Oklahoma tragedy—a seemingly random response to politics in a nation thirty years older but just as tempestuous.

The eleven-page indictment for McVeigh and Nichols was made Thursday, August 10, 1995, and released to the media. The indictment charged the two with conspiracy to use a weapon of mass destruction to kill people and destroy federal property, and listed all those murdered by the blast. It also brought charges for each of the federal law enforcement officials who were killed, including six Secret Service agents. The indictment provided a chronology on how McVeigh and Nichols allegedly collected materials for the bomb, stored them, and later assembled the explosive. It also said McVeigh made telephone calls in late September 1994, looking for detonation cord and racing fuel, and that Nichols stole explosives from a storage locker in Marion, Kansas.

In a separate indictment, Michael Fortier was charged with knowing of McVeigh's and Nichols's plans and concealing the information from authorities, lying to the FBI, and involvement in a robbery that helped finance the blast. His plea of guilty found him facing a possible sentence of twenty-three years in prison and up to $1 million in fines. McVeigh and Nichols faced the death penalty, as predictably announced by U.S. Attorney Patrick Ryan. Attorney General Janet Reno was quoted by the *Washington Post* as saying that leads would still be pursued in the case, "but we have charged everyone involved that we have evidence of at this point." On John Doe #2, FBI Director Louis Freeh was noncommittal. "So he still is an active suspect? I would characterize him as that." Freeh said that the circulated sketch of the #2 suspect was not being withdrawn from the public. Lead prosecutor Joseph Hartzler commented that, "The grand jury found probable cause to believe that there are others involved. We will continue the investigation."[25] But that wasn't the last word from this grand jury. One juror was unhappy with the way the government had run the proceedings. His fifteen minutes of fame were yet to come.

That weekend, back in Pendleton, Jennifer McVeigh had two problems to worry about: being related to Tim and being known as a Jell-O wrestler. She attended the Pendleton Field Days at the Wendelville Volunteer Fire Hall grove. According to former classmate Brian Haines, Jennifer was recognized at the event by a few intoxicated men who had some idea in mind.

Everyone was at the field days. When these three guys saw her, they kind of went after her. Three older men—I don't think they were angry. She's just a very attractive girl and they, well—that's the way things are for her. They went after her and she jumped a fence to get to her truck, and yelled, "Leave me alone!"[26]

With the indictment handed down, it was time for Stephen Jones to tackle his biggest case yet. Answering the charges would come later. First, Jones had to make sure an impartial judge would hear his client's side of the case. U.S. District Judge Wayne Alley was assigned August 11 to the still unscheduled trial by Magistrate Ronald Howland. Alley, sixty-three, a retired army brigadier general, was nominated to the federal bench by President Reagan and confirmed by the U.S. Senate in 1985. Alley had been a military judge from 1968 to 1975, with service in Vietnam, Hawaii, and Virginia.* Before he became a federal judge, Alley was a law professor and dean of the University of Oklahoma law school for four years.

About a week after not-guilty pleas for both Tim McVeigh and Terry Nichols were filed, McVeigh's attorneys asked Judge Alley to step down from the case. Stephen Jones filed a motion August 22, saying Alley and all other Oklahoma Western District judges should not participate. While Alley was not in the Murrah or the federal courthouse across the street during the bombing, his chambers were damaged and a member of his office staff was slightly injured. Jones's motion cited a 1975 case where there had been a plot to bomb the courthouse itself. Then Oklahoma Judge Fred Daugherty transferred the case to a judge in Kansas. Jones and fellow defense team members recreated the April 19 bombing scene in their papers, describing the horror—buildings in the city shook,

---

*He upheld the murder conviction of Lt. William L. Calley, Jr., in 1973. The lieutenant was involved in a massacre of civilians at My Lai, South Vietnam. Several officers and enlisted men were tried for similar war crimes, but Calley was the only man convicted.

windows shattered, and office equipment tumbled to the floor, while in the streets terrified people scattered, screaming. Jones intended to show how all eight Oklahoma federal judges would have perceived what was happening and how they could not now hear such a case and be objective. Jones, in an attempt to focus attention away from his client, also attacked the possible Oklahoma trial venue, the plan to hold a single trial for both McVeigh and Nichols, the motives of witnesses, and, of course, the death penalty. In his effort to have Judge Alley step down, Jones said:

> Judge Alley, like all the judges in the federal courthouse, are victims of the Oklahoma City bombing. To deny that there has been a traumatic physical and psychological impact on what one judge has called the court "family" is to belie reality. . . . If recusal was appropriate in 1975, then it's mandatory in 1995.

Judge Alley, though, apparently had a strong interest in hearing the bombing case. He filed a declaration with his court clerk stating that he lost no family or friends in the tragedy and that he would be a fair judge. The document said, in part:

> [I intend to] conduct a trial in a fair, objective, and dignified manner in full realization that the rights of all parties should be scrupulously observed. None of my personal property was destroyed or damaged except for minor nicks on two or three items.

Terry Nichols's attorneys, meanwhile, were also seeking judges outside of Oklahoma City. According to an August 24 *Washington Post* report, El Reno prison warden R. G. Thompson had declined to allow Terry's wife, Marife, to visit him—a meeting Nichols's lawyers argued was essential to his defense. The reason for the refusal was not made known in the report other than to say that the requested "contact visit" would have been in a private room. The attorneys made calls to the Justice Department, the

Washington solicitor general, and contacted Washington Judge Joyce Green, hoping to get the El Reno warden's decision on the visit overruled. Nothing worked. Nichols's co-counsel, lawyer W. Gary Kohlman of Washington, D.C., told the newspaper that his team also planned to join McVeigh's crusade to disqualify every Oklahoma judge from hearing the bombing case.

Two reports about McVeigh were made as one of the hottest Augusts on record came to an end. On the twenty-sixth, *Los Angeles Times* reporter Richard Serrano quoted an attorney from Oklahoma who claimed that shortly before the April 19 blast occurred, he saw a man who looked like McVeigh driving a car around the Murrah building. The claims from James R. Linehan conflicted with the government's version of events and the previous witness accounts placing McVeigh in the Ryder truck just before the bomb exploded. Linehan, a Social Security and Worker's Compensation claims specialist, was reportedly interviewed by the FBI, but not the grand jury. He recalled that on April 19, he was at a red light at the south side of the Murrah. Linehan recounted the scene to the *Los Angeles Times* as if it were happening as he spoke:

> That's when I notice a yellow vehicle beside me. The driver of this vehicle is hunched over the wheel. It's a white person because there's a white hand showing. I cannot see a face because there's either hair or a hood covering his head because the driver is hunched over the wheel and looking up at the Murrah building. The next second, this vehicle just peels out—peels out across the intersection. I thought I'd missed the light, but the light was still red. He goes to the middle of the street. He then turns right and whips it into the bottom . . . of the federal parking [lot] under the Murrah building. That's the last I see of it, the yellow vehicle disappearing into the parking area.[27]

Linehan also said the car he saw had no license plate. He claimed he saw the composite drawings of the suspects after the bombing and thought the McVeigh likeness looked "familiar," so he called the FBI and offered his story of "that yellow vehicle." Linehan added that the car he saw on the television film of the site where McVeigh was arrested was the car he saw April 19. He also said that the man he saw that day in the car had the same profile as McVeigh—the man he saw being led out of the courthouse on the evening news shows of April 21. Both prosecutors and defense attorneys declined to comment on Linehan's statements. If accurate, Linehan presents a problem for the prosecution because his scenario of April 19 differs from the government's. Linehan could also be a problem for the defense because his story would place McVeigh at the site of the bombing that day. Whether he will be called to testify is unknown, but Linehan told the *Times* that he was interviewed twice by the FBI and once by an investigator working for Stephen Jones.

The other strange media report that rounded out August detailed a possible security breach at El Reno, where McVeigh and Nichols had been housed since late April. Certainly, the two men were not the most popular individuals to ever stay at the federal facility, and rumors circulated whether they would both live to see their own trial. Stephen Jones had compared McVeigh to Lee Harvey Oswald when discussing safety matters. Notorious convicted killer Jeffrey Dahmer had died at the hands of a fellow prison inmate in a beating death that made national headlines just one year before.

On August 28, the *Daily Oklahoman* reported that syringes were found on food trays going to the unit where McVeigh and Nichols were held. Inmates had access to the trays, the newspaper said, and a correctional supervisor was suspended with pay. After the problem was discovered, El Reno Warden R. G. Thompson said security at the installation was "not at all" in jeopardy and the syringe incident was "an internal, personnel matter." Thompson declined further comment on the embarrassing situation.[28]

On September 5 and 6, a federal panel, including Kevin

DiGregory from the Justice Department's criminal division and Seth Waxman, an associate deputy attorney general, worked at reviewing U.S. Attorney Patrick Ryan's request for the death penalty for McVeigh and Nichols. The three-member panel historically weighs defense-presented mitigating circumstances with prosecution-presented aggravating circumstances. The latter may include using weapons of mass destruction and the destruction of government property, both of which apply in the bombing. After the panel completed its work, its recommendation went to Attorney General Janet Reno for her final decision.

Nichols's lead attorney, Michael Tigar, attended a closed-door session of the panel and argued that the death penalty should not be sought because, Tigar said, his client is innocent. And while he was also invited to the review, Stephen Jones declined to go, saying the process was a charade and a sham because Attorney General Reno had already announced her decision. Attorney Richard Burr even asked that the review committee delay its meeting and requested that the entire Justice Department remove itself from the case. Burr wrote to the committee, "We believe that the process of deciding whether the government will seek the death penalty against Mr. McVeigh cannot be meaningful unless that process is conducted independent of the Justice Department." But who would Burr have in place of the highest prosecutors on American soil for a crime that occurred on American soil? The UN? The Canadians?

McVeigh's attorneys also filed a supplement to their original request to have Judge Alley step down from the case. They said in essence that even Alley's court clerks were biased, citing a T-shirt (one of several) that had been sold in the office. The shirt read, "Those lost will never leave our hearts or be forgotten, April 19, 1995 . . . United States District Court, Western District of Oklahoma." McVeigh's lawyers had a point this time. A federal office, above all others, should not have such frivolous collectibles circulating, much less being sold by the employees during business hours. The Associated Press reported that court employees claimed the shirts were privately made by a staff member to raise money for charity.

In an unexpected move, prosecutors sided with defense attorneys on September 8 in asking Judge Alley to excuse himself from this case. The response in support of the defense's original motion contended that Alley was "too close to the case" because his office was damaged in the blast. Stephen Jones told *Tulsa World* of the prosecutors' intent. "I understand that the government will join in our motion that all [Oklahoma] judges be recused."[29] The prosecution further stated that the upcoming trial should be moved to Tulsa, Oklahoma. Still hoping to remain on the case, on September 14, Judge Alley ordered the trial moved to Lawton, about ninety miles from Oklahoma City, and set a trial date of May 17, 1996. He declined to step down and said in his decision:

> [Lawton] is close enough to be convenient for local witnesses and for affected persons who want to be spectators. It is far enough to provide a trial setting appropriate for detached and dispassionate deliberation. I have tried cases in Lawton and from those experiences have formed a high regard for the quality of jurors in that area. The allegations of bias and the appearance of lack of impartiality presented by the defendants are lacking. Preparing for and trying this case will be a difficult task in the coming months, and I can not merely ask another judge to shoulder that burden when the law does not require that.

Michael Tigar joined McVeigh's attorneys on September 27 in asking that Alley step aside. Tigar filed his motion with the Tenth U.S. Court of Appeals in Denver, citing the same reasons as Jones and the prosecution. Tigar went so far as to call Alley a victim of the explosion who shouldn't oversee the trial. One day later, Tigar filed a motion asking that the judge who eventually hears the case not sequester the jury. Jurors in the O. J. Simpson case were forced for many months to stay in hotel rooms and have no contact with the outside world so the media hype surrounding the ex-football star's case would not taint their future decision regarding his guilt. McVeigh co-counsel Rob Nigh filed a similar request on behalf of Timothy. Tigar said the jurors could avoid reports on the case if not sequestered.

> When jurors are separated from their families, and [are] in a "pressure cooker" atmosphere, relationships and hostilities develop that may prevent the jury from coming together. In counsel's experience jurors follow their oaths. They try diligently not to see or hear media coverage.[30]

Apparently unhappy with the prosecution's work in investigating the bombing, grand juror Hoppy Heidelberg allegedly spoke to reporters from the *Daily Oklahoman* and the conspiracy-oriented magazine *Media Bypass*. Heidelberg, though not mentioned by name, reportedly told both presses that federal prosecutors refused grand jury requests to interview witnesses and ask questions. *Media Bypass,* in separate reports, has alleged that many "witnesses" were not interviewed by the grand jury—"witnesses" that claimed to have information about the mysterious John Doe #2, and others who may have been involved in the bombing. Heidelberg told *Media Bypass* that he and others on the twenty-three-member grand jury were suspicious of the government's case and that other conspirators exist. But, the grand juror added, he believed Nichols and McVeigh were involved in the bombing plot.

While grand jurors are legally prohibited from revealing details of cases they hear, Heidelberg was apparently so disappointed with the proceedings that he shared his extensive notes and opinions with certain reporters, including Lawrence Myers of *Media Bypass.* He said he thought the grand jury was supposed to have a more investigative role in the case than merely accepting the government's information at face value and making the decision to indict.

McVeigh's lawyer, Stephen Jones, used the opportunity to pounce on the government's case. Jones filed a motion October 13 asking that McVeigh's indictment be dismissed because grand jurors are forbidden from disclosing testimony. Jones also said, based on Heidelberg's claims, that prosecutors "purposely did not bring to the grand jury evidence which would establish the role of others or a larger conspiracy . . . [because it] was under intense pressure for a quick indictment." An October 14 Associated Press report said that some grand jurors had wanted to interview the person who drew the sketches of the John Does, and ask questions about #2.

Five days later, Attorney General Janet Reno announced her expected decision to seek the death penalty against McVeigh and Nichols. She "agreed" with the recommendations made by her subordinates on the review committee and U.S. Attorney Patrick Ryan. The decision by Reno was formally made six months after the bombing. Jones responded to Reno's announcement with an argument he would likely use in court once McVeigh faced a jury of his peers:

> The news hardly comes as a surprise. The attorney general and the president announced they would seek the death penalty before they even knew who the defendants were. We will mount our attack on the obvious prejudgment of the case.[31]

The heat was turning up on Hoppy Heidelberg, too. Heidelberg's attorney, John DeCamp, said in an Associated Press report that he believed federal agents were investigating Heidelberg over the story in *Media Bypass*. "I've instructed him from this point on to speak to nobody without calling me," DeCamp said. Heidelberg, who was threatened with contempt of court and imprisonment, was dismissed from the grand jury on Thursday, October 26. He said that because he was self-employed he didn't fear jail. The importance of getting to the bottom of the case and finding John Doe #2 outweighed his personal well-being. Heidelberg told

ABC's "Good Morning America" that having John Doe #2 out there somewhere meant a continuing danger of terrorism.

> I'm not satisfied that the two people indicted were all the people involved. It's my impression that a grand jury investigation is an investigation. In an investigation, you don't know your destination. It's whatever you discover, and we didn't discover much. If we don't get to the bottom of this one, there could be more. I think the indictments [of McVeigh and Nichols] are valid.[32]

Speaking out and facing contempt, Heidelberg added, is the price you pay for the truth. He indicated that the others on the grand jury did not talk to the press as he had because they feared losing their jobs. But, Heidelberg said, the grand jury should have been allowed to show the John Doe #2 sketch to others it felt should have been interviewed. Stephen Jones also spoke with "Good Morning America" that day. While Heidelberg did not help Jones by announcing to the world that the indictment of McVeigh was "valid," he did present more procedural ammunition to the defense. Jones said the indictments should be dropped and the grand jury process started again.

> I can agree with [Heidelberg]. His basic allegation is that the government kept the grand jury away from anybody other than the two who were indicted. I agree that's a serious matter and should be investigated and while I'm sure the Justice Department and the FBI [are] investigating the matter, the truth of the matter is they are not supposed to keep their evidence away from the grand jury. It's silly and ridiculous to call a ten-year-old boy [Joshua Nichols] and the sister [Jennifer McVeigh] of my client [to testify] and not call the people who could identify John Doe #2.[33]

The indictments did say there may be "others unknown" involved in the bombing plot. On October 27, the existence of a

John Doe #2 was again enforced—this time by the government. The Associated Press ran a story on the national wire that a shadowy figure in the passenger side of the truck may be another man involved in the plot. The videotape of the truck was shot by a surveillance camera at an ATM just minutes before the blast. A law enforcement source said in the report that the investigators remained convinced that John Doe #2 is still at large. "No one knows who he is," the source said. "It's like he walked into a wall and vanished."[34]

Stephen Jones had University of North Carolina psychiatrist Seymour Halleck interview his client. Jones told *USA Today* and the *Daily Oklahoman* that McVeigh was found to be competent and an insanity defense would not be used in the upcoming trial. Jones spoke with *USA Today* on November 16, and claimed that McVeigh was "as sane as any lawyer or news reporter." Jones also cited positive school and military records kept on his client. Reaching into a time when McVeigh was a different man, Jones said, "We have thirteen years' worth of school records that show a person of exemplary character, a conscientious young man. Damn, we could bring in a dozen teachers to testify to it." Jones did not mention those others out there who knew an angry McVeigh many months before the bombing, a McVeigh who asked the *Union-Sun & Journal* if blood would have to be shed to reform the current government system. That McVeigh did not fit the character Jones was developing for the media or for a trial jury.

Jones continued his crusade to soften the public's perception of McVeigh by giving a speech November 16 at the University of Oklahoma, and responding to questions by the *Daily Oklahoman,* the newspaper that had for so long covered the stories of the victims. It had three reporters—Nolan Clay, Randy Ellis, and Diana Baldwin—covering this story. In outlining the defense plan Jones said not only that McVeigh would testify, but also that his client was more than capable of doing so: "There is no mental defect.

We're not pleading insanity, incompetency, or anything like that. It's a straight, factual defense. I have said he would testify. That's the present plan."[35]

The fact that Tim McVeigh could testify in his own defense was no great surprise. In the history of American justice, people like Ted Bundy and Mark David Chapman testified on their own behalf. It didn't help in either case: Bundy, a former law student, just showed how intelligent he was, but failed to prove himself innocent; and Chapman, the convicted murderer of John Lennon, impressed no one by reading from *Catcher in the Rye* by J. D. Salinger and saying that the book explained his actions. Maybe McVeigh would read from *The Turner Diaries*. That should impress the audience. In other issues covered by Jones in the university speech, he said:

- The trial should be moved from Lawton because of court-authorized polls and safety concerns. The polls taken in Lawton found that most people thought McVeigh was guilty. He said the Lawton courthouse only had minimal security. "I understand the government's reasons for wanting to stay in Oklahoma. I do not believe the government can convict Mr. McVeigh based upon the facts and evidence . . . if the case is held outside Oklahoma, but they most assuredly can convict him in Oklahoma, probably no later than the first day of the trial," Jones said, citing the alleged bias on the part of Oklahomans because the bombing was in their home state.

- The FBI investigated threats against Jones's life. Jones also said he had a recurring dream "of either someone parking a Ryder truck outside my home and blowing it up or my being shot in the hallway outside my office."

- Federal trials are not televised. Jones opposed victims, who cannot attend the trial, watching the trial by closed-circuit television, saying someone could tape the proceedings and

sell them. The viewing was originally suggested by prosecutors.

• Many politicians are using the McVeigh case to boost their
political careers. Jones alleged that the Clinton administration wanted a conviction and the death sentence before the
1996 presidential election. "This offers [those in] the Clinton administration the opportunity to prove themselves or
attempt to prove themselves as tough on crime."

Jones, according to the *Daily Oklahoman* report, showed how
his thinking at times mirrors McVeigh's. For instance, Jones
claimed that the Oklahoma City bombing gives the police and the
FBI greater power "to infiltrate, power to gather intelligence,
power to tap our telephone lines and to collect information about
each of us." He indicated that the attack on the government, as the
bombing had been dubbed, had "simply given the government
even greater license to expand its intrusive powers." Statements
like that will not set McVeigh free. In fact, they may convict
McVeigh faster because they attempt to explain or justify the
April 19 bombing, which in rational circles will never be justified.
If the government is issued increased investigative powers in light
of the bombing, maybe incidents like the one in Oklahoma will be
prevented in the future. (New federal antiterrorism legislation
was prepared almost immediately after the bombing, but only recently a watered-down version of the original bill was signed into
law by President Clinton.) Without power to investigate such violent acts, the United States will be placed in the same precarious
position as the once terrorism-plagued countries of Ireland and
England, where car bombings were so commonplace that residents came to believe they were part of everyday life and sympathy can be found for perpetrators trying to effect political change.

On November 21, Stephen Jones and Michael Tigar asked
that the trial be moved out of Oklahoma completely. Jones had

previously said Judge Alley's choice of Lawton, Oklahoma, was an unsafe location for the defendants and their attorneys. "It would be impossible for us to adequately protect ourselves in that environment," Jones said. This time Stephen Jones argued that the media in Oklahoma state had already "tried, convicted, and sentenced" his client. He provided thousands of pages of exhibits to the court to illustrate his point. The exhibits included local television news transcripts and newspaper articles about the case. "The fevered passion of the community of Oklahoma has been escalated by local news reports concerning the case. Timothy McVeigh had been tried, convicted, and sentenced to death by the media in Oklahoma," Jones said in a report he filed with the court. Assistant U.S. Attorney Steve Mullins countered: "I think that you're going to find that this case has had extensive coverage all over the country."

Though their wish to move the case was not immediately granted, defense attorneys scored a small victory when Judge Alley was finally asked to remove himself from the case. The Tenth U.S. Circuit Court of Appeals in Denver ruled on December 2, 1995, that Alley should be removed from the case because his chambers had been damaged in the blast. "We conclude that a reasonable person could not help but harbor doubts about the impartiality of Judge Alley." He formally stepped down on Monday, December 4, saying, "The judge who succeeds to this case will have to bear a dreadful burden, and I wish him or her well."[36]

On that same day the appeals court appointed U.S. District Judge Richard P. Matsch, sixty-five, of Colorado, to the bombing case. The son of an Iowa grocer, Matsch is known for his love of family, horse-riding, and the various athletic teams of the University of Michigan. Matsch's love for the law developed while working as a college intern for an attorney who frequented the Matsch family store. Matsch graduated from the University of Michigan in 1951 and went to University of Michigan Law School. He earned a law degree in 1953 and served three years in the army, performing counterintelligence in Korea after hostilities in that region ended. In 1958, he married Elizabeth Murdock, daughter of the longtime chief judge of U.S. Tax Court. Matsch joined the U.S. attorney's office in 1959. Six years later, he was named a referee in Denver bankruptcy court. In 1974, Matsch was appointed to the Denver bench by then-president Richard Nixon.

An intensely private man, Judge Matsch had served on the bench during high-profile and controversial cases including one case that had ties to groups with beliefs similar to Timothy McVeigh's. Matsch was the presiding judge at the prosecution of four members of the white supremacist, anti-Semitic group called The Order. The four were charged in the 1984 machine-gun slaying of talk-show host Alan Berg; the controversial, Nazi-baiting radio personality was killed that year outside his Denver apartment. During the three-month trial which ended with the conviction of two of the defendants and acquittals for the remaining two, security was very tight but Matsch declined to have bodyguards, even though he was a familiar figure in his black western hat and cowboy boots.

Prior to the nationally publicized Berg case, Matsch had presided for twenty years over the massive desegregation lawsuit that brought busing to public schools in Denver.

Known for his efficiency and directness, fellow lawyers have called Matsch the perfect judge to oversee the Oklahoma bombing case. One attorney said in the *1995 Almanac of the Federal Judiciary,* "If you make a stupid argument in front of him, he will take your head off." Denver lawyer Jon Holm told the Associated Press that "the last thing you'll see from Dick Matsch will be an O. J. trial." Of his appointment to the bombing case, Matsch told the *Dallas Morning News* in December, "It isn't a matter of wanting it or not. I was assigned and I understand the responsibility of that."[37]

The earlier May 17, 1996 trial date was scrapped. Judge Matsch met the defendants for the first time at a December 13 hearing in Oklahoma City. McVeigh and Nichols, for the first time since they separated sometime in April 1995, sat just ten feet apart during the hearing. The hearing concerned surveys of potential jurors, and exchanges of evidence and sealed documents. During the three-hour session, Nichols's and McVeigh's eyes never met. Stephen Jones downplayed the cold silence between the two men by indicating their silence went along with both defense teams' desire for separate trials. "It's not a personal rift," Jones told the Associated Press. "It's a legal division with respect to strategy and other matters." McVeigh smiled often and even laughed a couple of times during the hearing, while Nichols was serious, except to smile at a few of his family members who were present.

Judge Matsch laid down the rules of his court to the attorneys, and made note of his decision to drop the May 17 trial date. The judge set a January 30, 1996, hearing date for defense motions to move the trial. He also left a warning to the lawyers: "If there aren't agreements on things I expect there to be agreements on, that'll rile me a bit. The fact that I vacated the trial date does not mean we're going to proceed in a leisurely manner."[38]

As Matsch prepared himself for the biggest case of his life— one with legal ramifications that could have far more social impact than anything emerging from the O. J. Simpson trial—Stephen Jones was again at work defusing the public's perception that his client might be the most notorious American murderer of all time. What better way to deflect attention away from McVeigh than to refocus the public's eye on conspiracy theories. A poll by the *Los Angeles Times* released at about this time said that 10 percent of Americans surveyed believed that the government was somehow involved in the Oklahoma bombing—that the United States bombed one of its own buildings to brainwash citizens into thinking terrorists were at work here and that stricter gun and weapons laws were therefore needed. People who believed this would be the only ones in America who would ever have any sympathy for McVeigh. And if Jones was going to find an audience or an almost believable scenario that would lessen the anger felt toward

McVeigh and have any chance of reducing the penalty his client faced, this would be it. To lessen the burden on McVeigh, John Doe #2 needed to be caught and a wide-ranging conspiracy had to be alleged. Claiming the leg found at the site was the "real bomber" didn't work, so Jones had to pursue other avenues.

McVeigh defense team researcher Ann Bradley was sent to Amsterdam in the Netherlands to meet with a lawyer representing Daniel Spiegelman, a U.S. citizen in custody at a high-security Rotterdam prison since June 1995 on a mysterious charge of "trading in stolen manuscripts." His extradition was sought on other charges of weapons smuggling and falsifying passports. How exactly the Dutch newspaper *De Telegraaf* found out about the meeting between McVeigh's researcher and the lawyer was not made known, but the paper ran a story about the meeting and Spiegelman's resemblance to John Doe #2. Bradley told *De Telegraaf* that Spiegelman looked like the second John Doe. Spiegelman's lawyer, Abraham Moszkowicz, had a strong interest in his client remotely looking like McVeigh's mystery partner. If this were to be believed by Dutch authorities, Spiegelman could avoid being brought back to the United States to face the weapons charges because the Netherlands will not extradite suspects who face a possible death penalty. So, Moszkowicz alleged wholeheartedly that his client is a suspect in the bombing.[39] A January 7 Associated Press story said U.S. authorities had repeatedly denied that Spiegelman was wanted in connection with the Oklahoma investigation. The *De Telegraaf* article also cited no evidence that would link Spiegelman with the bombing. Spiegelman himself denied any link, the AP report said.

Jones continued his international bombing-conspiracy campaign during the weeks that followed, alleging ties to neo-Nazi groups and other countries. The attorney's allegations fueled a general and historical interest that will continue for many decades after the McVeigh/Nichols trial is complete, just as the conspiracy theories surrounding John F. Kennedy's assassination are the impetus for hundreds of books and articles. People like to believe in conspiracies because they cannot fathom that one or just a few people could have such an impact on society, as they did in Texas and in Oklahoma.

Since the April 19 bombing, conspiracy theories had developed faster than the Ebola virus, and were shared on the Internet—the new wave of amateur communications—as well as talk radio, TV, faxes, and at meetings of certain militias. Michigan Militia members Norman Olson and Ray Southwell, claiming to possess exclusive information from a California computer expert with intelligence ties, had said early on that the Japanese were to blame for the bombing. They subsequently resigned from their posts in the militia because of the public embarrassment of being so incorrect. But others bitten by the conspiracy bug rushed in to fill the void. Here are just a few scenarios:

- The Oklahoma bombing and the Waco incident involving David Koresh killed two former bodyguards of President Clinton who knew too much about the president and planned to go public with their spicy stories. Secret Service Agent Alan Whicher was killed in Oklahoma and BATF Agent Robert William was killed at Waco. Clinton attended Whicher's funeral, and William had worked for the BATF in Little Rock, Arkansas, when Clinton was governor. Twin Falls, Idaho, resident Bill Trowbridge told the Associated Press after a militia meeting there, "that makes four different bodyguards killed. Three in Waco, and this one. Sure did benefit Bill Clinton, didn't it? Check that out."

- The United Nations helped in the bombing plot. The John Birch Society, the *Spotlight* newspaper, and other paranoia-fueled groups have warned of a partnership between the United Nations and U.S. foreign policy makers to absorb the United States in a form of world government called a New World Order. Gate Keepers information service representative Pam Beesley told the Associated Press that "this is what the UN does when they go in and overthrow a country. They produce unrest in the country first." The Kansas City-based information service she's part of tries "to put information out to the common folk."

- The bomb was an "electrodynamic gaseous fuel device" that could not have been made by novices like McVeigh and Nichols. It had to have been made by U.S. officials possessing "high-level," "top-secret" information. That theory comes from former FBI agent Ted Gunderson, a favorite of the *Spotlight* newspaper. Gunderson claimed that John Doe #2 was "vaporized by design" and McVeigh was a "throwaway" or an expendable asset. The *Spotlight* called its story with Gunderson "an exclusive." It didn't say why he no longer worked for the federal government. But, from the claim made, one could determine why he's a former fed.

- Two bombs destroyed the Murrah. On April 19, the U.S. Geological Survey in Oklahoma recorded two major events 11.9 seconds apart at the time of the bombing. Copies of the seismograph were released and fanned out all over the nation, inspiring people to believe there were two bombs set off—one possibly by the government. Oklahoma chief geophysicist James Lawson explained that the second "tremor" was the federal building collapsing, not another bomb. Despite the explanation, he told the Associated Press he still gets calls from the confused. "A lot of them are anxious to explain to me that our government committed mass murder. They are disappointed that I'm not saying it was two blasts."

- At least three people (names withheld here) have tried to tell me that the government was involved in the Oklahoma bombing. No matter what I told them, or for how long I tried to tell it, they would not change their minds that the government was involved. Distrust in public officials has reached the point of delusion, where Americans create their own explanations for events they cannot understand. One of the people who spoke with me went so far as to say he'd obtained a photograph of the bombed-out Murrah (ordered through a late night AM radio show) that "proves two bombs were set off. McVeigh was led to Oklahoma by his nose, by the government."

- An advertisement in the conspiracy-oriented magazine *Media Bypass* offers a $24.95 video called *Oklahoma City: What Really Happened,* available through the Tree Top Fulfillment company of Evansville, Indiana. The ad poses these questions: "Was there more than one bomb?" "What happened to John Doe #2?" "Was there a Middle Eastern connection?" and "Did some occupants of the building have prior warning?" A lot of money can apparently be made satisfying the mental thirst of Amerinoids.

Federal authorities tried to calm the concerns of thousands who were crying conspiracy soon after the bombing occurred. The *Washington Post* quoted numerous senior law enforcement officials in July, saying that "the most exhaustive investigation in recent history has not turned up anything like an organization with a defined structure and clear, centralized leadership."[40] The feds said prosecutors would argue that McVeigh and Nichols, with help from one to three others, carried out the plot because of anger with the government over issues the suspects believed were evidence of the government overstepping its legal bounds. Despite the rejection of a multilayered conspiracy, Amerinoids would continue to believe what they wanted. How could the government tell them there was no broad conspiracy when the government was part of it? Stephen Jones stops short of accusing the government of participating in the bombing. Jones does allege, however, that investigators and prosecutors participated in a coverup by declining the grand jury's wish to pursue the John Doe #2 angle.

On Monday, January 29, 1996, Jennifer McVeigh and a male

friend made the twenty-hour drive from Pendleton, New York to Oklahoma City. Jennifer wanted to attend the Tuesday court hearing at which time Judge Matsch would hear arguments on where the trial would be held. Defense attorneys wanted to use the hearing to show Matsch that the sense of community in Oklahoma is strong and a fair trial would be impossible in that state; while the prosecution would tell him that the victims' families could not travel out of state to attend the trial. Assistant U.S. Attorney Steve Mullins said, "There is no statistical difference between the jury pool in Oklahoma and the jury pool in any other major city in America." Prosecutors suggested Tulsa as a site, which would be favored under the Victim's Rights Act, which requires that relatives of people killed in the bombing have easy access to the trial.

On January 30, after being mobbed by television cameras and reporters on her way into the change of venue hearing, Jennifer McVeigh sat in the same courtroom with the families of victims forever metaphorically tied to Timothy McVeigh and Terry Nichols. After spending the previous night at a jail in the city, away from El Reno, McVeigh and Nichols were escorted by U.S. marshals to the courthouse and into the courtroom. Caught on CNN's cameras at the courthouse, both defendants were wearing bulletproof vests and were handcuffed at the front. Those who had relatives who died in the bombing gathered outside the courthouse, carrying photos of the dead, braving the bone-chilling zero-degree weather.

During the hearing, defense attorneys showed television film clips that included erroneous information; footage of tearful calls from families for the death penalty for perpetrators of the bombing; coverage of memorial services; and promises from President Clinton, Attorney General Reno, and Governor Keating of Oklahoma that the death penalty would be sought. As the films were being shown, victims' family members in the court broke down and cried. An Associated Press report by Paul Queary said that Tim McVeigh smiled as the films were shown, and Richard Serrano of the *Los Angeles Times* reported that McVeigh "appeared relaxed and at ease in court." I spoke with Jennifer later, during a call to her hotel room in Oklahoma. She attempted to explain Tim's happiness in court.

> He wasn't smiling in reference to anything. He was smiling at me. And you know that if he wasn't smiling, they'd criticize him and if he was smiling they'd criticize him. You know what happened the last time when he wasn't smiling.[41]

During the hearing, McVeigh defense attorney Rob Nigh said the press coverage illustrated that the feelings in Oklahoma were too intense to pick a jury there and have a trial. "The media coverage in Oklahoma has included demonizations of Timothy McVeigh and Terry Nichols." Prosecutors countered with a researcher who told the court that 60 percent of potential jurors in Lawton, Oklahoma, had no bias about McVeigh and 73 percent had no opinion of Nichols's guilt or innocence. Researcher Donald Vinson also pointed out that people polled in Lawton, Tulsa, Denver, Kansas City, and Albuquerque did not differ. In all, the five cities had a 63 percent average absence of bias for McVeigh and a 76 percent rating for Nichols. Vinson said, "My research overwhelmingly convinces me that these two defendants can receive a fair trial in Lawton, Oklahoma, and if not Lawton, then certainly in Tulsa."

When day one ended, Jennifer McVeigh, accompanied by Stephen Jones, spoke during a news conference at which she explained why she chose to attend the proceedings: "No matter what, he's still my brother and I'm still going to be there for him. He's just a normal person. He's not this evil thing they've painted him." That night, Jennifer visited Timothy at the city jail before going back to her hotel to call her father in Pendleton.[42]

University of Houston political science department chairman Kent Tedin testified on Wednesday, the second day of the hearing. Tedin, speaking on behalf of the defense, said he surveyed 2,400 people in cities including San Francisco, and found that those in

Lawton and Tulsa think about the bombing every day or several times a week. But only about 8 percent of those in either Denver or San Francisco think of it. He said it was "extremely unlikely" that the two suspects could get a fair trial in Oklahoma. "They recall a lot more in Tulsa and Lawton about what they saw in the media," Tedin said. Judge Matsch made it clear that Lawton was out of the question as a potential trial venue because $1 million would be needed to upgrade the courthouse there before the trial could even proceed.

In a related matter, the Associated Press reported Thursday morning that Edye Smith of Oklahoma, who lost her two sons, Chase, age three, and Colton, age two, in the bombing, filed a lawsuit against McVeigh and other "unknown individuals" for $30 million. The civil suit for wrongful death would not be deliberated until after McVeigh's murder trial. About five other such suits have been filed. Smith attended the hearing, telling reporters that she wants the two defendants tried in Oklahoma so they can see the survivors and families of the victims in court.

On Thursday, February 1, Stephen Jones and Michael Tigar asked Judge Matsch to consider moving the trial to his home state of Colorado, while prosecutors argued that Tulsa would allow the families of victims access to the trial. Judge Matsch announced Friday, the final day of the hearing, that he reserved decision on the venue and would not make a choice before February 27.

With a break in the proceedings in Oklahoma, Jennifer McVeigh returned to Pendleton, and Stephen Jones was back trying to improve his client's image and discussing possible "international conspiracy" theories. He told the *Sunday Times* of London that his team was looking into other countries for leads and that the U.S. government may be doing the same. Jones said he hired the London firm of Kingley Napley to pursue possible leads, such as German and English neo-Nazi connections to the bombing. Jones stated in the February 6 Associated Press report that international connections to the bombing could be significant.

We are certainly pursuing an investigation of that line and have been for some months. The attorney general herself (Reno) said the FBI would certainly be justified to look at a European connection. We believe that the evidence may suggest a broader, deeper, more sophisticated conspiracy.[43]

The *Sunday Times* article connected the April 19 bombing to that same day's execution of American neo-Nazi Richard Snell in Arkansas. McVeigh's lawyers were quoted as saying the execution was being avenged by neo-Nazis. But Snell's widow said she had no reason to believe her husband's supporters had anything to do with the explosion.

Jennifer McVeigh was back in the news in mid-February when the announcement of her appearance on "Dateline NBC" was made. Interviewed at a Buffalo hotel by Jane Pauley, Jennifer said she would have to testify for the prosecution at the upcoming trial and regretted statements she had made to the FBI. A reporter with federal and defense connections in the case told me during each discussion we had about Jennifer that "the girl could send her brother to the electric chair" because of the incriminating information she knows about him. Of her early statements to the FBI, Jennifer told "Dateline":

I think he knows I really didn't have a choice but . . . I still wonder, still have a lot of guilt. I talked to them and maybe I somehow hurt him. That's really the biggest thing that bothers me every day—that I love my brother to death and want nothing more than to support him and be on his side. Yet I really had no choice and if I get called to testify, it will be for the prosecution. It's tough. You'll be in trouble if you don't talk to them, or you talk to them and you're going to get your brother in trouble.[44]

When the interview aired on February 13, Jennifer's words probably did more to hurt than help Tim's case. She spoke of her sympathy for the Branch Davidians and Waco—again tying her family to the government's reasoning for the bombing—revenge.

She also made the biggest mistake of her life when she suggested that the American people needed to "understand" the reasons behind the Oklahoma bombing. Attorney Richard Burr attended the interview and conferred with Jennifer before she answered Pauley's questions about the bombing itself. Even after the conference with Burr, Jennifer made a deeply damaging statement that will likely be linked to her brother at the trial. Pauley asked Jennifer if she thought the bombing was evil. Jennifer replied:

> Yes. I think . . . I don't know. I think it's evil in a sense that a lot of people . . . lives were torn apart, a lot of people died . . . innocent people. [She confers with Burr and continues.] I think the act itself was a tragedy for everyone involved, but maybe there's some sort of explanation to be had—I really don't think anything could justify the consequences—just understanding would help.[45]

Jennifer McVeigh mentioned "the consequences" after being prodded a bit by Pauley, but it's conceivable that she may have left that statement out. The most important part of the interview came when Jennifer suggested that the bombing needed to be understood and an "explanation" could be made. If she had made that statement publicly before going to Oklahoma, she may have had to fear for her life in the city where her brother is most unwelcome. Certainly the 168 people who died in the blast would not accept an explanation, and their families, forever doomed to remember April 19, 1995, would not even attempt to understand a motive other than blind rage by an American-turned-monster consumed with anger, confusion, and frustration directed toward a government he believed to be corrupt and evil.

Chapter 10

Motherless Child

In great pain, tears flow from the heart, not the eye.
—Russian proverb

"What are you doing?"

"You won't believe it. I'm just so busy."

It was reassuring and homey to hear her husband's phone voice every morning, while he began his day. He sounded busy, too, and a little anxious, office machines clattering in the background. She was on her break at work and not quite ready to get back at it.

"I haven't even gotten a chance today to look at my e-mail," Ricky Tomlin told his wife.

"Oh, really?" Tina Tomlin chuckled.

Click. The line was dead. It was as if he was on call waiting and had pushed someone else in. Tina waited a few seconds but Ricky never came back. As she hung up the phone, she heard shouting from up the hall in her office. The voice was frantic and frightening. "Oh, my God! The federal building's been bombed!"

The statement registered in Tina's mind and she doubled over, grabbing at her stomach, "Ricky! Ricky . . ."

Ricky L. Tomlin, forty-six, division program specialist for the U.S. Department of Transportation office in the Alfred P. Murrah Federal Building, was killed, along with the many others whose stories of the bombing would never be told.

Perhaps the most horrifying were those stories of the parents of children—the toddlers who had attended the day-care center in the building. The lives that would never have a chance at a beginning. The parents who could never let go, like the mother fox in the woods, carrying the body of her stillborn infant, waiting for it to wake up and wondering why it won't. The parents will carry that memory of terror forever, still thinking there may be a chance, even after the heartbreaking funerals for their dead children, and even after the building in Oklahoma was finally torn down.

The moment after the building was hit, Oklahoma City plunged into chaos.

"Where is my baby?" a woman screamed outside, minutes after the blast. She was shaking and holding a white towel. The woman grabbed her friend and held on as if that person was the railing of a ship going down. "My baby was in there."

And they waited. The streets were filled with firetrucks, ambulances, and bloody faces, like the faces you see on the evening news in places like Sarajevo and Beirut. This was not America, this was hell. Judgment day had come for thousands who thought April 19 was going to be just another day at the office, at home, in friendly Oklahoma.

"I haven't seen my son," pled Anthony Cooper, another man outside the site, hoping to hear something about or, God willing, be reunited with his two-year-old son. "I haven't seen my wife." And finally, total surrender to what he (like so many others) didn't understand. "I don't know," he said.

America's Kids Day-Care Center in the Murrah building drew

the world's attention because the bomber may have targeted the children. Initial stories about Timothy McVeigh quoted witnesses as saying he staked out the area and saw the children days before the blast, while other reports claimed he was unaware the children were there.

Tabloids were all over the Oklahoma story, while O. J. Simpson, with glowing photos and inside scoops, was pushed to the inside pages. *Star* magazine reporters Peter Kent and Melissa Key told the story of victim Phillip Allen.[1] The year-and-a-half-old boy called P. J. was taken to Children's Memorial Hospital after the bombing. The tiny, innocent face stares out of the photos with glazed eyes and a heart he carries on his shoulder, like an aura you can see that lets you know there really is a unique energy to man that makes all humans part of the same family.

When the bomb went off, the *Star* reporters detail, P. J. and other children were finishing breakfast at the day-care center. A deafening crack hit, followed by a series of spine-tingling thuds and crashes. And P. J. was falling through time. He plunged eighteen feet when the floor gave way, landing on the stomach of a worker from another office. P. J. landed in fate's hands as the man he landed on broke the fall, saving the little boy's life.

Later P. J.'s family members went driving from hospital to hospital in Oklahoma City, like so many other families, looking for their loved ones who were immediately ambulanced away from the bombing site. There were so many dead, so many injured, and so many rescue workers who responded that there really was no time for notification of families by authorities. In a split second, Oklahoma City had been turned into the land of the lost souls.

Little Phillip's family arrived at Children's Hospital and were informed that the hospital did have a P. J. Johnson there, but the child was listed as a female, and dead.

P. J.'s grandfather, Willie Watson, thought it to be too much of a coincidence and pressed the hospital workers to keep looking. "Turns out they had him listed under the last name of the guy he dropped on," Watson said.

P. J. landed on Calvin Johnson, a Social Security officer who, after regaining consciousness and strength in the wreckage, picked the child up and carried him to an ambulance.

After the confusion was settled at Children's, the workers told Dolores Watson that her grandson P. J. was badly burned over 55 percent of his body and had lost his mop of curly hair on his head. She broke down. "I just kept thinking, 'Oh, God, not my P. J. Why didn't you take me?'" Mrs. Watson recalled.

Twenty-three-year-old Sherri Prather, a part-time helper at P. J.'s day-care center, was off work the day of the bombing. The *Star* reported that an ill co-worker had attempted to call Sherri to ask her to fill in, but apparently she doesn't own a phone.

"If I had taken that call, my daughter, Hannah, and I would have been in the center that morning. I thank God every day that I didn't have a phone and didn't get the message," Prather said.[2]

Prather heard the news of the bombing and rushed to the area to help. She said she hoped she could identify the children at the center to aid rescue efforts. Sherri ended up at Children's Hospital, where she found P. J.

"They took me up to the intensive care unit where I saw P. J. I couldn't even recognize him at first. But when I saw his eyes and realized it was P. J., that's when my heart sank. I went over to his bedside and told him, 'P. J., it's Ms. Sherri. Everything is going to be okay.' I was crying," Prather stated, "and I didn't want to leave him because he's only a baby."

Sherri Prather was touched deeply by the tragedy and by seeing P. J. lying in the hospital bed, clinging to life. Not only was Sherri a worker at the day-care center, but she also left her eight-month-old daughter, Hannah, there from time to time due to college scheduling. Prather worked afternoons at the center and attended Oklahoma City College in the mornings.

The bombing happened on a Wednesday. Prather said, "If it had been Thursday, I would have dropped Hannah off in the morning and gone to school, and she might not be here now."

P. J.'s grandfather Willie said, "The doctors told us P. J. landed headfirst. He's still breathing. He wouldn't have been if he hadn't landed on some guy. P. J. is Oklahoma's miracle kid."

The thirteen-room day-care center was added to the Murrah six years ago, on the second floor. It was about thirty feet from the explosion. Of the three adults and twenty-one children who were there on April 19, only six lived, and all were children. The six, including P. J., happened to be in a windowless room at the center of the building with day-care worker Wanda Howell. Wanda, thirty-four, was killed along with a two-year-old she was found holding, Dominique London.

Christopher Nguyen, five, son of Thu and Phong Nguyen, was in the restroom of the day-care center just before the blast. He was playing with water in the sink, a penchant of Christopher's that always had him seeking fountains, sinks, and bathtubs.

Thu arrived on the bombing scene that morning looking for Christopher. Meanwhile, Phong was hearing of the explosion from a co-worker at York International.

Mr. Nguyen rushed out and by the time he got to the ravaged building, he found that Thu had been reunited with Christopher. "We couldn't recognize him."

Thu and Phong live with the rest of their Vietnamese family in Norman, Oklahoma. At Children's Hospital with Carla Hinton, a staff reporter from the *Daily Oklahoman,* the Nguyens were thankful for their son's fascination with water.

"That's what I think saved his life," Mr. Nguyen said. "He was in the bathroom playing with water."

That, yes, and a little help from truckdriver Richard McKnight.

At 8:50 A.M. on April 19, McKnight and his wife, Lisa, were leaving traffic court, a few blocks from the federal building. They were on Interstate 35 and "I felt the explosion in the car," McKnight recalled. He looked in the rearview mirror, saw the smoke coming from the building, and turned back toward it. McKnight wound up at the south entrance of the Murrah, where rescuers were handing out people from a crater. A firefighter handed Christopher to McKnight and the six-foot, three-hundred-pound man carried the injured child to the nearest ambulance.

McKnight saw Christopher on a local newscast the next day and went to see the boy in the hospital. To Mr. and Mrs. Nguyen, McKnight was a hero.

"Christopher was the only child I held in my arms," McKnight said later. "I will always, always remember Christopher and Christopher's face."[3]

Christopher's best friend at the center, Aaron Coverdale, five, wasn't as lucky. Aaron died with his brother, Elijah, two. Thu said the Coverdale's grandmother, Jannie, called her on April 25 and offered Christopher a new bicycle that Jannie had wanted to give to Aaron.

Thu also talked of Edye Smith, whose two boys, Chase, three, and Colton, two, died in the explosion. "She went home with empty arms. . . . We just have tears for each other," Mrs. Nguyen said.

Thu spent many days at the hospital with her son, who was in a light coma and had to recover from burns.

All reports of what happened after the blast tell an almost identical story. The Oklahomans caught up in the middle of the chaos rushed to help one another instead of running from the area to safety. They ignored their own injuries and dug in to aid the others while they waited for those faraway sirens to finally arrive.

A man who was working in an accounting office on the third floor, though not named in a report from *Globe International*, recalled what happened the second Oklahoma City became Oklahoma Hell, USA.

"There was a roar," the accountant said. "It was unbelievable. I blinked and was on the floor. I thought this must be what death is like . . . except I woke up. A lot of people didn't."

The man pulled himself out of the debris that covered him and saw a woman, badly cut by flying glass, heading toward an area where windows had been moments before. The man thought she would just dazedly keep going and plunge to her death. "I managed to get to her just as she began crawling along the edge," the man recalled. He asked her to reach out to him and she did. He led her out and safely down a stairwell.[4]

Rescue workers and ambulance crews arrived with firemen to the worst devastation imaginable. The size of the exposed portion of the building was enough to throw their stomachs into spins, like when the roller coaster takes its final plunge. But that plunge never ended, it just kept going as the hours turned into days, and then into the months and lifetimes that followed 9:02 A.M., April 19, 1995.

The world saw many photos and heard countless stories of struggle, care, and grief. But nothing—not the demonic initial film clips of Timothy McVeigh, not the photographs of the bloodied faces and weeping parents, or the tales of heroism by the police, firemen, and hospitals—could come close to the impact of two heartbreaking shots taken within moments of each other.

Baylee Almon celebrated her first birthday on April 18, one day before her death and international fame. Her head covered in blood, her limp body, broken limbs, and her little yellow socks are captured forever in the photo that was published in almost every newspaper in the world.

Baylee was carried out of the rubble by Police Sgt. John Avera, who handed her to firefighter Chris Fields. Fields thought the little girl might be beyond help.

"Come on, little darling, breathe, you can do it, little one. Don't die on me here. Please, I beg you. Breathe," he said to the tiny face that was the pride of her mom, Aren. He carried her for about twenty seconds before he reached the emergency medical station set up near the site. Baylee was aided by the rescue team and placed in an ambulance where she let out a small breath and then died.

"It was the longest walk of my life," recalled Fields. "This little girl will haunt me for a long time."

The photographer who captured the moment in photos, that may be used to break the hearts of juries for the McVeigh/Nichols and other trials, said at times he wished he had never taken them. Charles H. Porter IV, who would win a Pulitzer for his photo, then met his subject's mother, Aren. Aren told him, "We never would have known she was treated so good if you hadn't taken those pictures."

A rescue dog had made it to the basement of the Murrah tomb and sensed life under a pile of debris. The rottweiler, visibly upset, led its master across the twisted rubble, sniffed something sticking out of what looked like a wall and nipped it, then pulled back from the foot, startled. Bronte's master was alone with the dog and couldn't free the person by himself, so he ran out, dragging the barking dog, looking for help.

"We've got a live one!" the man screamed over and over, drawing the attention of rescuers outside. "We've got a live one."

Dr. Rick Nelson, a general surgeon who'd just left Muskogee, Oklahoma, to see how he could help, heard the rescuer's cry. Inside, Nelson and the others, fearing for their own lives in the shaky structure, found a teenager wrapped within pipes, wires, and concrete.

"It was like pickup sticks," Nelson recalled in an interview with *People*. "If you moved one piece the wrong way, the whole thing could come crashing down." For three hours they worked to extract fifteen-year-old Brandy Ligons. Finally Brandy could move her hand. She reached out and Nelson met her and held on.

"For the last twenty minutes, she was fading in and out and getting shocky," the doctor said. She was talking, though, and Nelson wanted to get her mind in a better place. "Once we're through this, I'm taking you to dinner. Hold on."

Brandy was eventually listed in fair condition at Children's, along with Christopher Nguyen. Her dream of becoming a lawyer has come closer with the help of her new friend, Dr. Nelson, who not only visits her regularly, but has also started a trust fund for her education.[5]

Days wore on for the rescuers, and the sun, shining brightly the day 168 people were slaughtered, went away. Its absence brought bitter cold and rain, making the search effort at the Murrah even tougher.

Relief from the agony of seeing, thinking, and sleeping only the Murrah graveyard came by way of dogs, taken to the site by a service known as Therapy Dogs International. The more than twelve hundred workers were touched by the dogs used to comfort stressed and grieving people. Thirty dog owners brought their trained animals to the Murrah, and let them walk around for people to hold, hug, and pet.

Volunteer Larri Sue Jones said, "It's something warm to hold. God knows people can use that."

The dogs seemed to soak up the grief like psychological sponges, while giving to the humans those caring eyes, dog smiles, and wagging tails that indicate, as dog owner Pat Kelley was told by a worker: "I saw this dog and knew everything was going to be okay." Dogs also comforted the hundreds of families in search of answers and peace.

Dalmatian owner Peggy Brawner offered this: "I think the dogs are really providing a diversion and some hands-on kind of hugging, letting people get their emotions out a little bit more. This is kind of a nontouch society we're living in now, but you don't have to worry about that with the dogs."[6]

There's a famous quote that reads, "In peacetime, sons bury fathers. In wartime, fathers bury sons." Those responsible for the bombing took children from parents, parents from children, grandparents from families, and any sense of stability Oklahoma City people once had away forever. If guilty, Timothy McVeigh did indeed change the course of history—because of the passage of new federal terrorist legislation, the attention the crime received by the media, and the questions raised about what American "rights" and "freedoms" actually are (and if they should be changed or altered).

Trudy Rigney, thirty-one, never came home April 19 from her internship job at the Oklahoma Water Resource Board. The board was located across the street from the Murrah. Her death from the explosion was not confirmed until April 23. The draftswoman's son, Jonmichael, eleven, had lost his best friend. With his father absent from the family, and only his aunt and grandmother to care for him, Jonmichael is another lost soul created by the tragedy.

Christopher Sullivan of the Associated Press interviewed Jonmichael and his aunt Paula.

The child, who looks much like his mother, with glasses and soft features, declined to talk about Trudy. Aunt Paula spoke of their future plans to raise the boy in Broken Arrow—plans that would have to follow their own course with the constant reminder that Jonmichael's best friend was taken from him at the hand of a stranger.

The people of Oklahoma City have attended funeral after funeral, numerous memorial services, and counseling groups. Many have turned to God. Some ask why and seek the religious answer, while others, sick of not hearing answers from the heavens, blame God.

"God did not do this," said Preacher Rex Haymaker at the funeral for Ashley Eckles, four, of Guthrie. "Evil people did."

Whether they feel they know the answers or not, the people of Oklahoma City will always be victims of a man-made crime. The 168 people killed have relatives who will never forget the names of those who are going to trial, nor will the five hundred injured, or the hundreds of thousands touched by the tragedy.

While many Americans focus their rage on Timothy James McVeigh and wish his death would be worse than that of the victims, some harbor misplaced anger for the parents who gave him life and the home from which he came.

His father, William McVeigh, was packed and ready to leave for Reno, Nevada, on a bowling weekend with buddies until he learned from the FBI that his son was charged. The media seemed to learn of the connection as fast as the federal agents, and were knocking on Bill's door April 21.

Bill was devastated like the victims' families, but had the tragedy rubbed in his face, not only by the media, but by that select group of people in America and in his Niagara County hometown who feel the accused are guilty until proven innocent.

"Father of Baby Killer" greeted Bill when he finally went back to work at Harrison Radiator and tried to put his belongings in his locker. An angry co-worker had spray-painted the slogan across the front of his locker while he was away. He received odd mail and so many telephone calls from news agencies begging for "exclusive" interviews that Bill had to get an unlisted number. A simple man, Bill was not ready for a crush of reporters that would last for almost three weeks.

"Bill is thick-skinned. [He] has a lot of friends and relatives and will get through this," Father Paul Belzer said.[7] Getting through may not be that easy. As with any major crime, a major trial follows, as do follow-up reports. Bill will never be left alone because of the notoriety his son attracted. After all, how would the father of one of the most hated men in recent American history ever live down what the Heartland will never forget, or forgive?

Bill McVeigh wasn't the only victim of angry, bitter Americans. His neighbors in Pendleton and the children at Starpoint School also found out they weren't just a bunch of small-town folks anymore—they were from McVeigh land. Starpoint Spartan runner Mike Heitzenrater told *USA Today* of the problems students had after the world learned the name McVeigh. "They call us 'The Bombers' or they call us 'The McVeighs' or they tell us we have explosive starts."

Neil Haseley, a sprinter for the track team, told *USA Today* reporter Erik Brady of similar experiences. "You walk by and it says 'Starpoint' on your chest and people look a second time," Haseley said. "They stare, like there might be something weird about you. It feels weird."

In Oklahoma, and in other parts of the country where Tim McVeigh stayed or lived, some citizens found themselves victims of the media's new pushiness where some TV reporters do anything to get "the story," which today includes rigging explosion devices in Ford trucks to show viewers they are not safe or manufacturing a fake grave of Nicole Brown Simpson to get on film for effect.

The *Daily Oklahoman* newspaper editorialized on how many of the world's reporters who visited were responsible. Yet some were not. "Reports that one TV talk-show star and her staff behaved insensitively toward families of critically ill children at a local hospital add to the deeply ingrained impressions of media insensitivity," the paper wrote.

In Pendleton, New York, at Jennifer McVeigh's college, the television media also overstepped its bounds, according to Niagara County Community College Dean Jane Haenle. Haenle told me about a woman from CNN who expected her to "gather up all of Jennifer's teachers and classmates" for comment when the news agency graced the campus. A former reporter herself, Haenle did no such thing and, in fact, went out of her way to protect Ms. McVeigh.

In Oklahoma City, life remained stagnant. The city was still in shock, trying to dig out . . . trying to help themselves. J. E. McReynolds, an editor at the *Daily Oklahoman,* eloquently wrote a week after the disaster that the city was still united.

"When a bomb destroyed the Murrah Federal Building in downtown Oklahoma City, the entire state—and soon, much of the nation—sprang to action. In the hundreds of hours of frenetic horror and abiding grace that followed, there have been many memorable events.

"But perhaps Oklahoma's most defining post-bombing moment came yesterday [April 26] at 9:02 A.M. when all across this land of red earth, blue skies, and goodness, our disparate yet unified people paused to remember, in the silence of their hearts, those we lost on April 19. For one minute, rescuers rested, businesses stopped, school teachers and students were quiet, tongues were silenced, and automobiles on the Broadway Extension pulled to the side—as, generally people here still do when a motorcade funeral drives by.

"Each one in his or her own unique way, citizens stood still, to remember the possibilities and promise of those who died—and to promise the future that these loved ones will not have died in vain.

"The world will not soon forget the days Oklahoma lifted itself from the terror and despair to the promise of joy. Those who survived will never forget the day Oklahoma stood still."[8]

An editorial cartoon accompanied the piece. It showed a bewildered, balding man on a trail at the edge of a sudden and wide river. Across from the river, the trail continued, accompanied by an arrow sign at the side that directed the walker "Back to Normal." On the river were two words, shimmering, that read, "The Tears."

Little Girl Lost:
An Exclusive Interview with
Jennifer McVeigh, Sister of
Timothy McVeigh

I think the interview is the new art form. . . . Once you say
something, you can't really retract it. It's too late. It's a very ex-
istential moment.

—Jim Morrison*
Los Angeles, 1968

Timothy James McVeigh wasn't home for Christmas 1995. His
younger sister, Jennifer, and father, Bill, celebrated together in
their hometown of Pendleton, New York. Even after the New
Year, the small ranch home on Campbell Boulevard was littered
with opened gifts, as the two Siamese cats slept on discarded
wrapping paper on the floor. "Sorry," Jennifer said to me during
a meeting at the home. "We still haven't cleaned up from the hol-
iday. Busy, I guess."

Ms. McVeigh, now twenty-two, smoked a cigarette and offered me a soft drink. She also had a glass and commented that she

*Jim Morrison, *Wilderness,* vol. 1 (New York: Vintage Books, 1988).

wished people would remember good things about her brother, that the thousands of reports issued about him were dehumanizing and many times completely incorrect. A portrait of a smiling Tim, from 1985, watched over the conversation from a wall in the kitchen. In fact, that portrait was really the only wall-hanging in the kitchen. It was kept company by a calendar and a magnetic notepad nearby, with the name and phone number of Dennis Sadler scrawled in black. One would think that the Christmases of the other McVeigh relatives in upstate New York and the two in Florida would have been similarly fragmented and tainted with a degree of sadness, but not because of Tim's absence. No, the family had been living different lives for years.

Since late April 1995, when she became internationally known as the devoted sister of Timothy McVeigh, alleged mass murderer, I have felt a little sorry for Jennifer McVeigh. Not because of accusations that she was somehow mixed up in the plot to bomb a building in Oklahoma, but because she is a child. Give an intelligent youth the wisdom of the world, or that which we perceive it to be, and you have Jennifer McVeigh. She is a country girl—attractive, subtle, weak. Much like brother Tim, she sought attention after the breakup of their parents' marriage. And Tim was there to give it to her, while at the same time feeding her endless messages carried for years by a radical Christian, prejudiced, and lonely minority that feels it has some type of claim to the land we share.

Jennifer McVeigh is the first sister of an alleged American terrorist to share that individual's ideas, but apparently not share the desire to take strong action. She is the daughter of a nation of people who are sick of being taxed, investigated, and led astray in a land that was originally founded by people hoping to avoid those government intrusions. But Jennifer is twenty-two, and as this is being written, she still doesn't understand that her brother will forever be remembered as the madman of Generation X, the lost soldier, and the man who killed 168 people on April 19, 1995.

Who could fault her? At twenty-something, fiction often becomes reality, but not to the extent of the Heartland's tragedy. Jennifer McVeigh could not have prevented the terrorist act in Oklahoma any more than Jackie Kennedy could have stopped her husband's death. Jennifer was near the catastrophe, she was not a part of it. She pressed no buttons. Jennifer is not a victim either. Jennifer McVeigh is one of us.

What follows is my interview with Jennifer McVeigh, recorded Thursday, December 28, 1995, at the family home in Pendleton, New York.

Brandon: Lana Padilla said in her book, *By Blood Betrayed,* that Terry Nichols picked a wrong friend in your brother. When you read that line, which she attributes to her son, that transfers all the blame onto Tim.

Jennifer: First of all, I'd say, in that sentence she's assuming them both guilty. I mean there hasn't even been a trial yet and that's the one thing that irritates me. All the articles written, everything, assumes them guilty. Just by the way that they speak and something like that—"You picked the wrong friend"—that's saying he did it. That irritates me. It irritates me that I don't think she even knew him that well, and she's trying to say (pause, Jennifer sighs) I don't want to say the wrong thing. You know.

Brandon: I understand. You don't think . . .

Jennifer: I don't think she has the right to judge in that way, in her position.

Brandon: Have you ever met her or talked to her?

Jennifer: No, I haven't, but I don't think she has the right to judge my brother in that way. I mean, she's (Terry Nichols's) ex-wife. How well could she know (Tim), first of all, and then . . .

Brandon: She seems in the entire book to be trying to say, "Tim is the one." She even attributes that to her son, "Tim did it."

Jennifer: Right.

Brandon: She keeps trying to repeat this over and over again. Then she says something like, I'm only selling this story so I can send my kid to college. What do you think about her doing this book?

Jennifer: (long pause) It's her way of making money off of it, I guess. That's how I see it. I mean, because it sounds to me like she's trying to clear her husband and implicate Tim in that book, throughout the whole book, I mean you see it, you've read part of it. . . . There hasn't even been a trial. You know . . . (Tim) is accused, not convicted, and that's wrong of her to pass that judgment. She is not the judge, she is not the jury. She has no right to make that judgment. She has the right to have an opinion, but if you're going to have an opinion, I would hope it would be an educated one.

Brandon: Did Tim ever tell you anything about her, what he thought of her or anything like that?

Jennifer: No, I never heard of her before.

Brandon: She's someone who's kind of an outsider . . .

Jennifer: But to me it sounds like she's trying to clear her and her husband—or her ex-husband—by putting all the blame on my brother. You know, if he did or didn't do it. Either way.

Brandon: She talks about Tim and President Kennedy. And then she says the date, November 22, 1994. She says, "I squirmed in my seat, knowing that Terry probably remembered that date for another reason. It was the date his present wife's two-year-old son, Jason, had mysteriously died the year before, suffocating in a plastic bag in their home in Kansas. Tim McVeigh had discovered the body." And then she leaves it at that, as if we're supposed to be led to believe something.

Jennifer: I don't like how that's put either. . . . I think it's cruel of her.

Brandon: It's kind of sick.

Jennifer: Sick of her to put that in there, because from what I understood beforehand—before she wrote this book—was that Tim found him and tried to save him or something. I guess everyone was sleeping. I don't know the exact story. I can't tell you the exact story, but I guess Tim found him and did try to save him. But implying that he would hurt a little kid like that, I mean, he has a niece, you know, he likes kids.

Brandon: She also mentions in the book that Tim used to tell people he hated kids. Tim has never said he didn't like kids?

Jennifer: Not that I know of, no. He never said that. He would never do anything to intentionally harm a child like that. He would have no reason to. It sounds to me like she's playing on what the media is playing on.

Brandon: Because Tim once saved someone's life, on the road.

Jennifer: Right, right.

Brandon: When he was on his way home from Fort Riley.

Jennifer: Right. But see, the media is playing on the death of children in this bombing. It seems to me like . . . (Lana's) playing on the same lines with Tim. Like the media said, all these kids are killed to get the people all mad and upset at one person, which would be Tim, and when . . . (Lana's) playing along the same lines.

Brandon: She's trying to use an unrelated situation and work it in.

Jennifer: Right, implying.

Brandon: Do you remember Terry visiting or anything?

Jennifer: No, I don't think I was living here at the time. Either that, or I was away or something, because I never met him. I never met Terry.

Brandon: Did your dad meet him before?

Jennifer: I think he may have.

(Tape interrupted—begins again at Jennifer McVeigh discussing Timothy McVeigh and the historic videotape of him leaving the courthouse in Perry, Oklahoma, and being met by an angry crowd of people who know he's been identified as a bombing suspect.)

Jennifer: . . . that makes me sick because they were going to know, all those people were standing out there, they're not thinking—they're still in shock. They're going to react on whatever. I mean, Harvey Oswald, look at what happened to him, he never . . . he just got shot and killed. Same thing would happen to Tim. I mean, he hasn't been to trial yet, but I mean, these people aren't thinking about that. . . . They don't know who he is or if he did it.

Brandon: And they're all screaming at him as if he did it.

Jennifer: Right, exactly. Who knows what they're gonna do. And if they refused him (a bulletproof vest) that I think is sick. If they did. I don't know if that's true or if it isn't. But if it is, that's pretty sick, because they should know the risks with all those people, crowds standing there, when a big tragedy happens like that.

Brandon: That film is very famous now. People always say, "Look at that cold face . . . there's no emotion after what he's done." What do you think about people who say something like that? I mean, he's probably in shock . . . he doesn't even realize what's going on . . .

Jennifer: I think the sun was shining in his eyes, first of all. He was squinting. I think that's part of it. How would you like it if a bunch of people were staring and screaming "Baby killer"? I mean, Tim was serious at times but we all look serious at times, and I don't think you can just assume a reason for everything.

Brandon: Jump to conclusions?

Jennifer: Yes, you can't just assume a reason for the way some-body looks at all times. About that picture, you were saying . . . (Tim) walking out (of the Perry courthouse). What would they have said about any look he had? I mean, what do they want? You want him to walk out with a big smile on his face? What would they say about that? What kind of look do they expect from some-one who has just been charged with a crime like that?

Brandon: Are you doing well in school?

Jennifer: I took a leave of absence for a year. I'm going back in the fall. They have [special circumstances] where you can take off, but not actually withdraw so that you don't have to reapply and send all those applications. So, I'm going back in the fall.

Brandon: To Buffalo State [College]?

Jennifer: Yes.

Brandon: Is everything okay? I mean, are you just taking a mental health break?

Jennifer: Yes, exactly. I was having a little bit of trouble concentrating. I mean, if I'm going to do my best, I'm going to get As, I'm not going to slump through it. I'm not like that. I want to learn, you know, and do my best if I'm gonna be going. But I just couldn't do it this semester. You know, I couldn't put my all into it. I didn't have my all to put into it. I have so much . . . well, I'm sure you can understand. I have so much on my mind, but I couldn't concentrate on art history and things like that. Art history just seems so irrelevant right now, you know?

Brandon: It seems irrelevant to concentrate on art history when you are history.

Jennifer: (laughs) I mean I'm one of those people who finds everything interesting. I like to learn about everything and this semester I couldn't get into anything. There's just so much other stuff that's going on in my mind and I want to keep up with the news. I want to, for my own records, for myself.

(I explain my negative encounter with a talk-show host's talent scout who sought an interview and called many times, becoming an annoyance to me.)

Jennifer: Well, they've all got something to get out of getting the big story. They've all got something in the form of a promotion or big paycheck, you know. . . . But it's not comfortable for me here anymore. I'm here to sleep but that's about it. Just knowing they broke down the door one day.

Brandon: Who?

Jennifer: The FBI . . . one day when we weren't here. My dad offered them a key. I don't care if you put this in your book or not, I guess. But he offered them a key and he went away on vacation.

Brandon: This was after the Friday (April 21) when they were here.

Jennifer: I'm not sure what day it was. He offered them a key and they said, "No, we won't need to go back." But they ended up coming back and, you know, they broke in the door and they fixed it, but the doorknob fell off later and we had to change it. I just don't feel safe here anymore, you know. Like the whole world knows where we live. What if someone decides, "Well, we think Tim did it so we're going to go after his family"? Where are they going to come? They're going to come right here because . . . we're the only ones of his family they know. They know what our house looks like. They know where we live.

Brandon: And they can't get to Tim.

Jennifer: Right, they can't get to Tim. They know where we live and every night I swear I get up twice to make sure the doors are locked. I'm not comfortable at home anymore. I'm sure my dad will stay here. He built this house. I'm sure he'll be here. I'm going to be home for college, I'm sure. It's cheaper for me that way. But if this were my house, and my dad was out of the picture, if it was just my house, I would move. Yes.

Brandon: Dan (Kane), at the paper, has a lot of respect for you. I said to him one day, "Dan, if Jennifer wanted to—because she's so young—she could do whatever she wanted with this situation. She could go on television shows and have money and pay for college and everything else, because that's the way the media is these days. 'We'll pay you such and such an amount if you give us an interview,' or whatever," and Dan said, "She has too much class for that."

Jennifer: I'm not into that. I'm not looking to make money off this. That's what I think . . . (Lana Padilla's) doing in writing this book and all her interviews. I'm just working. I don't want all that. All it is, is disrupting our life . . . all the attention. Because, if you go on one show, all of a sudden they're all over you again. Or when the trial starts. They're going to be all over us again. And there's always . . . you say one thing and they write another thing.

Brandon: Have people done that to you before?

Jennifer: I think that irritates me the most. For *Time,* they wanted to know some things about Tim's family life. And they wrote a good article about it. They wrote what we said. Everything was accurate. It's not just them. I probably shouldn't even mention them because they wrote a good article, but they wanted stories about Tim's past and that's what we told them. But it's always—well, you know, you're a writer, the first and last paragraph is "Tim McVeigh, blah, blah, blah . . ."

Brandon: Is charged with such and such . . .

Jennifer: . . . and then the last paragraph, same way. But I guess that's how they have to write it because that's their job. But the image people get is the first and last paragraph and everything in between might as well just be nothing. You know what I mean?

Brandon: Yeah. The reason that's done . . .

Jennifer: . . . to let you know who he is . . .

Brandon: They're not doing it to rub it in.

Jennifer: I know. I know, because I like to write, too, and I know if I'm writing a paper or something, your first paragraph is what you're writing about and your last paragraph sums it up, and everything in between is just in between. It's like a bad light on everything good you try to say. And I understand it has to be that way . . .

Brandon: If somebody was to ask you, who's John Doe #2, you'd say, "I have no idea," wouldn't you?

Jennifer: (laughs) I'd say that's going to be one of the FBI's biggest problems, having this John Doe #2 in the first place, because that kind of discredits Tim being John Doe #1. Because if they say there's this guy and this guy, and all of a sudden this guy doesn't exist, well how good is the portrayal of the first guy? How credible is this guy [Tim], if this guy [John Doe #2] doesn't exist anymore? How credible is the first sketch, who they say is Tim? To me, that doesn't make sense. I don't think there is a John Doe #2. But I also think that . . . I don't know. It's not good for the prosecution or the FBI.

Brandon: It hurts the case. It's the missing link.

Jennifer: And it should, because that's not credible evidence anymore. It can't be if one's so far off and the other is you know. You know what I'm saying.

Brandon: That's what Hoppy Heidelberg (a dismissed grand juror who spoke to the press) was saying, also. He said he was on the grand jury and he thought a grand jury investigates the case, but what he was told when he was on this grand jury was, "Here's the information, go with it." Instead of actually doing what the grand jury is supposed to do. That's also going to help Tim and hurt the prosecution, because a grand jury is assigned to take the information, use it, and find more or whatever.

Jennifer: . . . so they can make an indictment if they find enough evidence.

Brandon: And these guys said, according to this Heidelberg fella, just take this info and we'll use that. It seems pretty shoddy.

Jennifer: Toward the end of my time (in front of) the grand jury, I felt like I was on trial. They weren't even asking me about Tim anymore. They were asking me my opinion of this, my opinion of that. I felt like they were putting me on trial in front of the grand jury that is supposed to be investigating a bombing in Oklahoma City. Now what does my opinion have to do with the facts about the bombing or the facts about my brother? I don't get it. You know, if they're investigating . . . you know what I'm saying. I felt like they were putting me on trial in the grand jury and that bothered me. A lot. It really made me angry toward the end. Some of the things they were asking me made me really angry.

Brandon: They showed you pictures of the victims.

Jennifer: That was the FBI, showed me the dead, burned people and kids.

Brandon: You wonder what they expect to get from you out of that. (sarcastically) "I know Tim did it. Thank you for showing me these pictures. They made me realize something."

Jennifer: (laughs) Yeah.

(I mention situations of police entrapment shown on the television show "Cops.")

Jennifer: That's what I believe (about) Randy Weaver, too. They were after him, undercover to sell them a sawed-off shotgun, bugging him, bugging him, bugging him. And to me, that was entrapment in the first place.

Epilogue

The Chess Game

Public works crews in Oklahoma City removed barricades that had blocked traffic near where the Murrah building once stood. The blockade had been at the site nearly a year, and today, February 17, 1996, was just another day in the city. But Fourth Street, south of where the Murrah had been, was now open again. The fence blocking off the bomb site was sparsely decorated with a teddy bear, some withered flowers, and a few small American flags. Damage was still clear on numerous other buildings in the area.

Three days later Judge Matsch announced that the bombing trial would be held in Denver, Colorado, at the glass and granite federal courthouse where he had heard so many cases before. In making the decision, Matsch ruled that McVeigh and Nichols could not get a fair trial in Oklahoma because of the tragedy's impact on the state and its citizens. Matsch cited pretrial publicity, though, as the ultimate reason for his decision to move the case. He noted that McVeigh and Nichols were "demonized" in the

Oklahoma news media and prejudice against the defendants pre-
cluded a fair and impartial trial in that state.

The chosen Denver courthouse stands on the northeastern
edge of downtown, near a large homeless center. Denver Police
Chief Deputy Thomas Sanchez told the Associated Press that the
security measures would be beefed up at the courthouse because
of the "antigovernment sentiment" surrounding the case and the
suspects. Mayor Wellington Webb traveled with U.S. marshals to
Oklahoma City to see how security officials there had already prepared for the trial, in the event that Matsch had chosen their city.
But the judge had not. News reports quoted many Oklahomans as
saying they were upset the bombing trial was moving so far from
the city in which the crime had occurred. Many would not be
able to make the trip to see the trial. They had hoped to meet
McVeigh and Nichols in a courtroom.

To add insult to injury for one family, Oklahoma state medical
examiner Dr. Fred Jordan revealed on February 24 that twenty-
one-year-old air force pilot Lakesha Levy, killed in the bombing,
had been buried with the wrong left leg. The leg, which McVeigh
defense attorney Stephen Jones indicated could be the real
bomber, had been incorrectly traced to Levy. Dr. Jordan said it
probably belonged to one of the eight other victims who had been
found with missing legs. Levy was exhumed so Dr. Jordan could
test the leg. With such a mass casualty incident, Jordan's office
was probably so overloaded that a mistake like this could happen.
But the explanation was of no comfort to the victim's family when
she finally was removed from a crypt in New Orleans on March
15. Jones's request to Judge Matsch to be present when the body
was exhumed was rejected. In his ever-increasing ploy to show
distrust of the government, Jones claimed, like his client, that defense attorneys needed to be present at the exhumation to moni-
tor government investigators. Prosecutors said Mrs. Levy's family did not want the defense present when the victim was removed
from her crypt. Jones's team was allowed in the following day.

Jordan also announced that there may have been only 168 victims in the bombing since the leg had originally been listed as belonging to someone unknown, before being traced to Mrs. Levy. Since then, the death toll in the bombing has been listed as 168.

In late March, Stephen Jones continued his flirtations with the media, offering a glimpse of his claimed "investigation" into the case. Subscribing to the conspiracy theories pondered by the paranoid, Jones saw that possibly the only way to convince a jury of McVeigh's innocence or his minor role in the bombing was to point elsewhere, as often and as loudly as he could. As in the O. J. Simpson case, when Simpson's defense attorneys clouded the issue with racism, Jones hoped to take the heat off McVeigh by suggesting, again, that international conspirators acted out the Oklahoma bombing plot.

Jones told the Associated Press's Paul Queary on March 25, 1996, that:

> What I think we are investigating most actively is a possible Middle-Eastern role. There is evidence now existing that we have received that certain foreign countries made specific threats against the United States. And one of those threats was in Oklahoma City.

It's important to note that since Jones was appointed to represent McVeigh, his defense expenses have been funded by the taxpayers. They will not be revealed until the trial is over, but "fact-finding" trips for Jones's team are expected to add up on a scale unlike any other defense expense. Also, how many threats against the U.S. government have been made in this country's history? Probably too many to count. And the fact that Jones stresses one "threat" allegedly made on Oklahoma City shows the extent to which he will have to go in the trial to "exonerate McVeigh or reveal him to be a bit player," as Queary wrote.

Maybe because conspiracy theories are often invented by lawyers looking to cloud a case, the paranoid who have access to a press, and historians who see their craft only for personal gain and opportunity, in a not often-seen move, prosecutors in the Oklahoma bombing case responded to Jones's claims in a brief filed March 27 in U.S. District Court. Prosecutors said their research and evidence "continues to point to McVeigh as the killer and to Nichols" as his aide and abettor. "There was and is, in contrast, no evidence that the . . . bombing was the work of foreign terrorists." The game of knight and king is expected to continue even beyond the trial as the fate of McVeigh and Nichols is handled by the players of law on both sides of the case.

Timothy McVeigh and Terry Nichols were awakened at about 4 A.M. on March 30 while in their cells at El Reno Correctional Facility in Oklahoma. It was moving day. While details were kept secret from the press and many in law enforcement, members of a hostage rescue team and officials from the U.S. marshal service flew the two defendants in a Department of Defense jet to Jefferson County Airport, northwest of Denver. They were then taken by helicopter to Englewood Federal Correction Institution, the metropolitan area's only federal jail facility. Located south of Denver, it houses about one thousand men who are serving sentences for drug offenses or robbery. McVeigh and Nichols were given six-by-ten-foot cells.

McVeigh's co-counsel, Richard Burr, told the *Union-Sun & Journal* during an interview that his client looked "forward to a change of scenery" and that he expected McVeigh to be treated better at Englewood because the staff there is more distant from the bombing than those in Oklahoma.

As the one-year anniversary of the Oklahoma City bombing approached, President Clinton and First Lady Hillary visited the city on April 5. They remembered the victims in a ceremony at the site. Mrs. Clinton held the hand of Brandon Denny, a child who was in the day-care center when the blast occurred, but was one of the few who survived. The Good Friday ceremony was high-lighted by Clinton placing a huge wreath of seasonal flowers where the Murrah building once stood. He declared April 19 as a National Day of Remembrance and requested that Americans observe a moment of silence at 9:02 A.M. on that day to mark the moment of the tragedy. The president said the following in his weekly radio broadcast:

> Sometimes it takes a terrible tragedy to illuminate a basic truth: In a democracy, government is not them versus us. We are all us, we are all in it together. Government is our neighbors and friends helping others pursue the dreams we all share: to live in peace, provide for ourselves and our loved ones, and give our children a chance for an even better life.

McVeigh and Stephen Jones used the approaching date of April 19 to further their press relations campaign by granting an interview to *Time* magazine correspondent Patrick Cole. The April 15 edition of *Time* was available on store shelves as of April 6. The interview was conducted, according to *Time,* on March 29, the day before McVeigh was transferred to the Denver facility. It also included two photographs of a smiling, perceivably happy Tim McVeigh. Asked in the brief half-page interview if he ever built a bomb, McVeigh answered, "I never had my hand on one. I used to watch other people do it. I won't go into that." McVeigh also said he would like to testify. Richard Burr told the *Union-Sun & Journal* in an April interview that no formal decision had been made on whether McVeigh would testify and it would not be made until the trial. Even then, Burr said, the decision could be subject to "revisiting."

McVeigh and Nichols, accompanied by their legal teams, attended a hearing at the Denver Courthouse on April 9. The two former army friends sat a few feet apart and barely glanced at each other.

Judge Matsch announced that if the lawyers wanted separate trials for McVeigh and Nichols, they should submit their requests in July. Matsch set an August 27 hearing date on the matter.

On April 11, Tim's father, Bill McVeigh, was shown for the first time in a television interview. Peter Jennings questioned Bill at length about his son. Jennings filed a fairly comprehensive report on McVeigh and Nichols's personal lives through interviews with relatives and friends. But Jennings had to do his best on this piece since he was the top television journalist who had made an embarrassing mistake on April 21, 1995, by identifying Tim McVeigh as being from Pendleton, Michigan, instead of New York. *Buffalo News* television critic Alan Pergament reflected on Jennings's misreport in his column, saying, "It may have made viewers wonder briefly if there could have been two McVeighs and two Pendletons."

Jennings's April 11, 1996, show revealed that Bill McVeigh didn't know his son the way you'd think most fathers and committed family men would. Jennings told Bill, "Listening to you, I hear you describing someone you don't recognize quite so easily anymore." Bill said that the Tim he remembers best is the youth captured in the high school yearbook photo, which hangs in the kitchen at the McVeigh home in Pendleton. Jennings did not ask if Bill McVeigh thought his son was innocent or guilty. Bill told the *Union-Sun & Journal* on April 12, that Jennings was not allowed to ask that question by the attorneys involved in setting up the interview.

Tim gave a cryptic interview to the *Sunday Times* of London also in April. He revealed that his thoughts are as they were when in 1992 he wrote a letter to the *Union-Sun & Journal,* asking if blood would have to be shed to change America's political direction. To the *Sunday Times,* McVeigh said, "When they [the government] govern by the sword, they must reckon with protest by the sword." In addition, he claimed he is not alone in his thinking.

For a long time, I thought it was best not to talk about my political views. But millions share them, and I believe it is gravely wrong that I should allow the government to try and crucify me just for believing what I do.

On April 19, 1996, CNN and other networks ran all-day coverage of the memorial services in Oklahoma City. At 9:02 central time, thousands gathered at the former Murrah site to pause with many throughout the nation for 168 seconds of silence, honoring the number of people believed killed in the blast exactly one year earlier. American military jets flew overhead with a deafening boom in honor of the dead. In the quiet moments of the service, a baby at the site wept loudly and continuously as it was comforted by its mother.

Appendix

The Bombing Victims

The following is a list of those who were victims of the April 19, 1995 bombing of the Alfred P. Murrah Federal Building in Oklahoma City, Oklahoma, according to the government indictment of suspects and reports in the *Daily Oklahoman*. Their ages and places of employment (if applicable) are included.

Lucio Aleman Jr., 33, Federal Highway Administration (FHA)
Teresa Alexander, 33
Richard Allen, 46, Social Security Administration (SSA)
Ted Allen, 48, Housing and Urban Development (HUD)
Baylee Almon, 1
Diane Althouse, 45, HUD
Rebecca Anderson, 37, nurse
Pamela Argo, 36
Sandy Avery, 34, SSA
Peter Avillanoza, 56, HUD
Calvin Battle, 62

Peola Y. Battle, 56
Danielle Nicole Bell, 15 months
Oleta Biddy, 54, SSA
Shelly Turner Bland, 25, Drug Enforcement Administration
    (DEA)
Andrea Blanton, 33, HUD
Glen Bloomer, 61, U.S. Department of Agriculture (USDA)
Lola Bolden, 40, Army recruiting
James Boles, 51, USDA
Mark Bolte, 27, FHA
Cassandra Booker, 25
Carol Bowers, 53, SSA
Peachlyn Bradley, 3
Woody Brady, 41
Cynthia Brown, 26, Secret Service (SS)
Paul Broxterman, 43, HUD
Gabreon Bruce, 4 months
Kimberly Burgess, 29, Federal Employees Credit Union (FECU)
David Burkett, 47, HUD
Donald Burns, 63, HUD
Karen Gist Carr, 32, Army
Michael Joe Carrillo, 44, FHA
Rona Linn Chafey, 35, DEA
Zackary Chavez, 3
Robert Chipman, 51, Oklahoma Water Resources Board
Kimberly Clark, 39, HUD
Peggy Clark, 39, HUD
Anthony Cooper II, 2
Antonio Cooper, Jr., 6 months
Dana Cooper, 24, America's Kids Day-Care
Harley Cottingham, 46, Defense Department (DD)
Kim Cousins, 33, HUD
Aaron Coverdale, 5
Elijah Coverdale, 2

Jaci Rae Coyne, 14 months
Kathy Cregan, 60, SSA
Richard Cummins, 55, USDA
Steven Curry, 44, General Services Administration (GSA)
Benjamin Davis, Sgt., 29, Marine recruiting
Diana Day, 38, HUD
Peter DeMaster, 44, DD
Castine Deveroux, 49
Sheila Driver, 28
Tylor Eaves, 8 months
Ashley M. Eckles, 4
Susan Jane Ferrell, 37, HUD
Chip Fields, 48, DEA
Katherine A. Finley, 44, FECU
Judy Fisher, 45, HUD
Linda Florence, 43, HUD
Donald Fritzler, 64
Mary Anne Fritzler, 57
Tevin Garrett, 18 months
Laura Garrison, 61
Jamie Lee Genzer, 32, FECU
Margaret Goodson, 54, SSA
Kevin Gottshall II, 6 months
Ethel Griffin, 55, SSA
Juretta Guiles, 59, HUD
Randy Guzman, 28, Marine recruiting
Cheryl Hammons, 44
Ronald Harding, 55, SSA
Thomas Hawthorne, Sr., 52
Adele Higginbottom, 44, USDA
Anita Hightower, 27
Gene Hodges, Jr., 54, HUD
Peggy Holland, 37, Army
Linda C. Housely, 53, FECU

George Howard, 45, HUD
Wanda Lee Howell, 34, America's Kids
Robbin Huff, 37, FECU
Dr. Charles Hurlburt, 73, dentist
Jean Hurlburt, 67
Paul Ice, 42, Customs Service (CS)
Christi Jenkins, 32, FECU
Norma Jean Johnson, 62, DD
Raymond Johnson, 59, SSA
Larry Jones, 46, FHA
Alvin Justes, 54
Blake R. Kennedy, 18 months
Carole Sue Khalil, 50, USDA
Valerie Jo Koelsch, 33, FECU
Carolyn Kreymborg, 57, HUD
Teresa L. Lauderdale, 41, HUD
Kathy Leinen, 47, FECU
Carrie Ann Lenz, 26, DEA
Donald Leonard, 50, SS
Lakesha Levy, 21, Air Force
Dominique London, 2
Rheta Long, 60, USDA
M. Loudenslager, 48, GSA
Donna Luster, 43
Robert Lee Luster, Jr., 45
James McCarthy, 53, HUD
Kenneth McCullough. 36, DEA
Betsy McGonnell, 47, HUD
Linda McKinney, 47, SS
Cartney McRaven, 19, Air Force
Mickey Maroney, 50, SS
J. K. Martin, 34, FHA
Gilberto Martinez, 35
Claude Medearis, 41, CS

Claudette Meek, 43, FECU
Frankie Ann Merrell, 23, FECU
Derwin Miller, 27
Leigh Mitchell, 64
John C. Moss III, 51, Army
Trish Nix, 47, HUD
Jerry Lee Parker, 45, FHA
Jill Randolph, 27, FECU
Michelle A. Reeder, 33, FHA
Terry Smith Rees, 41, HUD
Mary Rentie, 39, HUD
Antonio Reyes, 55, HUD
Kathryn Ridley, 24
Trudy Rigney, 31, Water Resources
Claudine Ritter, 48, FECU
Christy Rosas, 22
Sonja Sanders, 27, FECU
Lanny Scroggins, 46, HUD
Kathy Lynn Seidl, 29, SS
Leora Lee Sells, 57, HUD
Karan Shepherd, 27, FECU
Chase Smith, 3
Colton Smith, 2
Victoria Sohn, 36, Army
John T. Stewart, 51, HUD
Dolores Stratton, 51, Army
Emilio Tapia, 50
Victoria Texter, 37, FECU
Charlotte Thomas, 43, SSA
Michael Thompson, 46, SSA
Virginia Thompson, 56
Kayla M. Titsworth, 3
Rick Tomlin, 46, Transportation Department
LaRue Treanor, 56

Luther Treanor, 61
Larry Turner, 43, DD
Jules Valdez, 50, HUD
John K. VanEss III, 67, HUD
Johnny Wade, 42, FHA
Bob Walker, Jr., 52
David Walker, 54, HUD
Wanda Watkins, 49, Army
Michael Weaver, 45
Julie Marie Welch, 23, SSA
Robert Westberry, 57, DD
Alan Whicher, 40, SS
JoAnn Whittenberg, 35, HUD
Frances Williams, 48, HUD
Scott Williams, 24
W. Stephen Williams, 42, SSA
Clarence Wilson, 49, HUD
Sharon Wood-Chesnut, 47, SSA
Ronota Woodbridge, 31, FHA
Tresia Jo Worton, 28, FECU
John "Buddy" Youngblood, 52
Others Unknown

Bibliography

Boorstin, Daniel J. *The Lost World of Thomas Jefferson.* Chicago: University of Chicago Press, 1981.

Bugliosi, Vincent, with Curt Gentry. *Helter Skelter.* New York: Bantam Books, 1975.

Campbell, Walter E. *Across Fortune's Tracks: A Biography of William Rand Kenan, Jr.* Chapel Hill, N.C.: University of North Carolina Press, 1996.

Carlin, Christopher. *Protecting Niagara: A History of the Niagara County Sheriff's Office.* Ransomville, N.Y.: Aegis Press, 1994.

Crockett, Art, ed. *Serial Murderers.* New York: Pinnacle Books, 1990.

Dees, Morris, and James Corcoran. *Gathering Storm: America's Militia Threat.* New York: HarperCollins Publishers, 1996.

Ellis, Bret Easton. *American Psycho.* New York: Vintage Contemporaries, 1991.

George, John, and Laird Wilcox. *Nazis, Communists, Klansmen, and Others on the Fringe.* Amherst, N.Y.: Prometheus Books, 1992.

315

George, John, and Laird Wilcox. *American Extremists: Militias, Supremacists, Klansmen, Communists, and Others.* Amherst, N.Y.: Prometheus Books, 1996.

Hansen, Jon. *Oklahoma Rescue.* New York: Ballantine Books, 1995.

Kaufmann, Walter, ed. *Basic Writings of Nietzsche.* New York: Modern Library, 1968.

Lay, Shawn. *Hooded Knights on the Niagara: The Ku Klux Klan in Buffalo, New York.* New York: New York University Press, 1995.

Linedecker, Clifford L. *Massacre at Waco, Texas.* New York: St. Martin's Press, 1993.

Macdonald, Andrew [William Pierce]. *The Turner Diaries.* Hillsboro, W.Va.: National Vanguard Books, 1978.

Michaud, Stephen G., and Hugh Aynesworth. *Ted Bundy: Conversations with a Killer.* New York: Signet, 1989.

Mill, John Stuart. *On Liberty.* Indianapolis, Ind.: Bobbs-Merrill Company, 1983.

Morrison, Jim. *Wilderness,* Volume 1. New York: Vintage Books, 1988.

Oates, Joyce Carol. "American Gothic." *New Yorker* (May 8, 1995): 35.

———. "Oates Defends Articles." *Union-Sun & Journal,* June 14, 1995, p. 2.

———. *Zombie.* New York: Dutton, 1995.

Padilla, Lana, with Ron Delpit. *By Blood Betrayed.* New York: HarperPaperbacks, 1995.

Project Vote Smart. *The Reporter's Source Book.* Corvallis, Ore., 1994.

Reavis, Dick J. *The Ashes of Waco.* New York: Simon and Schuster, 1995.

Speck, Christopher W. *Lockport: An Anecdotal History.* Lockport, N.Y.: Lockport Tourism Advisory Committee, 1989.

Stickney, Brandon. "Oates Says Area Lacks 'Community.' " *Union-Sun & Journal,* May 30, 1995, p. 9.

Notes

Chapter 1. Amerika

1. "Report from Ground Zero," *Media Bypass* (June 1995): 27.
2. Jon Hansen, *Oklahoma Rescue* (New York: Ballantine Books, 1995), pp. 7–8.
3. Ibid., p. 8.
4. "Report from Ground Zero," p. 27.
5. Hansen, *Oklahoma Rescue,* pp. 8–9.
6. Ibid., pp. 9–11.
7. James Dalrymple, "All-American Monster," *Sunday Times Magazine* of London (September 3, 1995): 34.
8. "Report from Ground Zero," p. 27.
9. Gazette wire reports, appearing in *Niagara Gazette* (April 23, 1995).
10. Hansen, *Oklahoma Rescue,* p. 17.

Chapter 2. The Gambler

1. *Buffalo News*, May 14, 1995, p. A-10.
2. Edward Tracy, authorized interview with author, May 1995.

3. Jerry F. Boone, "Yearbook Didn't Hint of Future," *The Oregonian,* May 4, 1995.

4. Julianna Jacoby, "McVeigh's Aunt Recalls How Nephew Changed," *Union-Sun & Journal,* July 17, 1995, p. 9.

5. Leo LaPort, Jr., authorized interview with author, February 1996.

6. Author's authorized interview with source, May 1995.

7. Leo LaPort, Jr., authorized interview with author, February 1996.

8. Kathleen Ganz, "Tim McVeigh Recalled as 'Go-Getter,' " *Union-Sun & Journal,* April 22, 1995, p. 1.

9. Ibid.

10. Justin Genter, authorized interview with author, May 1995.

11. Dan Kane, authorized interview with author, February 1996.

Chapter 3. Our Town

1. Christopher Carlin, *Protecting Niagara: A History of the Niagara County Sheriff's Office* (Ransomville, N.Y.: Aegis Press, 1995).

2. Henry Louis Taylor, Jr., *Buffalo Magazine* (February 25, 1996): 8–9.

3. Ibid.

4. Clifton Gibson, authorized interview with author, March 1996.

5. Marian Christy, "A 'Woman of Letters' Who Speaks from the Heart," *Boston Sunday Globe,* May 20, 1990, p. B55.

6. Sherwood Anderson, *Winesburg, Ohio* (New York: Penguin Books, 1976), p. 36.

7. Mary Wozniak, "First Defendants of Federal Probe," *Niagara Gazette,* n.d., p. 4A.

Chapter 4. Changes

1. Richard Pierce, authorized interview with author, September 1995.

2. Dan Kane, authorized interview with author, December 14, 1995.

3. Author's authorized interview with source, December 1995.

4. Author's authorized interview with source, November 11, 1995.

5. Richard Pierce, authorized interview with author, September 1995.

6. Chris Brennan, "McVeigh's Mother Dispels Some Myths," *Fort Pierce Tribune,* May 7, 1996, A1, 5.

7. Justin Genter, authorized interview with author, May 1995.

8. Peter Jennings reporting, "Rage and Betrayal: The Lives of Timothy McVeigh and Terry Nichols," ABC News (April 11, 1996).

9. "The Road to Oklahoma," CNN, November 19, 1995.

10. Brennan, "McVeigh's Mother Dispels Some Myths."

11. Richard Pierce, authorized interview with author, September 1995.

12. Kathleen Ganz, *Union-Sun & Journal*, April 22, 1995.

13. Lawrence Myers, "Biography: McVeigh Part 2," *Media Bypass* (March 1996): 20.

14. Pam Widmer, authorized interview with author, May 1995.

15. Author's authorized interview with source, May 1995.

16. Justin Genter, authorized interview with author, May 1995.

17. Pam Widmer, authorized interview with author, May 1995.

18. Author's authorized interview with source, May 1995.

19. *Buffalo News*, April 23, 1995.

20. Myers, "Biography: McVeigh Part 2," p. 21.

21. Ibid.

22. John Kifner, "Oklahoma Bombing Suspect: Unraveling of a Frayed Life," *New York Times,* December 31, 1995, p. A24.

23. Jennings, "Rage and Betrayal."

Chapter 5. Unknown Soldier

1. Robert McFadden, "Life of Solitude, Obsession and Anger," *New York Times,* May 4, 1995, p. A10.

2. "The Road to Oklahoma," CNN, November 19, 1995.

3. Robert Sheaffer, "Reichean Disciples, Restless Statues," *Skeptical Inquirer* (March/April 1996): 1.

4. Pam Widmer, authorized interview with author, May 1995.

5. "The Road to Oklahoma."

6. Lawrence Myers, "Biography: McVeigh Part 2," *Media Bypass* (March 1996): 22.

7. Dr. William Pierce as "Andrew Macdonald," *The Turner Diaries* (W.Va.: National Vanguard Books, 1978), p. 2.

8. Ibid., pp. 71–72.

9. *Response* (Summer 1995): 2.

10. Myers, "Biography: McVeigh Part 2," pp. 23–24.

11. Dan Kane, authorized interview with author, December 14, 1995.

12. Ibid.

13. McFadden, "Life of Solitude," p. A10.

14. Ibid.

15. Ibid.

16. Ibid.

17. Stone Phillips, "Comrades in Arms," "Dateline NBC."

18. Myers, "Biography: McVeigh Part 2," p. 24.

19. Peter Jennings reporting, "Rage and Betrayal: The Lives of Timothy McVeigh and Terry Nichols," ABC News (April 11, 1996).

20. McFadden, "Life of Solitude," p. 11.

21. Jonathan Franklin, "Timothy McVeigh, Soldier," *Playboy* (October 1995): 88.

22. McFadden, "Life of Solitude," p. A10.

23. Phillips, "Comrades in Arms."

24. Julianna Jacoby, "McVeigh's Aunt Recalls How Nephew Changed," *Union-Sun & Journal,* July 17, 1995, p. 9.

25. David Hackworth, "Talking 'Soldier to Soldier' Behind Bars," *Newsweek* (July 3, 1995): 27.

26. Phillips, "Comrades in Arms."

27. Ibid.

28. Steve Komarow and Kirk Spitzer, "Unraveling McVeigh," *USA Today,* May 2, 1995, p. 2A.

29. Dan Herbeck and Mike Vogel, "Suspect Examined at Hospital Here After Gulf War," *Buffalo News,* April 28, 1995, p. A1.

30. Phillips, "Comrades in Arms."

31. McFadden, "Life of Solitude," p. A11.

32. Ibid.

33. David Hackworth and Peter Annin, "The Suspect Speaks Out," *Newsweek* (July 3, 1995): 34.

34. James Dalrymple, "All-American Monster," *Sunday Times Magazine* of London (September 3, 1995): 34.

35. McFadden, "Life of Solitude," p. A11.

36. Ibid.

37. Ibid.

38. John Kifner, "Oklahoma Bombing Suspect: Unraveling of a Frayed Life," *New York Times,* December 31, 1995, p. A24.

Chapter 6. American Psycho

1. Brian Haines, authorized interview with author, January 9, 1996.

2. Joseph Treaster, "For Figure in Oklahoma Inquiry, Ties of Blood and Something More," *New York Times,* August 4, 1995, p. A8.

3. John Kifner, "Oklahoma Bombing Suspect: Unraveling of a Frayed Life," *New York Times,* December 31, 1995, p. A24.

4. Dan Herbeck and Mike Vogel, "Suspect Examined at Hospital Here After Gulf War," *Buffalo News*, April 28, 1995, p. A6.

5. Author's authorized interview with source, May 1995.

6. Dan Kane, authorized interview with author, December 14, 1995.

7. Mike Vogel and Susan Schulman, "Understanding McVeigh Presents Challenge," *Buffalo News*, April 30, 1995, p. A8.

8. "The Road to Oklahoma," CNN, November 19, 1995.

9. Peter Jennings reporting, "Rage and Betrayal: The Lives of Timothy McVeigh and Terry Nichols," ABC News (April 11, 1996).

10. David Hackworth and Peter Annin, "The Suspect Speaks Out," *Newsweek* (July 3, 1995): 26.

11. "The Road to Oklahoma."

12. Jennings, "Rage and Betrayal."

13. Robert McFadden, "Life of Solitude, Obsession and Anger," *New York Times*, May 4, 1995, p. A10.

14. "The Road to Oklahoma."

15. Jennifer McVeigh, authorized interview with author, December 28, 1995.

16. James Heaney and Phil Fairbanks, "Arizona Town Is a Training Ground," *Buffalo News*, April 24, 1995, p. A8.

17. Daniel Girard and Peter Edwards, "Showdown with Militia 'Terrifying,' Mayor Says," *Toronto Star,* April 22, 1995, p. A17.

18. Associated Press wire report, April 27, 1995.

19. "The Road to Oklahoma."

20. "Allegations Unbelievable for Those Who Knew Youth," *Buffalo News,* April 23, 1995, p. A12.

21. John George and Laird Wilcox, *Nazis, Communists, Klansmen, and Others on the Fringe* (Amherst, N.Y.: Prometheus Books, 1992), p. 372.

22. Andrew Macdonald [Dr. William Pierce], *The Turner Diaries* (W.Va.: National Vanguard Books, 1978), p. 42.

23. Brandon Stickney and Julianna Jacoby, "Area Co-Workers Recall McVeigh," *Union-Sun & Journal*, pp. 1, 4.

24. James Dalrymple, "All-American Monster," *Sunday Times Magazine* of London (September 3, 1995): 39.

25. Associated Press wire report, August 9, 1995 (as requested and forwarded to the *Union-Sun & Journal* on October 24, 1995).

26. McFadden, "Life of Solitude," p. A10.

27. Kifner, "Oklahoma Bombing Suspect," p. A24.

28. Brian Haines, authorized interview with author, January 9, 1996.

29. Gregory Beals, "'Watch What You Say,'" *Newsweek* (May 22, 1995): 27.

30. Howard Pankratz, "Bomb Theory Swirls," *Denver Post,* March 11, 1996, p. 1A.

Chapter 7. Public Enemy

1. John Hanchette, "McVeigh's Odyssey Began in Kansas Motel, FBI Says," Gannett News Service, *Niagara Gazette,* April 23, 1995, p. 5A.

2. "The Road to Oklahoma," CNN, November 19, 1995.

3. Jennifer McVeigh, authorized interview with author, December 28, 1995.

4. Leo LaPort, Jr., authorized interview with author, February 1996.

5. Julianna Jacoby, "McVeigh's Aunt Recalls How Nephew Changed," *Union-Sun & Journal,* July 17, 1995.

6. Author's authorized interview with source, January 1996.

7. *USA Today,* May 2, 1995, p. 2A.

8. Lou Michel, "Love Remains, Says Father of Bomb Suspect," *Buffalo News,* May 4, 1995, p. A1.

9. *Pensacola News Journal* quote as printed in Joseph Treaster, "For Figure in Oklahoma Inquiry, Ties of Blood and Something More," *New York Times,* August 4, 1995, p. A8.

10. James Dalrymple, "All-American Monster," *Sunday Times Magazine* of London (September 3, 1995), p. 40.

11. *Union-Sun & Journal,* October 18, 1995, p. 1.

Chapter 8. Right-Wing Diary

1. Brandon Stickney, "Former FBI Man Probes Criminal Mind," *Union-Sun & Journal,* November 7, 1995, p. 9.

2. Dan Kane, "McVeigh Sent Letters to *US&J,*" *Union-Sun & Journal,* April 26, 1995, p. 1.

3. Dan Kane, authorized interview with author, February 1996.

4. John George and Laird Wilcox, *Nazis, Communists, Klansmen, and Others on the Fringe* (Amherst, N.Y.: Prometheus Books, 1992).

5. Christopher Shearer in a letter to Brandon Stickney, May 1995.

6. Jennifer McVeigh, authorized interview with author, December 28, 1995.

7. Jerry Zremski, "LaFalce Describes McVeigh's Pro-Gun Letter as Relatively 'Tame,' " *Buffalo News,* May 3, 1995, p. A11.

8. Reuters as published in the *Daily Oklahoman,* April 27, 1995, p. 12.

9. Susan Schulman, "Letters Offer Insight into Bomb Suspect," *Buffalo News,* April 27, 1995, pp. A1, 4.

Chapter 9. Before the Trial

1. Diane Plumberg, "Workers Pause to Find Closure," *Saturday Oklahoman & Times,* May 6, 1995, p. 1.

2. Julie DelCour and Brian Ford, "Ex-Tulsan May Aid McVeigh," *Tulsa World,* May 16, 1995, p. 1.

3. George Garties, Associated Press wire report (April 25, 1995).

4. John Parker, "McVeigh Ordered to Trial in Bombing," *Daily Oklahoman,* April 28, 1995, p. 1.

5. Ibid.

6. Brandon Stickney, "McVeigh's Arrest Shakes Pendleton," *Union-Sun & Journal,* April 24, 1995, pp. 1, 3.

7. *Union-Sun & Journal,* May 13, 1995, p. 1.

8. Dan Herbeck and Lou Michel, "Sister Fears FBI Charges in Probe of McVeigh," *Buffalo News,* May 9, 1995, p. 1.

9. "NCCC Faculty, Students Hash Out Bombing," *Niagara Gazette,* May 10, 1995, p. 5A.

10. Dan Herbeck, "Probe Puts McVeigh's Sister in Legal Limbo," *Buffalo News,* May 16, 1995.

11. Paul Queary, Associated Press, as printed in the *Buffalo News,* May 28, 1995, p. A5.

12. "McVeigh: A New Defense," *Newsweek* (May 22, 1995): 4.

13. Associated Press as printed in the *Niagara Gazette,* p. 1 (n.d.).

14. Gannett News Service as printed in the *Union-Sun & Journal,* June 9, 1995, p. 1.

15. David Hackworth and Peter Annin, "The Suspect Speaks Out," *Newsweek* (July 3, 1995): 23.

16. Associated Press as printed in the *Union-Sun & Journal,* June 26, 1995, p. 1.

17. Associated Press as printed in the *Union-Sun & Journal,* June 27, 1995, p. 1.

18. Ibid.

19. Associated Press as printed in the *Buffalo News,* July 19, 1995.

20. Associated Press as printed in the *Union-Sun & Journal,* July 22, 1995, p. 1.

21. Associated Press as printed in the *Buffalo News,* July 25, 1995.

22. *Time* report as reprinted by the Associated Press (August 14, 1995).

23. Associated Press as reprinted in the *Union-Sun & Journal*, August 8, 1995.

24. Paul Queary, Associated Press, August 31, 1995.

25. Associated Press, August 11, 1995.

26. Brian Haines, authorized interview with author, January 9, 1996.

27. Richard Serrano, *Los Angeles Times,* August 26, 1995.

28. *Daily Oklahoman* as reprinted by the Associated Press, August 28, 1995.

29. *Tulsa World* as reprinted by the Associated Press, September 8, 1995.

30. Associated Press, September 29, 1995.

31. *Daily Oklahoman* as reprinted by the Associated Press, October 2ʊ, 1995.

32. Stone Phillips, "Grand Juror," "NBC Morning News," n.d.

33. Ibid.

34. Associated Press as printed by the *Union-Sun & Journal*, October 28, 1995, p. 1.

35. Nolan Clay, Randy Ellis, and Diana Baldwin, "McVeigh Won't Use Insanity Defense," *Daily Oklahoman*, November 16, 1995, pp. 1, 2.

36. Associated Press, December 6, 1995.

37. Pete Slover, *Dallas Morning News,* December 9, 1995.

38. Associated Press, December 14, 1995.

39. *De Telegraaf* as reprinted by the Associated Press, January 7, 1996.

40. *Washington Post* as reprinted in the *Buffalo News,* July 17, 1995.

41. Brandon Stickney, "Jennifer Says She Talked with Timothy," *Union-Sun & Journal,* February 1, 1996, p. 1.

42. Ibid.

43. Associated Press as printed in the *Union-Sun & Journal,* February 6, 1996, p. 1.

44. Jane Pauley, "Dateline NBC," February 13, 1996.

45. Ibid.

Chapter 10. Motherless Child

1. Peter Kent and Melissa Key, "Smile That Hate Couldn't Kill," *Star,* May 9, 1995, p. 25.

2. Ibid., p. 26.

3. Ellen Wulfhorst, Reuters, as printed in the *Buffalo News,* April 27, 1995, p. A5.

4. "Heroes of the Heartland," *Lifestyles* (Florida: Globe International, undated).

5. Gail Wescott, "The Last Life Saved," *People* (May 15, 1995): 104.

6. Associated Press, April 29, 1995.

7. Lou Michel, "Love Remains, Says Father of Bomb Suspect," *Buffalo News,* May 4, 1995, p. A8.

8. *Daily Oklahoman,* April 28, 1995, p. 4.

Index